INTERPRETING EVIDENCE

INTERPRETING EVIDENCE
Evaluating Forensic Science in the Courtroom

by

Bernard Robertson

Department of Business Law,

Massey University

and

G A Vignaux

Institute of Statistics and Operations Research,

Victoria University of Wellington

John Wiley & Sons

Chichester, New York, Brisbane, Toronto, Singapore

First published in the United Kingdom in 1995 by
John Wiley & Sons Ltd,
Baffins Lane,
Chichester,
West Sussex,
PO19 1UD

National 01243 779777
International (+44) 1243 779777

Reprinted April 1997

Other Wiley Editorial Offices

John Wiley & Sons Inc., 605 Third Avenue,
New York, NY 10158-0012, USA

John Wiley & Sons Inc., Editorial, Administration & Marketing,
7222 Commerce Center Drive, Suite 240,
Colorado Springs, CO 80919

Jacaranda Wiley Ltd, 33 Park Road, Milton,
Queensland 4064, Australia

John Wiley & Sons (Canada) Ltd, 22 Worcester Road,
Rexdale, Ontario M9W 1L1, Canada

John Wiley & Sons (SEA) Pte Ltd, 37 Jalan Pemimpin #05-04,
Block B, Union Industrial Building, Singapore 129809

British Library Cataloguing in Publication Data

A catalogue record for this book is available from the British Library

ISBN 0 471 96026 8

Typeset in 10/12 Baskerville by York House Typographic Ltd, London.
Printed and bound in Great Britain by Bookcraft (Bath) Ltd.
This book is printed on acid-free paper responsibly manufactured from sustainable forestation, for which at least two trees are planted for each one used for paper production.

To our wives and parents

CONTENTS

PREFACE

This book started as part of a wider project, the examination of the applicability of logical and probabilistic reasoning to evidence generally. This has been the subject of vigorous discussion in the legal literature and is one of the main threads of the "New Evidence Scholarship".

Forensic science suggested itself as a case-study as there seemed to be some degree of consensus that forensic scientific evidence should be thought about in probabilitistic terms, but when we surveyed the field it appeared to be a mess.

- Some expert witnesses, such as fingerprint officers, make categorical statements that two impressions are from the same finger.

- Some experts, such as glass experts, would only say that a sample could have come from a particular source and then gave some straightforward sounding statistics about the frequency of glass of that type.

- Some types of evidence, such as DNA, seemed to involve statistical arguments of impenetrable complexity.

The law seemed in equal confusion.

- There was a rule preventing giving an opinion on the ultimate issue, yet courts regularly heard witnesses talk about the probability of paternity.

- A court would reject evidence in one case because it usurped the role of the jury and in another because it was not definitive and conclusive.

- Courts sometimes pointed out problems with evidence that the forensic science profession did little about and sometimes ruled evidence out for reasons that had little to do with its probative value.

It also seemed to us that courts and textbook writers were keener to bandy words such as "reliability" and "regard the evidence with caution" than to explain what ideas lay behind these phrases.

The time had clearly come for some fundamental re-evaluation of forensic science. As we studied the matter we realised that the application of a few basic logical principles solved the problems of description and prescription with which we were faced. That is not to say that solutions came easily; the application of these principles requires hard thinking and we cannot pretend to offer answers to all the questions. The results lead to advice about how to think about evidence of much more practical value than an admonition to "regard the evidence with caution".

While preparing this book we found some forensic scientists who had been thinking along the same lines and had published papers in the scientific literature. The most prolific current writer is Dr Ian Evett of the British Home Office Forensic Science Service. Gradually, and despite opposition from within the scientific and legal fraternities, these ideas have begun to appear in legal literature and to influence the giving of evidence.

The result is that while the insights in this book will seem to some readers as revelatory as they first did to us, this book is, in fact, part of a movement throughout the forensic scientific world to re-evaluate scientific evidence and, at the same time, to encourage a greater sense of unity and professionalism amongst forensic scientists. So far as we know, however, this book is the first to be written as a single book-length work on the subject.

Who is this book aimed at?

The task of convincing forensic scientists that they must rethink their interpretation of scientific evidence is one for scientists writing in scientific journals. At some point, however, the scientist has to communicate with a lawyer and perhaps with a jury. Likewise, the lawyer who understands the law and is an expert at communicating with juries has to be able to understand the scientist. It is evident that in the past there has been a sad failure of communication.

This book attempts to remedy that. It is designed to be read by both lawyers and forensic scientists so that each will better understand the other and they will be better equipped to work together to explain the evidence to the court.

We intend that the book will also be of value to academics and students. The basic logical principles we apply provide the intellectual tool-kit for re-evaluating the law relating to expert evidence, and indeed to evidence generally. We believe that this is a classic example of deep theoretical thinking appropriate to university courses providing far more practical solutions to practitioners' problems than the *ad hoc* reasoning which has been applied to expert evidence in the past.

In completing this task we have been helped and encouraged enormously by academic colleagues and forensic scientists including, through the wonders of electronic mail, those from the United States, and the United Kingdom. Particular mention must be made of Dr Evett, who has not only been of invaluable technical assistance but who chivvied us vigorously when we were slacking on the job. Valuable comments on drafts were provided in the later stages by Richard Friedman, David Kaye and Dennis Lindley and by David Wilson of John Wiley and Sons Ltd who supported us enthusiastically. We have also benefited from discussion at many conference and staff seminar presentations at our own and other universities, and from a presentational point of view we have even benefited from the outright hostility we have met on occasions. We have conducted thoroughly enjoyable (to us at any rate) Masters and Honours courses in which a number of enthusiastic students have contributed ideas and sharpened up our presentation. Some are mentioned by name at appropriate points in the book.

We have been generously supported by research grants from Victoria University of Wellington Internal Grants Committee, which have enabled us to employ several research assistants as the project ground through its various phases. Isobel Egerton, Andrew Fairfax, Victoria Heine, Michael Sleigh and Victoria Wicks-Brown have all contributed during vacations and term time.

Certain passages are adapted versions of papers which we have published elsewhere. More than one passage is extracted from our paper "Expert evidence: law, practice and probability" (1992) 12 OJLS 392; the passage on stylometry is adapted from "Stylometric Evidence" [1994] Crim L R 645, of which Isobel Egerton was co-author; much of chapter 7 is to be found, differently arranged, in "DNA Evidence: Wrong Answers or Wrong Questions" (1995) 96 Genetica 145; the section on fingerprints is adapted from "The Interpretation of Fingerprints" (1994) 3 Exp Ev 3. The assistance we have had from the editors and publishers of those journals is also gratefully acknowledged.

This book is based on a logical argument and the state of the law in any particular jurisidiction is not important for its thesis. Nonetheless, we have endeavoured to state the law correctly where we give examples and citations and hope that the law is correct as of 1 January 1995.

BERNARD ROBERTSON
Palmerston North

G.A. (TONY) VIGNAUX
Wellington

ABBREVIATIONS

Where no country is specified or obvious a series or institution is English.

A Crim R	Australian Criminal Reports
AC	Law Reports Appeals Cases
All ER	All England Law Reports
ALR	Australian Law Reports
Am J Hum Gen	American Journal of Human Genetics
Ann Hum Blg	Annals of Human Biology
BMJ	British Medical Journal
BULR	Boston University Law Review
CCC	Central Criminal Court (The Old Bailey in London)
Cal LR	California Law Review
CLR	Commonwealth Law Reports (Aus)
Cr App R	Criminal Appeal Reports
Crim LJ	Criminal Law Journal (Aus)
Crim LR	Criminal Law Review
Crim Lab Dig	(FBI) Crime Laboratory Digest
CUP	Cambridge University Press
DSIR	Department of Scientific and Industrial Research (now ESR) (NZ)
ER	English Reports

ESR	Crown Research Institute for Environmental, Health and Forensic Sciences (NZ)
Exp Ev	Expert Evidence
Fam	Law Reports Family Division
Fed Prob	Federal Probation
FLB	Family Law Bulletin (NZ)
FLQ	Family Law Quarterly (US)
For Sci Int	Forensic Sciences International
FSR	Fleet Street Reports
Harv LR	Harvard Law Review
HL	House of Lords
HOFSS	Home Office Forensic Science Service
IC Pol R	International Criminal Police Review
J Crim Law & C	Journal of Criminal Law, Criminology (and Police Science)
JFS	Journal of Forensic Sciences
JFSS	Journal of the Forensic Science Society
LQR	Law Quarterly Review
Med, Sci & L	Medicine, Science and the Law
NLJ	New Law Journal
NSWLR	New South Wales Law Reports (Aus)
NZ Rec LR	New Zealand Recent Law Review
NZFLR	New Zealand Family Law Reports
NZLR	New Zealand Law Reports
OJLS	Oxford Journal of Legal Studies
OUP	Oxford University Press
QB	Law Reports Queen's Bench
S Ct	Supreme Court Reports (US)
Sankhya	Sankhya, The Indian Journal of Statistics
SASR	South Australian State Reports
SC	Supreme Court (US or Aus States)

SPLR	South Pacific Law Reports
TLR	Times Law Reports
VR	Victorian Reports (Aus)
WLR	Law Reports Weekly Law Reports

TABLES

Cases

Legislation

Contents of Chapter 1

INTRODUCTION

Chapter 1

INTRODUCTION

The purposes of forensic scientific evidence include:

- to establish that a particular person was at a given place at a given time;
- to establish that a particular person carried out an activity, like signing a cheque, or breaking a window;
- to establish that something was done with a particular instrument, for example that a door was forced with a particular tool, a shot fired from a particular weapon, or a call made from a particular telephone;
- to establish a relationship between two people, for example in paternity disputes and incest or immigration cases.

There is a whole range of techniques used for forensic purposes and new methods are continually being added to the arsenal of the forensic scientist. Our purpose is not to discuss the technical details of these methods; our space is limited and our reader's time is short. We propose to concentrate on how such evidence should be interpreted and incorporated into the court process.

1.1 Two principles

The methods used all stem from two principles.
(i) Locard's Principle: Every contact leaves a trace. Whenever any two objects come into contact with one another they affect one another in some way.

This principle was annunciated by Edmond Locard (1877–1966), a French forensic scientist and fingerprint expert. Thus we might find skin and blood under a deceased's fingernails and infer that they come from the attacker. We might arrest a suspect on the basis of other evidence and find, on him or his clothing, fibres which might come from the deceased's clothes or blood which might come from the deceased. Alternatively, the accused may carry traces of particular soil and plant types which correspond with those at the scene.

(ii) Principle of Individuality: Two objects may be indistinguishable but no two objects are identical.

Whether we are talking about a human being or a single grain of sand the question simply is whether we have sufficient ability to distinguish between two objects with the information provided or with the measurement tools we have available.[1]

The combination of these two principles together is of enormous potential value to the forensic scientist. If no two people are identical then the impressions that people leave on objects with which they have been in contact will be different. The second principle, however, cuts the other way. If no two objects are identical then no two fingerprint impressions will be identical even though they are taken from the same person; no two samples of handwriting by the same author will be identical. The question becomes whether we have sufficient information to be able to judge whether two marks have the same source.

We describe these two statements as principles rather than laws because, using a standard definition of a law of science, neither can be elevated to that status. The philosopher Karl R Popper (1902–1994) proposed that for a law to be regarded as scientific it must be potentially falsifiable, *i.e.* it must be possible, at least in theory, to design an experiment which would disprove it.[2]

It seems to be impossible to design an experiment to refute either of our two principles. If an experiment fails to find an impression after two objects have been in contact (one might imagine two sheets of smooth metal) or fails to find a characteristic distinguishing between two objects, it may be that all that is revealed is the limitations of the detection process. Nonetheless, there is plenty of evidence to justify these beliefs; in particular the effect of the steady progress in forensic scientific technology is to bolster our belief by enabling traces and differences to be detected where none could be detected before.

1.2 A valiant start – *Bertillonage* or anthropometry

One of the first attempts to apply the Principle of Individuality scientifically was *Bertillonage* or anthropometry. Anthropometry simply means the measurement of humans. At a formal level anthropometry was a failure and to modern eyes even seems slightly ridiculous, having connotations of phrenology, but it was a rational approach to the problem of identification. It is also instructive to study such systems. If we can identify the reasons for the failure it may give insight into what it is we expect from scientific evidence.

Alphonse Bertillon (1853–1914), later the Parisian chief of criminal investigation, proposed a formal series of measurements that could be used to prove a

---

[1] Grieve, DL, "Reflections on Quality Standards – an American Standpoint" (1990) 15 *Fingerprint World* 108.
[2] Popper, KR, *Conjectures and refutations: the growth of scientific knowledge*, 5th ed (Routledge and Kegan Paul, London, 1989).

person's identity. His father, Louis-Adolphe, was the head of the Paris Bureau of vital (*i.e.* social) statistics and he was probably influenced by him and by his brother Jacques who was also a social statistician. By 1882 he had developed a system which was brought into use by the police in Paris and, subsequently, in London. *Bertillonage*, as it came to be called, required taking a photograph and recording a series of measurements of bone features which were known not to change after adolescence. Later, fingerprints were added to the features recorded. The basis of the system was that it would be unlikely that any two people would have the same measurements over the whole range of features.

Bertillonage suffered from a number of problems. Some of these were operational. The procedure was slow, and therefore expensive, and it was far from error free. The officers taking the measurements had to be specially trained; this involved more expense, and even then, at the levels of accuracy called for, no two would take the same measurements from the same series of features. The system could not be applied to juveniles.

There were more fundamental defects however. One was that the probability of another person having the same set of measurements was unknown. This would not be a problem where there was some reason, other than appearance, for believing that a person claiming to be A was in fact B because the coincidence of the measurements would be highly unlikely. As the database got bigger, however, the chance of a match by coincidence rose. If a person was found to match a record in the database how sure could we be that he was the same person? In other words, how many other people might share those measurements? An enormous investment in empirical research would be required to answer that question.

The greatest limitation of all was that the system was purely comparative. It could only specify whether or not a person had the same measurements as a person who had earlier been arrested. There is no doubt that this is often useful. An example is when someone is arrested on suspicion of failing to attend court or when a person being sentenced denies that previous convictions relate to him. However, *Bertillonage* could not help investigators by providing evidence that a particular person had been in a particular place.

Although fingerprints were taken as one of the *Bertillonage* measurements and Bertillon himself solved a crime using fingerprints in 1902, there was no formal classification system for them. Once such systems were developed (by Galton and Henry in England and Vucetich in South America) fingerprints alone became a far quicker and simpler method of identification. In the first full year of operation by the London Metropolitan Police, fingerprints identified three times as many persons as anthropometry and, two years later, 10 times as many. Not only were fingerprints far simpler and cheaper to obtain and record but they could also help investigators identify the perpetrators of crimes. *Bertillonage* was dropped.

1.3 Requirements for forensic scientific evidence

Measurement and photography are still used to help identify criminals and are recorded with the details of their convictions. They have a number of advantages. Photographs can be transmitted and reproduced easily and can enable people to be recognised at a distance. In most cases a photograph will settle a question of identity. Where this is seriously challenged, however, a photograph is of questionable value, particularly if much time has passed since it was taken.[3] Likewise, physical descriptions can be broadcast on police radios and even the most rudimentary description will eliminate a large proportion of the population. However, when identity is seriously challenged, descriptions and even eyewitness identification are of questionable value, perhaps because the question has become whether the perpetrator was the accused or someone else of similar appearance.

The failure of *Bertillonage* prompts us to consider the features of an ideal scientific identification system. These would include:

- that it identifies features unique to the individual;
- that those features do not change over time;
- that those features are unambiguous so that two experts would describe the same feature the same way;
- that it is able to place individuals at a crime scene; and
- that it is reasonably simple and cheap to operate.

Inevitably, few systems will satisfy all these requirements and in particular there may be a trade off between the last requirement and the others. Each of the systems that we examine later will have some of these features and lack others.

At any time there will have been developed some kinds of evidence and associated techniques with which we can distinguish between individuals, and other kinds with which we can only distinguish between groups. For example, the vast bulk of clothing is mass-produced and we may not be able to distinguish one garment from another in the same production run. Finding a thread from even a distinctive garment may, therefore, point at any one of a number of people.

With body tissues and fluids, on the other hand, current technology may allow us to find features which will identify an individual. In order to do this the tissue would have to have characteristics which are detectably unique to the individual and which preferably do not change during the individual's life. A century ago fingerprints were claimed to fit these requirements and no one has disproved this claim so far. The increasing sophistication of DNA testing has brought us to the

---

[3] At the trial of the alleged Nazi concentration camp guard Demjanjuk in Israel various techniques were used to try to show that the defendant in 1989 was the person in a photograph on a 50-year-old identity card.

point where it is possible to distinguish one individual's DNA from any other's (except, probably, an identical twin's).

If we can establish features which identify individuals in this way then we can maintain a database of such features. Thus, the police regularly record the weight, height, eye and hair colour, tattoos, accent, etc of offenders. All these features can be made to change, or appear to change, but will often be useful for identifying petty criminals.

Fingerprint collections have been built up for a century and the possibility now opens up of maintaining similar databases of DNA profiles. With such a database it may be possible not just to tell that we have arrested the right person but to identify suspects for investigation. A feature found at the scene of a crime may be compared with the database to find corresponding features. Does this mean that we have now found out who left the trace at the scene? In order to consider that question and others we need some knowledge of the types of scientific evidence but, more importantly, we need a thorough understanding of the principles of interpretation.

Unfortunately, knowing that a particular feature is unique and unchanging is not the end of the matter. The attention of lawyers is too easily concentrated upon the ability of a technique to satisfy these requirements. If the test can satisfy them, it is greeted as a panacea; if it cannot it is damned as "unreliable". This ignores the vital point that any technique will only function to a high degree of precision under controlled conditions. The conditions under which forensic scientists work are often far from ideal. Although the laboratory in a paternity case will have available fresh whole blood carefully taken from the parties, the forensic scientist will have to compare one such sample with a trace left at the scene which may be minute, old and contaminated.

It follows that in many instances a scientific witness will not be able to say that two samples definitely came from the same person. Often the evidence can only lead to an assessment of the probability that two samples came from the same person. The legal system has not been successful in dealing with this kind of evidence, and our purpose is to explain how such evidence should be given and integrated into the case.

Reliability

Rather than think rigorously about these problems, the legal system has been prone to ask questions such as "how reliable is this evidence?". This question is vacuous since "reliable" appears to have no fixed meaning. It is used at different times with at least four different meanings:

- *sensitivity* – can the technique be relied upon to produce usable results from the quantity and quality of material being examined?;
- *quality control* - are the factors which affect the outcomes of the tests understood, and were proper control procedures carried out to prevent outcomes distorted by unwanted elements, such as contamination?;

- *discriminatory power* – can this evidence, as used in forensic science, distinguish between individuals or only between relatively large classes of the population?;

- *honesty* - sometimes, regrettably, has the scientist told the whole truth about the tests, the observations and the inferences?.

Thus "reliability" is not a useful concept and we shall not use it in this book. We shall discuss sensitivity, quality control, discriminatory power and honesty as separate concepts.

1.4 What we will cover

We adopt a structure different from that of most other books on forensic scientific evidence. Those intended for scientists are usually built round the different techniques available. Those for lawyers are often structured round rules such as the Basis Rule, the Field of Expertise Rule, the Qualifications Rule and the Ultimate Issue Rule. That such a structure is unsatisfactory is shown by the extent to which these "rules" are intertwined. Courts sometimes refer to one, sometimes to another. Cases which are decided on the basis of one rule are often explicable by reference to another.

In this book we:

- explain the fundamentals of logical reasoning about evidence and show how these principles apply to all forms of scientific evidence in court cases. These principles explain how individual items of evidence should be thought about and how they should be combined with the other evidence in the case;

- discuss various misleading and fallacious styles of presentation of evidence, some of which are still in common use;

- argue that the same principles of reasoning are applicable to all forms of evidence;

- discuss some specific types of scientific evidence to show how the principles apply to particular problems they raise; and

- examine some of the more traditional legal questions in the light of our analysis and make recommendations for reform.

Contents of Chapter 2

INTERPRETING SCIENTIFIC EVIDENCE

Chapter 2

INTERPRETING SCIENTIFIC EVIDENCE

Expert scientific evidence usually involves the forensic scientist making an observation on some aspect of the case and, based on past experience, reporting inferences to the court. For example, the scientist may compare blood found at the scene with that of the accused and declare it to be of the same type which may be quite rare in the general population. Our task is to see precisely what inferences can and cannot legitimately be drawn from such an observation. There is a simple and logical solution to these questions that deals with many of the difficulties courts have perceived with expert evidence.

In later chapters we discuss how the expert should report such inferences and how the court should interpret them, what weight the court should give them and how they should be combined with other evidence to help the court to decide the issues before it. In this chapter we consider how to evaluate a single item of evidence that is offered as proof of part of a party's case.

2.1 Relevance and probative value

The first requirement that any piece of evidence tendered in court must satisfy is that it must be relevant. In order to be considered, an item of evidence must be one that might rationally affect the decision. If it cannot, then it is surely worthless. A typical definition of relevance which reflects that used in all common law systems is found in Rule 401 of the US Federal Rules of Evidence:

> " 'Relevant evidence' means evidence having any tendency to make the existence of any fact that is of consequence to the determination of the action more probable or less probable than it would be without the evidence."

Rather than the term "fact" in this book we will use the words "assertion" or "hypothesis" for what must be proved in either a civil or criminal case. If an item of evidence does not cause us to change our probability assessment for the hypothesis then we would not normally describe it as evidence either for or against it. Thus if an item of evidence is worth considering it is one that might cause us to increase or decrease our assessment of the probability of some fact which is of significance in determining the case.[1] "Good evidence", presumably, must have a substantial effect on our probability. What is it about a piece of evidence which enables us to change our probability assessment? To answer this question, we must consider some extreme cases.

Ideal and useless evidence

An *ideal* piece of evidence would be something that always occurs when what we are trying to prove is true and never occurs otherwise. If we are trying to demonstrate the truth of an hypothesis or assertion we would like to find as evidence something which always occurs when the hypothesis is true and never occurs when the hypothesis is not true. An example is the old proverb "where there is smoke there is fire". In real life, evidence this good is almost impossible to find. Suppose a blind person needed to determine if it were cloudy. Rain is not ideal evidence because absence of rain does not imply absence of cloud. If it is raining we can be sure there are clouds about but there may also be clouds if it is not raining.

At the other end of the scale, some information is certainly useless as evidence. Imagine a child being interviewed because of suspected sexual abuse. We seek factors which indicate abuse (or otherwise). If we looked at "all data" without discrimination we might note that she is breathing at the time of the interview. After many such interviews we conclude that all children who allege abuse are breathing at the time of the interview. We know, however, that this is useless as evidence of abuse simply because all other children breathe as well. In other words, the child is equally likely to be breathing whether she has been abused or not. Despite being a characteristic shared by all abused children, breathing is not any sort of evidence for abuse. It does not *discriminate* between abuse and non-abuse.

Likewise, a large proportion of the DNA in our cells is indistinguishable in all human beings. This is why we nearly all have two eyes, two legs etc. The presence of this material in DNA samples taken from the scene of a crime and from a suspect is useless as evidence of identification. Since everyone shares such characteristics the finding is equally likely whether or not it was the accused who left the mark.[2]

Typical evidence

In practice, however, ideal evidence is seldom found. Even if the evidence always occurs when the hypothesis is true it may also occur when it is not (for example,

---

[1] Montrose uses the term "material" rather than significant. See Montrose, JL, "Basic Concepts in the Law of Evidence" (1954) 79 LQR 527.
[2] Lempert, R, "Some caveats concerning DNA as criminal identification evidence; with thanks to the Reverend Bayes" (1991) 132 Cardozo LR 303–342.

rain as evidence for clouds). Alternatively, when the hypothesis is true the event may not invariably occur. Thus, in the real world, evidence is something that is more likely to occur when what we are trying to prove is true, than when it is not. Good or strong evidence would be something that is much more likely to occur when what we are trying to prove is true, than when it is not.

For example, during a career of interviewing, a doctor might observe that a high proportion of abused children display signs of stress such as nail-biting. This will be evidence of abuse if and only if abused children are more likely to bite their nails than other children. If it turned out that abused and non-abused children are equally likely to bite their nails then this observation is useless as evidence of abuse. If abused children are much more likely to bite their nails than non-abused then we have strong evidence of abuse. Suppose 80% of abused children bite their nails but only 10% of other children do so. Nail-biting would then be eight times more likely in the case of an abused child than in another child. If, on the other hand, 90% of other children bite their nails then nail-biting would point the other way and reduce the probability that the child had been abused (but only weakly).

There are two points to notice: first, the strength (or probative value) of the evidence depends not only on how many abused children bite their nails but also on how many non-abused children do so; secondly, and most importantly, all we know at this stage is the probability of the *evidence* in each case. We do not know how likely it is that the child has been abused.

The probative value of any piece of evidence can be assessed in the same way. A scientific test result is good evidence for a particular hypothesis if it is much more likely to occur if the hypothesis is true, than when it is not. We will know this only if we have seen the result of the test not only on a number of occasions when the hypothesis is true, but also when it is false. We cannot be sure of the strength of the evidence if we only observe cases when the hypothesis is true. However, what we will know at the end of this is how likely the *test* result is if the hypothesis is true and not how likely it is that the hypothesis is true.

A breath-testing machine

Consider a simple breath-testing machine designed to be used at the roadside for checking whether a driver is over or under the legal alcohol limit. It is supposed to show a red light if the driver is over the limit, a green light if he is under. It will have to be calibrated before being used to determine how accurate it is. We must guard against two types of error: a false positive and a false negative. A false positive – a red light shows when the person is actually under the limit – leads to someone being wrongly arrested and inconvenienced by being required to be tested by the more accurate device at the police station. A false negative – a green light shows when the person is really over the limit – leads to a drunk driver remaining on the road.

Unfortunately, reducing one of these rates by adjusting the settings of the device will inevitably increase the other. There is presumably a reason for each false reading and technical improvement would reduce the errors. However, bearing in mind that we are trying to produce a cheap and robust device we may not be able to afford to investigate all the causes. It may be impossible in practice to eliminate errors altogether and we simply have a choice of which errors to make. Which error is the more serious is a political question, but let us suppose some figures purely for sake of example.

Before using it, we calibrate the testing machine with samples of air with a measured alcohol content. Many such samples are tested. Suppose, as a numerical example, we test 1,000 samples with an alcohol concentration marginally below the legal limit and 1,000 samples marginally above. We adjust the device so that, of the samples over the limit, 950 read red and 50 read green, and, of the samples below the limit, 995 read green and 5 read red.[3]

An aside on probability and odds

This section breaks the flow of our argument, but the simple ideas of probability and odds form such a fundamental part of the argument presented in this book that it is important that the reader is reminded of them. This section is therefore a quick revision of the ideas of probability and odds before we go further. Readers already familiar with the concepts should therefore omit this section.

Probability is a rational measure of the degree of belief in the truth of an assertion based on information. The hypothesis, assertion, or premise is itself either true or false. For example, the assertion "The driver is over the drinking limit" is either true or false but we may not be sure of whether or not it is true. Our degree of belief about the truth of the assertion is measured by our assessment of its probability.

The value of all probabilities depends on the assumptions and information used in assessing them. Thus, we would assess a different probability for the assertion "the driver is over the drinking limit" if we had evidence of the result of the breath test, than we would without that evidence. All the evidence that is used to assess a probability is known as the *condition* for the probability. All probabilities are conditional on the evidence used.

Evidence is also described in the form of assertions. Thus "the light showed red", if true, is evidence for the hypothesis that "the person is over the limit" and would determine a different probability than would be assessed if the evidence "the light showed green" were true. That, again, would generally be different if we either had no evidence of the colour of the light or had additional evidence of erratic driving.

Probabilities take values between 0 and 1.[4] A probability of 0 means that (on the basis of the evidence listed in the condition) the assertion is impossible and we

---

[3] We must make two points about this exposition: first, the figures have been chosen simply for arithmetic simplicity and may well be wrong by orders of magnitude; secondly, the problem has been simplified. In fact, the probability of a false reading will decline as one moves away from the limit so that the chances of a false positive from a sample substantially under the limit will be negligible.

[4] The reasons for this are explained in our paper Robertson, BWN and Vignaux, GA, "Probability – the Logic of the Law" (1993) 13 OJLS 457.

therefore believe it to be false. A probability of 1 means that, given the condition, the assertion is true. Thus, my probability for the assertion "the sun will rise tomorrow", given my knowledge of the working of the solar system, is 1.

Most assessments of probability fall between these limits.[5] A probability of 0.5 for an assertion means that we are equally sure (or equally unsure) that the assertion is true and that its negation is true.

Probabilities can be represented as percentages by multiplying them by 100%. A probability of 0.5 could be described as a probability of 50%, one of 0.3 as a probability of 30%. We will often use percentages in this book.

We will also need to describe probabilities in the form of *Odds*. Many people are familiar with odds, if only from betting. They also recognise that they are a description of uncertainty, like probability. However, not everyone realises that they are only another way of representing probability and one can go from one form to another quite easily.

To get the odds from the probability of an assertion you calculate the ratio of the probability to (1 – the probability) and simplify as much as possible. Thus, a probability of 0.3 has equivalent odds of:

$$\text{Odds} = \frac{\text{Probability}}{(1-\text{Probability})} = \frac{0.3}{(1-0.3)} = \frac{0.3}{0.7} = \frac{3}{7}$$

This could also be written as odds of 3 to 7 (in favour of the assertion).

Odds corresponding to a probability of 0.5 are:

$$\text{Odds} = \frac{0.5}{(1-0.5)} = \frac{0.5}{0.5} = \frac{5}{5} = \frac{1}{1}$$

These odds would be described as 1 to 1 or *evens*.

Odds of less than evens are sometimes reversed and described as "odds against" the assertion. Odds of 3 to 7 in favour of an assertion might, instead, be described as odds of 7 to 3 *against*.[6]

To return from odds to probability is a little trickier. One calculates the fraction: numerator of the odds divided by the sum of the numerator and the denominator of the odds. Thus, odds of 3 to 7 would be the same as a probability of:

$$\text{Probability} = \frac{3}{(3+7)} = \frac{3}{10} = 0.3$$

[5] We are usually warned even to be aware of the possibility of an unexpected astronomical calamity which would prevent the sun rising tomorrow and, therefore, never to assess the probability of a "certain" assertion exactly as 1 but as a value minutely less.

[6] Odds are also sometimes described just as a fraction or its decimal equivalent. Odds of 3 to 7 might be stated as 0.43 = 3/7; evens as 1.0 = 1/1. This presentation always has the potential to be confused with a true fraction, however, and we will not use it.

Even odds (1 to 1) correspond to a probability of $1/(1+1) = 1/2 = 0.5$.

The breath-tester again

From the data from the calibration tests we can see that:

(i)   If the sample is over the limit there is a 95% probability (950/1000) that the device will indicate red and a 5% probability (50/1000) that it will indicate green – the odds are 19 to 1 that it will indicate red if the sample is over the limit.[7]

(ii) If the sample is under the limit there is a 0.5% probability that the device will indicate red and a 99.5% probability that it will indicate green – the odds are 199 to 1 that it will indicate green if the sample is under the limit.[8]

We can see from the calibration data that a red light on the breath test is pretty good evidence for the assertion that "the person is over the limit". If a person is over the limit there is a 95% probability of a red light; if a person is under the limit there is only a 0.5% probability of a red light. Thus, a red light is 190 times more likely to occur if the subject is over the limit than if under ($95/0.5 = 190$).

In contrast, a green light is good evidence *against* the assertion that "the person is over the limit". If a person is over the limit there is a 5% probability of a green light; if under the limit there is a 99.5% probability of a green light. A green light is about 19.9 times *less* likely to occur if the person is over the limit than if under ($5/99.5 = 1/19.9$). Therefore, depending on the light shown the tester can provide good evidence either for or against the assertion that "the person is over the limit".

However, let us re-emphasise that this is telling us only the probative value of the evidence and not the probability that the person is over (or under) the limit. We are sure that the breath-tester is a good piece of evidence, which means that it should cause us to change our assessment of the probability that the person is over the limit. But how exactly is this to be done?

2.2 The likelihood ratio and Bayes' Rule

The information at this stage is the "wrong way round". We knew the contents of the samples and we have determined the probability of getting a red signal, given that the sample is over the limit. However, when the device is used we want to know something quite different. If the device gives a red light what is the probability that the person is over the limit?[9]

Early in the history of probability theory attention was devoted to the difficulty that the evidence is the "wrong way round". This was known as the problem of inverse probabilities.[10] The solution of a particular case was discovered by the

---

[7] It is much clearer and more precise to express this in symbols: probability (red | over the limit) = 0.95 where the symbol "|" stands for "given the condition" or just "given". Similarly, probability (green | over) = 0.05.

[8] Probability (red | under the limit) = 0.005 and probability (green | under) = 0.995.

[9] What we want is probability (over the limit | red light).

[10] For some interestingly written history, see Gigerenzer, G *et al*, *The Empire of Chance* (CUP, 1989).

Reverend Thomas Bayes (1702–1761) and published posthumously in 1763. His work was extended by Pierre Simon, Marquis de Laplace (1749–1827). They proved, in what is now known as *Bayes' Rule*, that the value of a piece of evidence in testing a particular assertion against an alternative is determined by its *likelihood ratio*.

The likelihood ratio

We have already met the likelihood ratio in considering the evidence of nail-biting and the evidence of the breath tester in **2.1** above. In the child-abuse case the likelihood ratio for nail-biting is the 80% chance of nail-biting if the child *has* been abused, divided by the 10% chance of nail-biting if the child *has not* been abused, 80/10 or 8. In the breath test example above the likelihood ratio for a red light is:

$$\frac{\text{Probability of red if over limit}}{\text{Probability of red if not over limit}} = \frac{95}{0.5} = 190$$

where the probabilities are of getting a red light supposing the two conditions (over and not over the limit).[11]

The likelihood ratio, then, is the probability of the evidence supposing our assertion is true, divided by the probability of the evidence if the assertion is not true. The probability of the evidence supposing the assertion is true, is the *numerator*. The probability of the evidence if the assertion is not true, is the *denominator*. When we divide them we get a single figure, a ratio which tells us the strength of the evidence in supporting our hypothesis.

If the likelihood ratio is more than 1 the evidence tells in favour of the hypothesis. If the ratio is less than 1 (usually expressed as a decimal fraction) then it tells against the hypothesis. If the ratio is exactly 1 then the evidence is neutral. The strength of the evidence is measured by how much the likelihood ratio differs from 1, in either direction.

Bayes' Rule

Bayes' Rule is a logical theorem – there can be no doubt about its truth. It tells us how to update our knowledge by incorporating new evidence. We start with some knowledge about the hypothesis, expressed as odds in favour of it. These are known as the *prior odds*. The prior odds (our assessment without the evidence) must be multiplied by the likelihood ratio of the new piece of evidence to give the *posterior odds*.[12] The posterior odds are what we want to know – the odds in favour of the hypothesis after taking into account the new piece of evidence:

prior odds × likelihood ratio → posterior odds

[11] For a green light the likelihood ratio for these two assertions is (5)/(99.5) = 1/19.9.
[12] This is more formally presented in the Appendix where there is also a discussion of probability and odds.

Returning to the breath-tester, a red light makes the odds that the person was over the limit 190 times greater than we would have assessed them to be without it.

Therefore, we must first consider how likely the person was to be over the limit before we consider the evidence of the breath-test. In other words, what were the prior odds that the person was over the limit? If the driver was stopped for no particular reason (for so-called "random testing") these odds may just reflect the proportion of drivers at that time of day who are over the limit. There might be only 1 out of 100 drivers who are over the limit. The prior odds would then be 1 to 99. Usually, however, there will be evidence such as erratic driving which alerted the police and caused the the driver to be stopped. If, on the basis of such evidence, it is believed that there is a 50/50 chance (odds of 1 to 1, or evens) that the driver is over the limit before testing, the odds in favour of that proposition after seeing the red light become 190 to 1:[13]

$$\frac{1}{1} \times 190 = \frac{190}{1}$$

The effect of prior odds

With a different prior probability, one will get a different posterior assessment. Suppose that you knew that you certainly had not had a drink for over 48 hours but the device gave a red light when you blew into it. You would probably conclude that the device had given a false reading although there is a slight possibility that alcohol had been retained in your body for a long time. So, for example, you might have assessed the odds that you were truly over the limit as 10,000 to 1 *against* before taking the breath test – that is odds of 1 to 10,000 in favour of the proposition that you were over the limit. After taking a test with a likelihood ratio of 190, as we just calculated, you should now consider that the odds that you are over the limit are about $(1/10,000)(190) = 19/1000$. This is about 53 to 1 against being over the limit. It is still very improbable but not nearly so improbable as before.

The officer performing the test, not knowing your history, may have different prior odds. Even if he believes that there is only a 1 in 10 chance that you were over the limit prior to administering the test (*i.e.* odds of 1 to 10 that you were over the limit) he would now believe that the odds were $(1/10)(190) = 19$ to 1 in favour of that assertion.[14]

---

[13] Odds of 190 to 1 correspond to a probability of $190/(190+1) = 0.9948$.
[14] This paragraph emphasises that there is no such thing as a "true probability". The truth is that you are either over or under the limit. The reason we have to make probability assessments is that we do not have complete information and every probability assessment is dependent (or "conditional") on the information taken into account.

An HIV test

Very large or very small prior odds can give some startling effects. For example, in testing for HIV among potential blood donors, it is very important to avoid false negatives. That is to say someone with HIV should not be given a negative result (told that they don't have HIV) by mistake. In tests used in 1985, in order to avoid these false negatives, a false positive rate of 1% had to be accepted.[15] This meant that on average out of every 100 tests administered to those who are virus-free, 1 test wrongly said that HIV was present. Assume that the test gave no false negatives. A positive result was certain to occur if the subject carried HIV and had a 1% chance of occurring if the subject did not. In other words, a positive result had a likelihood ratio of $1/0.01 = 100$.

This sounds (and is) very accurate, but a curious result is obtained when we combine the evidence with the prior odds. At that time, probably fewer than 1 in 10,000 potential blood donors had the virus, so the prior odds that the person had HIV were 1 to 10,000. The likelihood ratio of the positive result is 100. Multiplying the prior odds in favour of infection by the likelihood ratio gives the posterior odds of 100 to 10,000 = 1 to 100 (*i.e.* 100 to 1 against). In other words *even given a positive test* it was still highly unlikely that the person had the virus.

To understand this more easily, imagine 10,001 tests, of 10,000 subjects without the virus and 1 infected. We expect to record the 1 real infection and to obtain no false negatives. However, we would also expect to record 100 false positives from those without the infection (with the remaining 9900 as true negatives).[16] Thus, we would expect 101 positive results, only one of whom actually carries HIV. Therefore, the posterior odds, of carrying HIV after considering a positive result, are 1 to 100 (or 100 to 1 *against* the subject being infected – as demonstrated above). This is why a second, independent test must be administered when a positive result occurs.

Using imaginary figures, if the second test result had a likelihood ratio of 1500, the posterior odds after both tests would be $(1/10000)(100)(1500) = 15$ to 1 in favour of the assertion of the presence of HIV. The problem of combining evidence in this way is discussed in more detail in chapter 5.

Transposing the conditional

We now mention one of the most common mistakes which is made in dealing with evidence. It is considered in more detail later in chapter 6. It is too easy – and quite wrong – to slip from the knowledge that there is only a 1% chance of a positive result if you do not carry the HIV virus, to the conclusion that there is only a 1% chance that you do not carry HIV if you get a positive test result. This is to

---

[15] Notice the similarity with the breath-tester. The data are taken from letters to the editor from Hall, GH (1985) 291 BMJ 1424 and Seetulsingh, D (1985) 291 BMJ 1647.

[16] In this calculation we use expected values only. In any particular group the numbers of false positives may well vary, for reasons which we cannot control – otherwise we could reduce the false positive rate.

ignore the prior odds – in other words, to ignore what we already know about the matter. Likewise the fact that there was a 95% chance of a red light if the subject is over the limit does not mean that there is a 95% chance that the subject is over the limit if there is a red light.[17] This common error is known as *transposing the conditional*[18] since the condition (the assertion that the subject is carrying the HIV virus) is swapped with the evidence (of the test result).

The error can be recognised clearly in a case where nobody would make a mistake. Consider the probability that a person, known to be over six feet tall, is a man. This is obviously high – most six-footers are men. Now, in contrast, consider the probability that a person known to be a man, is over six feet tall. This is obviously not the same since only a small proportion of men are over six feet tall. In one case we are considering the probability that "the person is over six feet" and in the other the probability that "the person is a man". The two cases also have different conditions. The confusion arises because the assertion in one statement is the evidence in the other (and vice versa).

To look at this numerically, suppose that 5% of men but only 0.5% of women are at least six feet tall. Knowing that a perpetrator is six feet tall should multiply our assessment of the odds in favour of their being a man by the likelihood ratio of $5/0.5 = 10$. Assuming that the number of men and women in the population are roughly equal, the prior odds that a person is a man is 1 to 1. If we are told that the perpetrator is over six feet tall then the posterior odds that they are a man are $(1/1)(10) = 10$ to 1.

Suppose we had originally been given the information that the six-foot person, whose sex we are considering, was a nurse. We know from the information above that the fact that someone is over six feet tall multiplies the odds that they are a man by 10. However, the fact that someone is a nurse gives us *prior* odds that they are a man equal to the small proportion of nurses who are men. If only 2% of nurses are men this gives prior odds of 1 to 49. The evidence that the person is over six feet tall multiplies these odds by 10. This gives posterior odds in favour of being a man of 10 to 49 (odds of about 5 to 1 against being a man). It is important to realise that the value of the evidence of height has not itself changed, but a six-foot nurse is still much more likely to be a woman than a man because of the huge imbalance of the sexes in that profession.

Giving evidence

If a case involving the breath-test device was contested in court a forensic scientist might give evidence about the result of the test. What evidence could he give? He could not tell us the probability that person was over the limit since to do so he would have to hear and consider all the other evidence to assess the prior

---

[17] This is equating probability (red | over limit) to probability (over limit | red).

[18] This phrase appears to have been coined in Diaconis, P and Freedman, D, "The persistence of cognitive illusions" (1981) 4 *The Behavioural and Brain Sciences* 333. Although it uses an adjective as a noun it is now the phrase in common use. The fallacy is discussed more fully, with some examples from cases in chapter 6.

probability, which is really the job of the court.[19] What he *could* tell us, in this simplified example, is that a positive test should multiply the prior odds that the person was over the limit by 190; that is, he should state the likelihood ratio *and that is all he should say.*

It follows that we cannot determine the probability of guilt (or presence at the scene, or paternity, or whatever else is to be proved) simply on the basis of the expert evidence. We must have the prior odds as well. However, the task of determining the prior odds is a task for the judge or jury and not for the expert, who is not privy to the rest of the evidence in the case.

Therefore, *expert evidence should be restricted to the likelihood ratio given by the test or observation* (or its components.) If an expert purports to give a probability for the hypothesis he must be assuming some prior. This is wrong in both law and logic.

2.3 Admissibility and relevance

As we have seen, an item of evidence will change the odds if it has a likelihood ratio different from 1. If the likelihood ratio is greater than 1 the evidence will cause our assessment of probability for the assertion to increase. If it is less than 1 our assessment of the probability should decrease. Hence, any piece of evidence giving a likelihood ratio other than 1 is relevant and, in principle, all relevant information should be used in coming to a rational assessment of the probability.[20]

To assess a likelihood ratio it is not essential to have precise numbers for each of the probabilities. The value of the evidence depends upon the ratio of these numbers. Therefore, if we believe that the evidence is 10 times more probable under one hypothesis than the other, the likelihood ratio is 10, whatever the precise values of the numerator and denominator may be. Often we will be able to assess this ratio roughly on the basis of our general knowledge and experience. Saying that evidence is relevant is just another way of saying that it is more probable under one hypothesis than another and, therefore, has a likelihood ratio different from 1.

Unfortunately, courts and commentators have often used the word "relevant" to mean something more complicated. There is always a cost in terms of money, time, multiplication of issues, or possible prejudice, of introducing any piece of evidence. The probative value of the evidence must be weighed against these costs. United States Federal Rule 403 provides:

> "Although relevant, evidence may be excluded if its probative value is substantially outweighed by the danger of unfair prejudice, confusion of the issues, or misleading

---

[19] We use the term "court" informally to mean "tribunal of fact" as opposed to the forensic scientist. In the small percentage of cases tried on indictment this will be the jury rather than the judge.
[20] " . . . unless excluded by some rule or principle of law, all that is logically probative is admissible." (Thayer, JP, *A preliminary treatise on the law of evidence*, (Little, Brown & Co, Boston, 1898) p 264).

the jury, or by considerations of undue delay, waste of time or needless presentation of cumulative evidence."

"Probative value" is clearly directly related to the likelihood ratio. The further the likelihood ratio is from 1 (in either direction) the greater is the evidence's probative value.

Evidence with a likelihood ratio not far from 1 (*e.g.* only 0.8 or 4), will have low probative value and might not be worth admitting if the cost (in the wider sense described) is too high. Some new types of evidence may have such low values of likelihood ratio. It is up to the proponents of these new types of evidence to demonstrate their likelihood ratio on the basis of independent tests.

Some people distinguish between relevance and probative value, while others refer to "degree of relevance". What is not helpful is to use "relevant" to refer to the outcome of this balancing of probative value against the cost of admitting the evidence. These two considerations must be kept separate, as they are by the US Federal Rules.

The problem for a judge is to determine the relevance or probative value of an individual item of evidence without examining the entire case. One of the objects of Rule 403 is to save time and expense, and this will not be achieved if, at an admissibility hearing, the evidence is canvassed as fully as in open court. Somehow, the judge must estimate what the probative value of the proposed evidence may be (that is, in our terms, what its likelihood ratio is) and balance that against the wider costs of admission. If the mere question of admissibility will cause substantial argument and expense and one believes that the probative value of the evidence will be low then this itself may be a reason for refusing to admit it.[21]

On the other hand, when examining forensic scientific evidence, there is a tendency to demand very high likelihood ratios. Sometimes, DNA evidence, as we shall see in later chapters, can have likelihood ratios in the millions. Hodgkinson refers throughout for the need for the evidence to be of "high probative value".[22] It seems that courts might regard the evidence as almost useless if the likelihood ratio is less than 100. In the Australian case *R* v *Tran*[23] aspersions were cast on the DNA evidence because the likelihood ratio may have been as low as 87; but in other cases courts have recognised that DNA likelihood ratios as low as 72 and 40 are relevant evidence.[24]

Values as low as that may actually compare quite favourably with much evidence that is traditionally admitted, such as eyewitness descriptions and identifications, although it may be difficult to obtain data to establish their likelihood ratios.

---

[21] For example, polygraph or lie-detector tests seem to produce likelihood ratios of only 1.5 to 3 and to be very weak evidence (Kleinmuntz, B and Szucko, JJ, "A field study of the fallibility of polygraphic lie detection" (1984) 308 *Nature* 449–450.

[22] Hodgkinson, T *Expert Evidence Law and Practice* (Sweet and Maxwell, London, 1990) 4.

[23] (1990) 50 A Crim R 233. This case also involved problems with confidence intervals which are dealt with in chapter 6.

[24] *Police Department of Rarotonga* v *Amoa Amoa* Court of Appeal of the Cook Islands CA 3/93, 11 August 1993, tbr SPLR.

There seems no special reason why forensic scientific evidence should be subject to any more rigorous conditions. Always assuming that the evidence does not fall foul of some other exclusionary rule, a blood-grouping test giving a likelihood ratio of only 4 or 5 should not be rejected on that ground alone. The question is whether there is sufficient other evidence to combine with it to attain the required standard of proof. Combining evidence is discussed more fully in chapter 5.

Prejudging the case?

To calculate the numerator of the likelihood ratio one has to assess the probability of the evidence supposing that the prosecution case is true. This has led some to believe that calculating a likelihood ratio involves assuming that the prosecution case is true.[25] This is misconceived. One is only considering how probable the evidence would be supposing (for the sake of argument) that the prosecution case is true and then comparing that with the probability of the evidence supposing that the defence case is true. This process requires no level of belief in either of these hypotheses. Furthermore, it merely makes explicit the logical reasoning process naturally applied to any piece of evidence. If a juror thinks that a particular piece of evidence is incriminating this can only be because the juror thinks that the evidence is more probable if the prosecution case is true than if the defence case is. If we were to make this objection to all evidence any sort of rational inference would become impossible.

2.4 Case studies

At the end of appropriate chapters we will discuss some real cases which illuminate points made in the body of the chapter. Here, we look at a case where a likelihood ratio was given in court, some problems with paternity cases, and psychological evidence in child sex-abuse cases.

A case involving DNA evidence

The New Zealand case *R* v *Pengelly*[26] provides an example which helps us to see what should be done with the evidence. The case concerned a murder in Auckland, in the course of which the assailant cut himself and left bloodstains at the scene. These were analysed using a DNA profile (see chapter 9). In court, the forensic scientist, Dr Margaret Lawton, described her results by saying:

"In the analysis of the results I carried out I considered two alternatives: either that the blood samples originated from Pengelly or that the … blood was from another individual. I find that the results I obtained were at least 12,450 times more likely to

[25] A recent example is Uviller, HR (1994) 43 Duke LJ 834, 836 *et seq.*
[26] [1992] 1 NZLR 545 (CA). The material quoted is from the trial at first instance and taken from the transcript in the Case on Appeal.

have occurred if the blood had originated from Pengelly than if it had originated from someone else.[27]

Question: Can you express that in another way?

Answer: It could also be said that 1 in 12,450 people would have the same profile ... and that Pengelly was included in that number.''

Although she did not use the term, the witness had stated the likelihood ratio for the evidence on the two hypotheses that the blood came from Pengelly and that it instead came from a randomly selected person. This likelihood ratio had then to be multiplied by the prior odds.

There are two ways to do this. One is to consider the DNA evidence as the first item of evidence and determine the prior odds by asking what is the population from which the perpetrator could have come? As the population of Auckland is approximately one million we would assign prior odds (that is prior to any evidence) of about 1 to 1,000,000 that Pengelly was the killer.[28] When we multiply those (conservative) odds by the likelihood ratio of 12450 we get for the posterior odds:

$$\frac{1}{1,000,000} \, 12450 = \frac{1245}{100,000}$$

These are odds of 1 to 80 that Pengelly is guilty (or 80 to 1 *against* his guilt). In other words, instead of being 1 out of one million people who might have committed the murder, Pengelly was 1 out of only about 80 who could have been guilty. The effect of the evidence is to change the odds that Pengelly is guilty from 1 to 1,000,000 down to 1 to 80. Further evidence was therefore needed before Pengelly could be convicted.

Alternatively, one could consider the other evidence first and come to a judgment of prior odds based upon that. The other evidence in the case pointed to quite a small group, including Pengelly, which probably contained the perpetrator, such that the prior odds were down to about 1 in 4. When these prior odds are multiplied by the likelihood ratio of 12450 we get for the posterior odds:

$$\frac{1}{4} 12450 = 3112$$

Thus, the posterior odds are over 3,000 to 1 in favour of the assertion that Pengelly is guilty. This is equivalent to a probability of over 99.9%.[29]

---

[27] It became clear in cross-examination that "someone else" meant "a randomly selected member of the population".

[28] We have not even yet taken into account that violent burglaries are carried out by able-bodied people (usually male) over about 12 and under 60, which would cut the odds down further.

[29] From the odds, $3112/(3113+1) = 0.9997$.

For reasons we discuss later Dr Lawton did not attempt to give the jury direct guidance on how to handle the likelihood ratio. However, the important point to note is that, correctly and consistently with the argument in this book, at no stage did she express an opinion as to the probability that the blood came from Pengelly. She summed up her evidence by saying that the likelihood ratio of 12450 "very strongly supports the premise that the two blood stains examined . . . came from Pengelly".

The probability of paternity

Experts commonly testify to the probability of assertions. This is particularly so in paternity cases where courts are used to hearing witnesses give a probability that X is the father of Y.

Thus, in the New Zealand case *Byers* v *Nicholls*[30] we find testimony that "evidence of the [tests] indicates that there is a 99% probability for [Byers] being the father of [the girl]". This typical statement follows a formula advocated as long ago as 1938.[31] It is still in common use in several jurisdictions despite having been exposed as fallacious by eminent US scholars.[32]

Experts who adopt this method of giving evidence commit three major errors. The first error is that they have assumed prior odds which have no connection with the facts of the particular case. Before we can state a probability or odds for any assertion, we must assess prior odds. These odds will depend upon the other evidence in the case. Experts in paternity cases have developed the habit of routinely assuming prior odds of 1 to 1 (evens) on the grounds that they know nothing about the case; with no information about a matter and only two hypotheses such odds may indeed be the appropriate assumption.[33] However, the experts certainly know something and the court probably knows more – that this is a case in which one person has fathered a child and that that person's identity is in doubt. Why take prior odds of 1 to 1? Why not take prior odds of 1 to the male population of the world (say, 1 to 2 billion) or 1 to the male population of the country? Unless the likelihood ratio yielded by the evidence is astronomically high (which, with modern DNA testing, it might well be) the assessment of the prior will substantially affect the eventual probability.

Secondly, the witness is assuming an alternative hypothesis, that if the father were not the defendant it was some randomly selected male from the population, again without reference to the facts of the individual case. This choice of alternative hypothesis is discussed in chapter 3.

[30] (1988) 4 NZFLR 545.
[31] Essen-Möller, E, "Die Biesweiskraft der Ähnlichkeit im Vater Schaftsnachweis; Theoretische Grundlagen" (1938) 68 Mitt Anthorop, Ges (Wein) 598.
[32] For example see Kaye, D, "The probability of an ultimate issue; the strange cases of paternity testing" (1989) 1 Iowa LR 75–109.
[33] The search for methods of determining uninformative priors has been a constant theme in the Bayesian literature since the time of Laplace. See, for example, Box and Tiao, *Bayesian inference in statistical analysis* (Reading, Mass: Addison-Wesley, 1973) and Jaynes, "Where do we stand on Maximum Entropy?" in Rosenkranz (Ed), *ET Jaynes: Papers on Probability, Statistics and Statistical Physics* (Dordrecht:Reidel, 1983).

Thirdly, and worst of all, the witness may conceal these assumptions by wrapping them up in a single probability. We shall also see in chapter 5 that it is quite impossible to take evidence given in this form and combine it with the other evidence in the case.

Sometimes the expert openly states what the assumed prior is and says (for example) "assuming a prior of evens, and considering the odds against a match by chance, on the basis of this evidence alone, I believe the odds in favour of X being the father of Y are 10,000 to 1 – that is a probability of 99.99%".[34] As it stands this is not incorrect but it introduces extraneous material and confuses the issues.

In some jurisdictions in criminal cases witnesses state in a similar way the probability that the accused left a mark found at the scene of the crime. Such evidence is sometimes called the "probability of contact" and is common in the United States. In a German case the witness gave a "probability of contact" but made clear that it was based on a prior of evens (in other words that without the evidence the accused was as likely as not to be the person who left the mark). The court said (in translation):

> The conversion of the probability of the characteristics of 0.014% into a probability of incrimination ... of 99.986% requires, as the expert witness Dr H has set out to the Supreme Court, the establishment of a prior probability. One can only reach a result of 99.986% if the prior probability of 50% is assumed. That means ... that before the DNA analysis the probability that the seminal fluid is from the accused is as high as the probability that it is not. The expert witness, who should only report about the result of this DNA analysis, could start from this (neutral) prior probability. The court had to be aware that the result of the expert witness's opinion only makes an abstract statement about the statistical probability of incrimination. This result is not allowed to be treated as the equivalent of the concrete incrimination of the accused.[35]

The court was left with no guidance about how to use this "abstract probability" as evidence. If it had been, it would have been to combine the likelihood ratio for the evidence with the prior which the *court* (not the expert) had assessed on the basis of the other evidence. This would have made the expert's prior redundant. The expert should simply have stated the likelihood ratio for the evidence.

Whenever expert witnesses purport to assess the probability of an hypothesis they should be questioned to establish the assumptions which have been built into their prior odds and to establish the true value of their evidence in the context of the particular case. The only exceptions appear to be evidence like fingerprints and handwriting where experts assert that two impressions did or did not come from the same source. The reasons for these exceptions are discussed later.

Although the courts have become accustomed to receiving such evidence (especially the "probability of paternity") they have such difficulty in dealing

[34] *E.g. Loveridge* v *Adlam* [1991] NZFLR 267, *Brimicombe* v *Maughan* [1992] NZFLR 476.
[35] BGH, Urteil vom 12.8.1992 – 5 StR 239/92 (L.G. Hannover), BDR (Germany) 1992 vol 10 988–989.

with it that it is in precisely these cases that they agonise over the relationship between "statistical" and "legal" probability. Thus, in the English case *Re JS (A Minor)* Ormrod LJ said:

"The concept of 'probability' in the legal sense is certainly different from the mathematical concept; indeed, it is rare to find a situation in which these two usages co-exist, although when they do, the mathematical probability has to be taken into the assessment of probability in the legal sense and given its appropriate weight."[36]

We believe that this distinction is artificial. It is the giving of evidence of a probability of contact or of paternity which leads to the belief that there is such a thing as a "mathematical probability" or an "abstract statistical probability" which plays no part in common sense reasoning. The solution is that experts should not give evidence in this fashion.

Child sexual abuse

The logic explained in this chapter can also help to untangle cases where evidence is not given in the form of numbers. The likelihood ratios we have seen above happen to have been derived from statistical surveys or series of scientific measurements but our aim is to make the best possible use of all the information we have, in order to decide a particular case, including evidence which is not statistical in form. The concept of a likelihood ratio for the evidence, even if we cannot state a precise numerical figure in every case, provides the appropriate logical tool for doing this.

In the New Zealand case *R* v *B* [37] a man was accused of sexually assaulting his adopted daughter. A psychologist gave evidence of a number of tests and observations which she had carried out while interviewing the girl. Some of these were formalised tests such as the Family Relations Test and the Rother Incomplete Sentences Test. Others were simply observations of the matters that the child talked about, for example her dreams and her self-image. In discussing each observation the psychologist made some comment such as:

"[this] is typical of sexually abused girls/children/young persons"

except for the dreams, about which she said

"dreams of this kind are frequently experienced by sexually abused young people."

The court regarded the psychologist's evidence as inadmissible for a number of reasons, one of which was:

"its admission must inevitably lead to the jury learning the expert's opinion on the very issue it is required to answer ... large parts of the ... evidence clearly reflect the

---

[36] *Re JS (A Minor)* [1981] Fam 22, 29, [1980] 1 All ER 1061.
[37] [1987] 1 NZLR 362.

psychologist's view that she was examining a child who had been sexually abused by her father."[38]

In another New Zealand case just two years later, *R* v *S*[39] a psychologist gave evidence of a number of characteristics presented by a child alleging sexual abuse, such as self-mutilation, lack of eye contact and an unwillingness to talk about home life. Before detailing these she had been asked the question:

"Did [the complainant] exhibit any characteristics which were consistent with what you had come to know as the characteristics of sexually abused children?"

to which she replied

"very definitely."

In the first case the expert is saying that she has examined a number of abused children and a high proportion of them exhibit these signs. In other words she was giving the probability of finding the behaviour supposing that the child has been abused.[40] Most explicitly, "dreams of this kind are frequently experienced by sexually abused young people". In *R* v *S* the expert was asked whether the child exhibited characteristics which she had come to know as the characteristics of sexually abused children. Again, this clearly means characteristics frequently met in abused children. The probability of these characteristics is high supposing that the child has been abused.

Of course, what the jury had to decide in each case was the probability that the child had been abused, given the psychologist's evidence and all the other evidence in the case.[41] We can now see that the psychologist has not provided all the information which the jury needs. First, there must be prior odds, although that is not the sole responsibility of the expert. The prior odds may be provided by other evidence or might simply be the result of a survey as to the occurrence of the relevant type of abuse. Secondly, the court also needs to know how probable the evidence is if the child had not been abused.[42] The Court of Appeal rejected the evidence for a number of reasons which missed the real issues, but it approached this point when it pointed out that "some at least of those characteristics ... may very well occur in children who have problems other than sexual abuse". In other words, there may have been alternative explanations for the evidence. Alternative explanations will be discussed in chapter 3.

[38] Per Casey J at p 372.
[39] [1989] 1 NZLR 714.
[40] Probability (behaviour|abuse).
[41] Probability (abuse|behaviour etc).
[42] Probability (behaviour|no abuse).

2.5 Summary

- A forensic scientist cannot tell us how probable the prosecution case is but only how much more probable the *evidence* is if the prosecution case is true than if it is not.

- The figure which expresses this comparison is the likelihood ratio.

- In principle, evidence will be relevant when the likelihood ratio is less than or greater than 1. A likelihood ratio of 1 means that the evidence is unhelpful and irrelevant.

- Although relevant, evidence may be excluded by an exclusionary rule or because its probative value (measured by the likelihood ratio) is not sufficient to overcome the cost of admitting it in terms of time, money, confusion or prejudice.

Contents of Chapter 3
THE ALTERNATIVE HYPOTHESIS

Chapter 3

THE ALTERNATIVE HYPOTHESIS

In chapter 2 we saw that the forensic scientific witness must not, and indeed can not, tell us the probability that something occurred, but should only give a likelihood ratio for the evidence (or its components). It is logically meaningless to suggest that any piece of evidence has any value in itself as support for any particular hypothesis. Its value depends entirely upon its ability to discriminate between one hypothesis and another. The first hypothesis will be the case which the prosecution has to prove. What is the second?

So far we assumed that the second hypothesis was just the negation of the first: "the person was over the limit", "the person was not over the limit"; "the person is guilty", "the person is not guilty". It is often difficult if not impossible to determine the probability of the evidence with a vague and ill-defined hypothesis such as "the person is not guilty". The value of the evidence will best be realised if the two hypotheses are well formed, positive and specific.

Some symbols

Despite the risk of intimidating readers by including symbols in the book we believe that, as they are such an important aid to clear thinking, they ought to be used. It is almost impossible to discuss abstract notions without such aids. We do not intend to go into the higher reaches of mathematics. We are only using the symbols as an efficient tool in our analysis of the legal problems. Here we introduce the symbols for hypotheses, evidence, and probability. They are described at greater length in the Appendix.

Hypotheses

H	stands for an hypothesis. An hypothesis (or premise or assertion) is a statement that is either true or false, such as "It rained today". Since we may have more than one hypothesis we will number them:
H_1	is usually what the prosecution is trying to prove, such as "The

| | accused was present at the scene''; |
| H_2, H_3 etc | stand for different alternative hypotheses. |

Evidence

| E | stands for some item of evidence. This is in the form of a statement that is true or false, such as ''The blood type of the accused matches that found on the scene''. There will be many items of evidence so they will be numbered: |
| E_1, E_2, E_3 etc | stand for different items of evidence. |

Probability

P( )	stands for the probability of the hypothesis written in the bracket, *e.g.* $P(H_1)$ means the probability that hypothesis H_1 is true. It will have a numerical value between 0 and 1. Thus, if H_1 = ''The murderer is the accused'', at some point in the trial we might say that $P(H_1)$ is 0.5. Since all these probabilities will require us to describe their conditions we add to the notation the symbol
$\vert$	meaning ''supposing'' or ''given'' so that
P(H|E)	means the probability of H supposing E is true. Thus, we might use $P(H_1\vert E_1)$ to mean the probability of H_1 given the evidence E_1 is true.

We do not use symbols more complicated than these.

3.1 Which alternative hypothesis?

Theoretically, there can be an infinite number of different explanations for an event; it would be impossible to compare the prosecution's hypothesis with all of them. In practice, we can usually identify a small number worth considering. For example, a robbery charge might be defended by denying that the incident took place or by denying that the accused was the person involved, and each of these has many variations.

During the course of the trial (and before the trial in civil cases) it will become clear what the grounds of the defence are. In the vast majority of cases the two most likely explanations will be those put forward by the prosecution and by the defence respectively. Therefore, although it is the task of the prosecution to prove its case (that is, its assertion or hypothesis) beyond reasonable doubt we can judge whether it has done so by comparing its case with a small number of alternatives and, frequently, with just the one offered by the defence (which we will often designate H_2).

Probative value and the alternative hypothesis

The likelihood ratio for a particular piece of evidence in distinguishing between two hypotheses can be written

$$\frac{P(E|H_1)}{P(E|H_2)}$$

where H_1 and H_2 are the two hypotheses to be compared. It follows that to determine the value of any particular piece of evidence for the prosecution case one has to identify the particular defence argument – the hypothesis that we are comparing it against. This can be illustrated by considering an extreme example. A person dies after being stabbed and a suspect is arrested nearby wearing bloodstained clothing. DNA testing is carried out and the scientist reports a likelihood ratio for this evidence (E) – that the evidence is at least 10,000 times more likely if the blood on the suspect came from the victim (H_1) rather than from a randomly selected person (H_2); indeed, powerful evidence in favour of the prosecution case.[1]

At trial, the accused states that he did not stab the victim but found him bleeding and rendered first aid, getting the victim's blood on his clothes. If this explanation (H_3) is the defence the DNA evidence immediately becomes valueless. Why? Because although the probability of the evidence given that the accused was the perpetrator[2] may be 1, so is the probability of the evidence given the defence story.[3] The ratio of these probabilities, the likelihood ratio, $P(E|H_1)/P(E|H_3)$, is 1 and so the evidence does not help us to choose between the prosecution and defence hypotheses. The DNA analysis is no longer relevant to the assessment that the court has to make.

In a less extreme case one just gets a less extreme result. Thus, the accused might instead confess to having had a fight with the murder victim's brother, getting his blood on him (H_4). To determine the likelihood ratio of the DNA evidence we must answer the question, "What is the probability of the DNA evidence if the blood on the accused came from the brother?"[4] The likelihood ratio, $P(E|H_1)/P(E|H_4)$, will be greater than 1 but almost certainly much less than the 10,000 figure, since two brothers' DNA analyses are much more likely to resemble each other than either is to resemble that of another person randomly selected from the general population.

Alternatively, the accused's blood might resemble that of the victim and so the hypotheses to be compared are that the blood found came from the accused (H_1) and that the blood is from the victim (H_5).[5]

Selecting the appropriate alternate hypotheses

One must think carefully to identify the appropriate alternative hypotheses and determine the correct likehood ratios to use. Frequently, the defence will be that the perpetrator was not the accused but someone else, not otherwise specified.

[1] The likelihood ratio is $P(E|H_1)/P(E|H_2) = 10,000$.
[2] $P(E|H_1)$.
[3] $P(E|H_3)$.
[4] $P(E|H_4)$.
[5] As in *Preece* v *HM Advocate* [1981] Crim LR 783.

We must then consider how probable the evidence is if the perpetrator was someone other than the accused.[6] There will usually be other evidence about the perpetrator, which will tend to narrow down the alternative hypothesis. For example, if there is good evidence that the perpetrator was of Vietnamese appearance we have to consider how probable the DNA test result is if the perpetrator was a Vietnamese other than the accused. There is not much point in considering how probable the evidence is if the perpetrator were caucasian.

How should the investigator determine what is the appropriate alternative hypothesis? Forensic scientists have often assumed in the past the alternative hypothesis that the perpetrator could have been any other member of the population.[7] The probability of the evidence will then be derived from the frequency of the characteristic in the population. It appears that only as an afterthought is the comment sometimes made that one may need to alter the likelihood ratio in the light of the facts of the particular case. This may be because the forensic scientist is not aware of all the evidence at the time. However, determining the appropriate alternative hypothesis is no mechanical task. The starting point should be the facts of the particular case and the explanation put forward by the defence. The decision to compare with a randomly selected person from the population (or a randomly selected member of a sub-group) should be regarded as a conclusion to be justified, rather than as a starting point.

It would be legitimate to compare the suspect with such a random person only when (i) there is no evidence to separate the perpetrator from the general population, or (ii) there is no explanation forthcoming for a mark on the accused, or (iii) the test used is such that results can be regarded as independent of variations in sub-groups, as in the case of some DNA testing methods.

Example

As an example of the complexity of identifying appropriate alternative hypotheses we can consider the facts surrounding the murder of the English tourist Marjory Hopegood in Hamilton, New Zealand in January 1992. A man of Maori appearance was seen running away from the scene and subsequently washing himself in the Waikato river.[8] Blood which did not belong to the victim was found at the scene and was analysed using a DNA test which produces results which vary in frequency from race to race. Suppose that, subsequently, a Maori was arrested and identified by an eyewitness as the man seen. The prosecution hypothesis is that this man was the perpetrator (H_1).

Two possible lines of defence might be imagined: first, that the accused was the person seen running away but was not the murderer (H_2) or, secondly, that the

---

[6] P(evidence|perpetrator is someone else).

[7] "Typically, forensic scientists use the concept here of a random man" Buckleton, JS and Walsh, KAJ "Knowledge-Based systems" in Aitken, CGG and Stoney, DA (eds) *The Use Of Statistics in Forensic Science* (Ellis Horwood, Chichester, 1991).

[8] *The Evening Post*, Wellington, Monday, 13 January 1992, p 3.

accused was not the person seen running away and the eyewitness identification was wrong (H_3).

In the first case if the defence story is true, the murderer was not the man seen running away and there is no information about the murderer. The relevant questions are then: (i) what is the probability of the DNA evidence if the murderer was the accused, $P(E|H_1)$? and (ii) what is the probability of the evidence if the murderer was a randomly selected person in New Zealand, $P(E|H_2)$? This will depend on the frequency of the DNA test result in the population as a whole.

In the second case, if the eyewitness identification of the accused is wrong, there would be some reason to believe that the murderer was of Maori appearance even if it was not the accused. The appropriate questions therefore are: (i) what is the probability of the DNA evidence if the murderer was the accused, $P(E|H_1)$? and (ii) what is the probability of the evidence if the murderer was a randomly selected man of Maori appearance, $P(E|H_3)$? This will depend upon the frequency of the DNA test result in the Maori population.

Suppose, to everyone's surprise, a European rather than a Maori was arrested and his defence is that the murderer was the Maori seen running away. In this case the relevant questions would be: (i) what is the probability of the DNA evidence if the murderer was the accused, $P(E|H_1)$? and (ii) what is the probability of the evidence if the murderer was a randomly selected man of Maori appearance, $P(E|H_3)$? – despite the fact that the accused is a European!

In chapter 2 we saw that an expert cannot, on the basis of one item of scientific evidence, state a probability of paternity, presence, occurrence, or whatever. The evidence should be given in the form of a likelihood ratio. We now see that not only can a single piece of evidence not justify a "probability of occurrence" but also that items of evidence do not have their own intrinsic "absolute" likelihood ratios. The likelihood ratio depends crucially upon the alternative hypothesis, which, in turn, will usually depend upon the nature of the defence.

3.2 Exclusive, exhaustive and multiple hypotheses

In order to be compared rationally, hypotheses have to comply with certain conditions.

Exclusiveness

The two hypotheses used in the likelihood ratio, say H_1 and H_2, must be mutually exclusive. That is to say, they cannot both be true. For example, the propositions that the accused was the perpetrator and that someone else was the perpetrator are exclusive. The propositions that the perpetrator was an American and that the perpetrator was an Afro-American are not exclusive because it is possible to be both. The likelihood ratio cannot sensibly be used with non-exclusive hypotheses. It makes no sense, for example, to compare the frequency of a DNA profile in

Britons of West Indian origin with the frequency of the profile in the population as a whole including those of West Indian origin.

Exhaustiveness

Although the hypotheses must be exclusive they need not be exhaustive; that is to say they need not account for all possible explanations. It is true that *odds*, by definition, are found only by comparing two exclusive and exhaustive hypotheses. The hypotheses, H_1 that the accused was present at the scene and H_2 that the accused was not present are exhaustive and these are the hypotheses that are frequently used in presentations of forensic scientific evidence. $P(H_1)/P(H_2)$ gives true odds. We might say that it was 100 to 1 that he was present.

It is impossible, however, to assess the probability that the accused would have, for example, blood on his clothing if he were not present at the scene. This hypothesis can be subdivided in so many ways that it has no graspable meaning. Any such probability is really just a sum of the probabilities of the evidence under each of these possible sub-hypotheses. Nearly all the probability in such an assessment will be accounted for by the one or two most likely explanations, and the others can safely be put to one side. What is required in practice is some positive explanation as to how this mark came to be on the accused. In the absence of any explanation we are forced to ask how likely it is that the ordinary person would have this blood on their clothing.[9]

When a positive and specific alternative hypothesis is being considered, the ratio of the probabilities of it and the prosecution hypothesis will not be true odds. For example, if H_3 is that the accused was at home with his family at the time, then the ratio $P(H_1)/P(H_3)$ will not account for all the possibilities. These hypotheses are therefore not exhaustive and do not give true odds that the accused was at the scene. However, provided that these hypotheses are the two most likely explanations, their ratio will usually be close to true odds. For example, there may be evidence placing the accused at the scene of the crime. The accused's family may testify that he was at home at the time. It seems that, although there are theoretically any number of other places he might have been, these are the two most likely and in most cases we can compare them alone and be confident that we are approximating the true odds for the first hypothesis.

Multiple hypotheses

If the hypotheses being compared are not exhaustive there must be more than two possible explanations. The prosecution hypothesis may have to be compared with several other hypotheses. However, when the alternative hypothesis changes, the value of the evidence changes. Evidence which may be of enormous value in distinguishing between one pair of hypotheses may not distinguish between

[9] We propose that this is the answer to the question raised by Zuckerman, AAS "Law, fact or justice?" (1986) 66 BULR 487, of how the jury should react to a failure by the accused to provide an explanation for such evidence. The distribution of bloodstained clothing in the general population was examined in the pioneering study by Briggs, TJ, "The probative value of bloodstains on clothing" (1978) 18 Med Sci & Law 79.

another pair at all. Any one piece of evidence will enable one to rank hypotheses according to how probable the evidence is (given each), but their rankings may well change when other evidence is considered.

In theory, the probability of the evidence given innocence (or, for that matter, given guilt) is the combination of the probabilities of the evidence given every possible hypothesis consistent with innocence and the prior probabilities of those hypotheses. In practice two factors make this much easier than it might sound. First, large numbers of these component hypotheses can be lumped together, for example in the breath-test case for a finding of guilt we are only concerned with whether the accused was over the limit, not in the precise blood alcohol content. Even when it comes to sentencing, we will probably be concerned with ranges of blood alcohol level. The second factor is that, for vast numbers of the theoretically possible hypotheses, the prior probabilities will be so low that they can be ignored. We will then be left with a manageably small number of component hypotheses.

In summary, the hypotheses being compared must be exclusive but need not be exhaustive. In most cases, comparing the two most likely hypotheses will give us a figure which, for practical purposes, will be the same as true odds.

3.3 Immigration and paternity cases

Paternity cases provide good illustrations of the effect of changing the alternative hypothesis. Applications for immigration may be made on the basis that one is the child of someone already resident in the country. In such cases, the applicant will be claiming to be the child of a particular person and the immigration authorities may be claiming that they are not. There will seldom be a named alternative candidate as parent. Some paternity disputes are also of this nature, where the mother alleges that the defendant is the father and the defendant simply denies this without naming an alternative candidate or group of candidates as father.

Consider a simple case where a relationship is claimed with a putative father (Father-1) of a child. The applicant's hypothesis, H_1, is that Father-1 is the father of the child. The child has a genetic characteristic, a particular blood group, not present in the mother. It, therefore, must have been transmitted by the father. Father-1 is found to have that characteristic. Thus $P(E|H_1) = 1.0$. How we proceed from here depends on whether or not there is a named alternative father.

No alternative father

If there is no named alternative father, as in most immigration cases, then there are two exclusive and exhaustive hypotheses to be compared; one, H_1 that Father-1 is the real father and the other, H_2 that "someone else" (unknown) is the real father.

If the characteristic occurs in 1% of the population then we can say that the *evidence* is 100 times more likely if Father-1 is the real father (since he certainly has the characteristic, $P(E|H_1) = 1.0$) than if someone else is the father (because then the probability of the evidence $P(E|H_2) = 0.01$). The likelihood ratio is $P(E|H_1)/P(E|H_2) = 1/0.01 = 100$.

A named alternative father

In another case we might have a named alternative candidate, Father-2, and have good evidence that the mother only had intercourse with these two men during the relevant period. Although the assertions that Father-1 was the father, H_1, and that Father-2 was the father, H_3, are not theoretically exhaustive, comparing them should give us a close approximation to true odds in favour of Father-1's paternity. We then have to consider what we know about Father-2. If we know his blood group then either he has the "wrong" blood-group and can be excluded as the father or he has the "right" bloodgroup in which case the evidence cannot distinguish between Father-1 and Father-2 (since the likelihood ratio would be $1/1 = 1$). In the latter instance the decision will depend entirely upon other evidence.

If we do not know his blood group then the best we can do is to treat him as a "random" member of the population and say that there is only a 1% chance that he has that group and therefore that the evidence is 100 times more likely if Father-1 is the father than if Father-2 is. This assessment, however, is highly unstable; that is to say, we know of a piece of evidence (the blood group of Father-2) which would cause us to change the assessment radically one way or the other if only we had it. Judges appear to be intuitively reluctant to use the population frequency of occurrence when a blood test of the alternative father is not available.[10] On the other hand, once DNA analysis has been completed courts will not order further testing even when there is a quantifiable, although a very small, chance that a further test might lead to an exclusion.[11]

Some tests do not merely exclude or include. Some will give probabilities for the evidence which vary according to which of two non-excluded men is considered. For example, a mother, a child and three putative fathers are tested for the PGM blood factor. Each of us has 2 PGM genes, so each of us has two of four possible factors, labelled 1-, 1+, 2-, 2+. The factors are inherited, one from each parent. The results of the tests (E) are as follows:

		H_1	H_2	H_3
Mother	Child	Father-1	Father-2	Father-3
1- 1-	1- 1+	1- 1+	1+ 1+	1- 2+

The child has a 1+ factor and the mother does not have one. Therefore, the father must be the source of the 1+ factor and therefore must have at least one 1+ factor.

Father-3 can be immediately excluded since he does not have the 1+ factor. Father-1 might have passed on either the 1+ or the 1- while Father-2 would

---

[10] *Loveridge v Adlam* [1991] NZFLR 267.
[11] *G v T* [1994] NZFLR 145.

certainly have passed on a 1+. Father-2 is twice as likely to pass on a 1+ factor as Father-1. More formally, the probability of the evidence if Father-1 is the true father, $P(E|H_1) = 0.5$, while for Father-2 it is $P(E|H_3) = 1$ (and for Father-3 it is 0). The evidence is twice as likely if Father-2 is the father than if Father-1 is. This gives us a likelihood ratio of 2, which does not sound very useful, but in paternity testing a large number of such tests are looked at and the results combined, as explained in chapter 5.

Knowing this, what do we do? We also have to consider the other evidence in the case, the frequency and timing of alleged intercourse, the credibility of the witnesses and so forth. On the basis of this evidence we have to come to some assessment of the odds in favour of the proposition that the defendant was the father. In a particular case it may be a matter of comparing the probabilities in favour of one candidate and another.

Example

The English case *Re J S (A Minor)* was such a case.[12] R accepted his girlfriend's baby (baby JS) as his own but J alleged that the baby was in fact his. J underwent a blood test but R refused to do so. The test showed that J was one of 1% of the European population who could not be excluded from being the father of baby JS.

The relevant question was, how much more likely was J than R to be the father of baby JS? One hypothesis (H_1) is that J was the father of baby JS. The alternative hypothesis (H_2) is that R is the father but that J nonetheless has that same blood characteristic. If R was the father there is nothing to separate J from a randomly selected member of the population. Assuming that the child had some characteristic shared only by 1% of the population and that the mother did not share it, the father must have had that characteristic. The evidence (E) was that J's blood had that characteristic. The probability of obtaining the evidence if J was the father is $P(E|H_1) = 1$ and the probability of obtaining the evidence (from J) if R was the father $P(E|H_2) = 0.01$. The likelihood ratio for the evidence is therefore $1/0.01 = 100$.

This must be combined with other items of evidence including that R refused the test. Another was that the mother had had intercourse much more often with R than with J over the relevant period. This must give a likelihood ratio in favour of R of (perhaps) the ratio of the numbers of instances of intercourse. This makes a crude assumption that there was an equal probability of conception on each occasion, but we have no information justifying any other distribution. Balancing this there was the fact that, after having lived with R for some time without conceiving, the mother had an affair with J and then conceived. This will weigh in favour of J being the father.

If R had allowed a blood test the picture would have been very different. Either he would be excluded (that is, he did not have the important characteristic), in which case the likelihood ratio would be infinitely large (since $P(E|H_2) = 0$), or he would have the characteristic and $P(E|H_2) = 1$. The likelihood ratio would be

---

[12] [1981] Fam 22 (CA), [1980] All ER 1061.

1 and the evidence irrelevant. All decisions are made with imperfect information but it is obviously undesirable to have to make a decision in the absence of an identifiable and easily obtainable item of evidence which will completely alter our assessments. This is an example of an "unstable" assessment as discussed above.

As it turned out the court decided on other grounds that J was quite unsuitable to have access to the child. The point is that, far from revealing any difference between probability theory and legal probability, careful attention to the principles of logical inference would have identified the relevant questions and shown how to use the evidence the scientist had given.

Correct presentation also solves the problem that Ormrod LJ raised in that same case of what weight to give the evidence.[13] The answer is that the evidence should be accorded *precisely* the weight it rationally merits and that is given by the likelihood ratio. This tells the court by what factor to multiply the odds in favour of guilt or liability given by the other evidence in the case.[14] In any case, the question whether a "mathematical probability" can discharge the legal burden of proof is a red herring. It is the totality of the evidence, including the prior, which must meet the standard of proof. This will be considered in chapter 5.

3.4 "It was my brother"[15]

In criminal cases where the evidence is of blood or DNA tests the lowest likelihood ratios will occur where the hypotheses being compared are that the accused or one of the members of his family, perhaps a brother, is the perpetrator. Ratios below 100 would be typical. Of course, there are fewer suspects in such a case but they are harder to distinguish. Ideally one would like samples from all the suspects, and it is worth considering whether a power should exist in such circumstances to take samples from people other than the person arrested.

One should never lose sight of the other evidence in the case. The "worst case" is that the DNA evidence fails to distinguish between the two brothers. If the non-defendant brother has not provided a sample, one can only assess the probability that the samples would fail to distinguish. The case will then rest on the remainder of the evidence which, one hopes, will enable us to make the distinction. If the prior odds based on the rest of the evidence in the case are high enough then it will not matter what the result of the DNA analysis might have been.

Let us re-emphasise that although the value of the evidence is decreased if the alternative perpetrator is a brother, so is the pool of possible suspects. In fact, specifying a brother as the alternative may reduce the prior odds from one in

---

[13] *JS (A Minor), In Re* [1981] Fam 22, 29 (CA). See **2.4** above.
[14] The analogy of weight can be pursued by substituting the logarithm of the likelihood ratio which can then be added to or subtracted from the logarithm of the prior odds. IJ Good even coined the term "the weight of evidence" to describe this measure. See *Probability and the Weighing of Evidence* (Charles Griffin & Co, London, 1950), chapter 6.
[15] With acknowledgement to Evett, I, "Evaluating DNA Profiles in a Case Where the Defence is 'It was my Brother'" (1992) 32 JFSS 5, where the problem is fully worked through.

several million to one in three or four. The combined effect of this and the blood evidence may even be to strengthen the case against the accused. This point is considered at greater length in chapter 5.

3.5 Marks at the scene and marks on the suspect

Remembering *Locard's Principle*, evidence may be left at the scene by the perpetrator or picked up by the perpetrator from the scene or the victim. Although the logical analysis is always the same there are different factors at work in these two situations.

Marks at the scene

In the Marjory Hopegood case we considered earlier in this chapter, a mark (the bloodstain, E) was left at the scene. The race of the *accused* was not relevant in establishing the alternative hypothesis. This is because, no matter what the defence offered, the second question assumed that it was someone other than the accused who left the trace. The alternative hypothesis (H_2) is that the perpetrator was someone else. Thus, it does not matter whether the accused is a member of the most tightly knit genetic sub-population. Of course, what may matter is any evidence relating to the *perpetrator*.

If there is no evidence about a perpetrator other than the analysis of a sample from the scene, an appropriate comparison is with a randomly selected person from the population of possible perpetrators, regardless of the race of the accused. If we have eyewitness evidence that the perpetrator was of Hispanic appearance and a suspect is arrested on the basis of evidence other than sample analysis, then the appropriate population is all those of Hispanic appearance and not the population of the suspect's particular sub-population.[16]

Thus, where a mark is left at the scene and alleged to have come from the accused, the two questions to be asked are:

- what is the probability of obtaining this evidence if it was the accused who left the mark, $P(E|H_1)$?

- what is the probability of obtaining it if someone else left the mark, $P(E|H_2)$?

Marks on the accused

A different situation arises when we consider a mark (such as a bloodstain) found on the *accused* and alleged to have come from the scene. In these cases the value of the evidence is determined by information about the accused as well as about the victim. The alternative hypothesis (H_3) is that the accused, although having

---

[16] Note that while, ideally, the alternative hypothesis should be that another person of such appearance committed the offence, the data available will be from surveys in which the people surveyed are usually asked to nominate their own race. There may be a difference between the self-identified race and the race that an observer would ascribe to an individual.

no contact with the scene, would have this mark for some other reason. Of course, there may be yet another defence which involved the accused being at the scene. The mark evidence would probably not distinguish between these two hypotheses.

In order to determine the probability of E supposing the accused had not been at the scene we need information about the accused's characteristics, lifestyle and movements. A demolition worker is more likely than others to have glass on his shoes, an habitual violent offender might be more likely to have glass or blood on his clothing, and the blood most likely to be on anyone's clothing is his own. If we have such information about the accused, whether provided by the accused or anyone else, it should be used.[17] If we have no such information about the accused, we may have to resort to regarding him as similar to a randomly selected member of the population.

The two questions to be asked in such a case are:

- what is the probability that the accused would have this mark on him if he was guilty as described, $P(E|H_1)$?

- what is the probability that, taking account of his lifestyle and occupation, the accused would have this mark on him although he is not guilty, $P(E|H_2)$?

The accused's race

This vital distinction between a mark at the scene and one on the suspect has often been missed, not least in comment about the analysis of DNA evidence.[18] In particular, the view has been put forward that the value of scene DNA evidence may be affected by the characteristics of the accused's race.[19] This is never true.

There may, of course, be some evidence that the *perpetrator* belonged to the same race or the same racial sub-population as the accused. The characteristics of this race may then be relevant when we are considering a mark left at the scene, but that is because the perpetrator belongs to it, not because the accused belongs to it. The only apparent exception to the rule that the accused's characteristics are not relevant is where, as with the siblings discussed in the last section, the fact that the accused has a particular characteristic is used to calculate the probability that someone else has it.

These conclusions stem, not from science, technology, or the intricacies of statistics, but from a simple logical analysis of the structure of the case.

3.6 Hypothetical questions

It is settled law that an expert may be asked hypothetical questions. In particular, forensic scientists are often asked whether the observations they have made are

---

[17] See Buckleton, Walsh and Evett, ''Who is random man?'' (1991) 31 JFS 463 for discussion of these problems.
[18] *E.g.* McLeod, N, ''English DNA Evidence Held Inadmissible'' [1991] Crim LR 583.
[19] Young, SJ ''DNA Evidence – Beyond Reasonable Doubt?'' [1991] Crim LR 264.

consistent with circumstances other than those forming the prosecution case.[20] These questions are obviously aimed at raising alternative hypotheses H_2, H_3, H_4, which (from a defence point of view) might yield a lower likelihood ratio. They recognise that the value of such evidence varies according to the hypotheses being compared. Evidence does not, of course, become valueless because it is consistent with more than one hypothesis. The important point is that the relative probability of the evidence under each hypothesis should be compared.

How hypothetical can a hypothetical question be? Hodgkinson cites US and Australian cases to support the argument that such questions do not have to be tied rigidly to facts proved at the trial but must bear some relationship to the evidence given.[21] He summarises by making three points:

> "First, no party should, without more [evidence], diverge in its hypothetical questions to an expert from the evidence of fact. Such a course should always be justified by elements in the evidence of fact ...
>
> Secondly, whether such a course is proper will also always depend upon whether the expert opinion which relies upon it is undermined by any such discrepancy.
>
> Thirdly, expert opinion is only admissible if it is relevant to matters in issue. If it is founded upon facts which have not been or will not be even approximately proved it should not be given."

This summary seems to be conditioned by thinking about civil cases in which both parties are obliged to commit themselves to statements of claim and defence. It is not so clear that these requirements apply strictly to the defence in a criminal trial, who, for the most part, are not required to produce evidence of anything. The governing proposition is obviously that "expert opinion is only admissible if it is relevant to matters in issue". Hodgkinson's final sentence can only fully apply to civil cases. When a criminal defence lawyer is cross-examining a prosecution witness no notice need necessarily have been given of the defence case and, indeed, defending attorneys might actually alter tactics depending upon the replies.

This is especially true where evidence of DNA or blood analyses is being considered. An expert might give an extremely high likelihood ratio strongly supporting the proposition that the mark came from the accused, H_1, rather than from a "randomly selected person", H_2, but the likelihood ratio for the evidence if the alternative hypothesis was that the perpetrator were the accused's brother, H_3, will be very much smaller.[22] There is no burden on the defence, however, to produce any evidence to support the contention that the perpetrator might have been the accused's brother; rather, the burden is on the prosecution to prove that it was not. This also means that the scientist must prepare to meet several defence hypotheses as it is extremely difficult, often impossible, to make these calculations while in the witness box, under pressure, and without access to data.

---

[20] What "consistent" means and what lawyers sometimes think it means are discussed in chapter 4.
[21] Hodgkinson, T *Expert Evidence: Law and Practice* (Sweet & Maxwell, London, 1990), p 148.
[22] Evett, I, "Evaluating DNA Profiles in a Case Where the Defence is 'It was my Brother' " (1992) 32 JFSS 5.

As we saw, each of the implied alternative hypotheses will have corresponding prior odds relative to the prosecution hypothesis, H_1, and these must be considered as well as the likelihood ratio.

This suggests three conclusions:

- there should be some reasonable prior probability in favour of the hypothesis advanced. This may be assessed from evidence adduced or to be adduced or from general knowledge and experience;
- the prior odds suggested by the new hypothesis must be taken into account as well as its effect on the value of the evidence;
- the defence should not be allowed to ask a series of hypothetical questions just to produce a barrage of different numbers to confuse the jury and cause them to believe that the evidence is in some sense "unreliable". The point that the value of the evidence will vary according to the hypotheses being compared should be made, but subsequent discussion should comply with the first two points above.

3.7 Pre-trial conferences and defence notice

We have seen that the value of a piece of forensic scientific evidence may depend crucially on the circumstances of the case. Likewise, its value may be altered not only by the defence's expert evidence but also by its general line of argument. Often the scientific witness will be kept unaware of these factors deliberately. Indeed, the popular perception amongst police and lawyers is that scientific witnesses should not be told the facts of the case so that they will be "unbiased". This supposes that scientific evidence can be viewed "objectively" and in isolation. Furthermore, the defence in a criminal case seldom has to reveal its line of defence in advance and, in some jurisdictions, does not even have to give notice of its expert evidence.

This provides a dilemma for reformers of legal, and especially criminal, procedure. It is already enacted in some jurisdictions (and proposed in several more) that there must be a pre-trial exchange of expert evidence even in criminal cases. Much more controversial are proposals to require the defence to reveal its general line of argument in advance.[23] The practical implications of this are considered in chapter 11.

In a criminal case the defence is, traditionally, entitled not to put forward any explanation for the evidence, even at trial. Where there is an unexplained mark on the accused this leaves the jury unable to distinguish between the accused and the general population. Likewise, the jury can only regard the perpetrator as a member of the general population in the case of a mark left at the scene. In these

---

[23] As the Royal Commission on Criminal Justice recommended in 1994. For reaction to these proposals see the index to (1994) NLJ.

cases the jury has no alternative but to fall back on the concept of the "random man", and of course, it does so.

Particular problems are caused when the defence produces at trial, as it is traditionally entitled to do, an explanation which has not previously been mentioned. Part of the stock-in-trade of the prosecutor is the ability to predict lines of defence, but, when the unexpected occurs, the scientific witness may be left in a difficult position.

There have been proposals for pre-trial conferences in criminal cases. These are intended to "narrow the issues" and to save time and money at trial. Such conferences would have the side effect of revealing lines of defence so that scientific witnesses for both sides can assess their evidence in the light of the appropriate alternative hypotheses.

3.8 Case studies

We now look at a case where a new hypothesis changed the course of a trial, discuss further child sexual-abuse cases and examine a case where a forensic scientist was unable to give all the relevant evidence.

The baby in the canal

That the strength of the evidence depends on the alternative hypothesis is intuitively realised by judges and is illustrated by the English case, *R* v *Harding* which concerned the death of a baby in a canal.[24] The baby had died of shock rather than of drowning and this was regarded as indicating that a large area of the baby had suddenly become immersed in water. From this it was inferred that the baby had been thrown into the canal by the mother (H_1). The defence was that the mother had fallen asleep and the baby must have rolled out of her arms into the water (H_2).

The Governor of Holloway Prison, who happened to be a doctor, was present in court. He believed that death from shock could have resulted from the sudden entry of cold water into the nostrils and he spoke to the defence after the case. The defence appealed, seeking to admit fresh evidence. It should be noted that this was not new information in the sense of new facts about the individual case, but new information about the world in general, capable of leading to a new *hypothesis*. The court admitted the evidence, saying (*per* Lord Hewart LCJ at p 196):

"... if evidence of that nature, ... had been in the hands of the defence at the Assizes, the course of the trial would of necessity have been different. The line of cross-examination would have been different; the addresses to the jury would have been different; and undoubtedly the summing up of the Judge, both as to what it says and as to what it does not say, would have been different. ... the crucially important view ...

---

[24] (1936) 25 Cr App R 190.

was entirely absent. It had occurred to nobody. It was suggested by nobody. It was not the subject of any observations.''

This case demonstrates vividly the importance of hypothesis selection and the effect of failure to consider an appropriate alternative hypothesis.

Alternate hypotheses in cases of child sexual abuse

In the New Zealand case R v B, discussed at the end of chapter 2, the Court of Appeal mentioned that there might be alternative explanations for the behaviour (E) observed. In other words, the court was asking what was the appropriate alternative hypothesis (H_2 = non-abuse). Should it be that the behaviour would be observed in a randomly selected child of the same age group? It might be expected that a child making allegations of sexual abuse comes from a stressful environment; so should the alternative hypothesis assume that the child comes from a stressful and dysfunctional family? If so, we might expect the value of the evidence to be sharply reduced because many of the signs reported, although perhaps not all, would be produced by a home life that was generally stressful.[25]

One could go further and ask whether step-children should be compared with step-children, orphans with orphans, children in day care with other children in day care and so forth. Any of these groups might display the behaviour to a greater extent than a "normal" child so that it would be a less valuable indicator of abuse for such children.

The second question is how the probability of the evidence assuming non-abuse, $P(E|H_2)$, is to be assessed. Survey evidence of the incidence of various characteristics may be very limited. Psychologists, on the whole, tend to study abnormal cases rather than the general population and there is little research data on the incidence of characteristics regarded as symptoms of stress. If the appropriate alternative hypothesis is that the child was randomly drawn from the population, perhaps the best we can do is leave the jury to make the assessment.

Not only was both evidence and the courts' handling of it unsatisfactory, but so was the reaction of the New Zealand Parliament. In 1989 a new section 23G was inserted into the Evidence Act 1908, which, *inter alia*, permits psychologists and psychiatrists to give evidence that "observed behaviour is consistent or inconsistent with the behaviour of abused children of the same age group". This is an unfortunate phrase.[26] It reflects the continued, and pointless, search for evidence which enables the expert witness to say "this child definitely has been abused" rather than evidence which supports the hypothesis of abuse.

It is unclear what the phrase means, but clearly it does not mandate giving evidence in the fashion advocated here since it ignores the possibility of the behaviour occurring in non-abused children. If its effect is to make admissible the kind of evidence given in R v B and R v S then it allows evidence which neither the jury nor anyone else will be able to evaluate.

[25] Levy, RJ, "Using 'scientific' testimony to prove child sexual abuse" (1989) 23 FLQ 383.
[26] Which we will discuss at some length in chapter 4.

Preece v HM Advocate

In this notorious Scottish case[27] the expert witness, Dr Clift, found that stains at the scene of a murder were of group A (secretor) and that the accused was group A (secretor). The prosecution hypothesis was that the accused committed the murder (H_1). In evidence, Dr Clift reported the match of the stains with the accused (E) and stated that the proportion of group A secretors in the population was some value, let us call it f. The implication was that the probability of this match occurring "by chance" was f. Thus, $P(E|H_2) = f$.

Unfortunately, he was unable, or not allowed, to bring one other vital piece of evidence to the attention of the court, although he did present the information in his written report which had been given to the defence. The victim was also group A (secretor)!

Immediately, a *third* hypothesis is introduced, (H_3). The stain came from the victim and the perpetrator did not leave any stain. The secretor evidence cannot distinguish between this and the prosecution hypothesis (H_1) since the probability of getting the evidence is 1 in both cases. Other information is needed to separate them, perhaps the shape and location of the stains, which we do not have available to us in looking at the case now.

If Dr Clift had been using the method of reporting advocated later in this book, but without a truly logical thought-process, he would, perhaps, have equivalently reported a likelihood ratio of $1/f$ to distinguish between the two hypotheses (H_1) that the blood came from the accused (the prosecution's hypothesis) and (H_2) that the blood was from the perpetrator, some unknown person from the population. These are the two obvious, exclusive hypotheses that were assumed.

However, to have reported a likelihood ratio in this way would have been to ignore the evidence of the victim's blood grouping. Since Dr Clift knew about that he would have had to take this information into account in assessing likelihood ratios. He would have had to consider, and counsel would have been unable to ignore, the question: "What are the appropriate alternative hypotheses?".

The upshot of this case was that a forensic scientist was severely criticised and even regarded as dishonest. However, Dr Clift did exactly what he had been trained to do (the classical techniques involved are examined more fully in chapter 7). Had he been trained, or either counsel been educated, in the logical method of assessing evidence advocated in this book, more useful questions would have been asked, the relevant factors would have been probed and the problems caused in this case would not have occurred.

3.9 Summary

- An item of evidence cannot, by itself, prove a hypothesis considered in isolation. Evidence can only help to distinguish between hypotheses.

---

[27] [1981] Crim LR 783.

- The value of any item of evidence as support for the prosecution hypothesis may be different for different defence hypotheses.

- The question must be asked: "What are the appropriate alternative hypotheses?".

- Where a mark is left at the scene of a crime and alleged to have come from the accused, the likelihood ratio is the probability of the evidence supposing the accused left the mark, divided by the probability of the evidence if "someone else" left the mark. Who the "someone else" might be will depend upon what is known about the *perpetrator* and what line of defence is chosen.

- Where a mark is found on the accused and alleged to come from the scene, the likelihood ratio is the probability of the evidence supposing the accused received the mark at the scene divided by the probability that the accused would have this mark although not present. The latter will depend upon what is known about the *accused* and the line of defence chosen.

- In considering the evidence based on body samples such as bloodstains at the scene of a crime, the race of the accused is not relevant. What is relevant is what is known of the race of the perpetrator.

- In paternity cases the value of the evidence will vary according to what is known about alternative possible fathers.

- Hypothetical alternatives may reasonably be put to expert witnesses provided they have some reasonable prior probability, but it may be difficult for them to calculate likelihood ratios when this happens.

- Two hypotheses being compared must be exclusive of each other.

- It may be necessary to compare the prosecution hypothesis with more than one defence hypothesis. Provided that the hypotheses considered are the most likely explanations for the evidence it will not matter that they are not exhaustive.

- In a rational procedural system all the hypotheses to be considered at trial would be known to the expert witnesses beforehand so that they could assess the value of their evidence in the light of these and make appropriate calculations.

Contents of Chapter 4

EXPLAINING THE STRENGTH OF EVIDENCE

Chapter 4
EXPLAINING THE STRENGTH OF EVIDENCE

How should the effect of scientific evidence be expressed to a judge or jury? Until recently, scientific evidence was usually given in a way that did not follow the structure explained in this book. Evidence was given of probabilities and of the results of statistical tests of different sorts instead of likelihood ratios, and of the probability of matching by chance instead of evidence tied to the background of the case. In the face of this barrage courts have retreated from the centuries-old *ultimate issue rule* and have agonised over the weight to give to "statistical evidence". Some argue that evidence presented in statistical form may be given undue weight or, conversely, that juries cannot understand numbers.

In this chapter we recommend a way of giving scientific evidence that complies with the logical structure and makes clear to the court exactly how much the evidence is worth. Some kinds of evidence are very difficult to consider in these terms and we discuss how they might be dealt with. We also reconsider the ultimate issue rule and come to some surprising conclusions.

4.1 Explaining the likelihood ratio

In the *Pengelly* case in chapter 2 we recall that the scientific witness said:

"I find that the results I obtained were at least 12,450 times more likely to have occurred if the blood had originated from Pengelly than if it had originated from someone else."[1]

It would comply with the logic of the previous chapters if this were left baldly stated, but it is clear that it would mean little to many people. In fact there is some risk that the listener will interpret it wrongly.[2] In *Pengelly* itself, counsel promptly

---

[1] [1992] 1 NZLR 545 (CA). It became clear in cross-examination that "someone else" meant "a randomly selected member of the population".
[2] See 2.2.

asked the witness to put it another way. She responded by saying that of every 12,450 people in the population one would have shared these characteristics. Even this information requires further manipulation before it will help us decide how much more probable it is that Pengelly was the perpetrator.

Part of the task of expert witnesses should be to explain how and why the court is helped by the evidence they are giving. Why should the witness not suggest by precisely how much it should help the court? The witness could say something like: "Whatever the odds in favour of contact or presence based upon the other evidence (which I have not heard) my evidence makes them R times higher", where R is the value of the likelihood ratio. It must also be clear that the scientist and the court are considering the same alternative hypotheses. This not only gives the correct value for the evidence but tells the jury what to do with it, whereas it is not self-evident what is to be done with a likelihood ratio.

It may be objected that this is telling the jury what to think or what to make of the evidence. There are a number of reasons why this is not a valid objection.

- First, the witness is not telling the jury what to decide but simply how to integrate the witness's evidence with the remainder of the case.

- Secondly, there should be no objection to jurors being taught how to think rationally in abstract, otherwise logicians, probabilists and others would have to be excluded from juries. If there is no objection to jurors understanding rationality in abstract there should not be any objection to their being shown how to handle a particular piece of evidence rationally.

- Thirdly, some other ways in which we shall see that experts currently give evidence constitute a far more outright attempt to usurp the role of the jury and yet they are countenanced by courts every day.[3]

- Fourthly, if other methods lead to wrong interpretations then a logical approach will minimise the risk of errors.

The expert may well have to explain further what the likelihood ratio means and how it was arrived at, particularly under cross-examination. This should be relatively easy as the basic concepts are clear and simple. The problem is to get over preconceptions frequently held by lawyers and lay people. The significance of background information and the assumptions which the expert has made need to be explained so that other experts can assess the value and appropriateness of the evidence for themselves. The likelihood ratio method should also help the expert to explain, either in relation to the facts of the case or in answer to hypothetical questions, how it is that the value of the evidence changes if the alternative hypothesis is changed.

Sensitivity tables

One suggestion that has been made is that the witness should explain the effect of the likelihood ratio by using a table showing the effect of the evidence starting

---

[3] *E.g.* the probability of paternity (qv) and see the discussion of the ultimate issue rule below at **4.4**.

from different prior odds. This is a sensitivity table as it shows the effect – the sensitivity – of the posterior odds to different priors. Thus if the likelihood ratio for the evidence was 1,000 the sensitivity table might show posterior odds assessments for priors as follows:

Prior odds	Likelihood ratio	Posterior odds
1 to 10	1,000	100 to 1
2 to 10	1,000	200 to 1
5 to 10	1,000	500 to 1
1 to 1	1,000	1,000 to 1

Once one sees that the prior odds are multiplied by the likelihood ratio to give the posterior odds, the table becomes elementary. It appears more complex if probabilities are used and this is one reason why we prefer always to present figures in odds form. Here the expert is going beyond presenting the strength of his own evidence and discussing how the jury should reason about evidence in general. If there is a place for such a presentation it is probably in counsels' or the judge's summing up.

We therefore recommend that witnesses give evidence in a way that makes clear that the role of their evidence is to affect the prior odds assessed on the basis of the other evidence in the case. For example, words to the effect of:

"Whatever the odds in favour of contact or presence based upon the other evidence (which I have not heard) my evidence makes them R times higher."

4.2 Words instead of numbers?

It is also often claimed that juries cannot handle evidence in numerical form and that some form of words should be used instead. There is also said to be a risk of the "dwarfing of soft variables",[4] which is to say that the jury may become fixated by the evidence given in the form of numbers and fail to give the correct weight to the other evidence in the case. Presenting the evidence as we suggest above should minimise this risk by focussing attention on the importance of combining the scientific evidence with the other evidence in the case. However, let us consider the use of words to represent the strength of the evidence.

There may be risks in the use of numbers but there are also dangers in the use of words. Words have different meanings to different experts, particularly those in different professions. Informal surveys have found that terms such as "almost

[4] Tribe, L, "Trial by mathematics" (1971) 84 Harv LR, 1329; and see also discussion of *R v Chedzey* at 5.7

certain" and "highly probable" mean quite different things to scientists on the one hand, and to lawyers and police on the other.[5]

The inconsistent meaning of "consistent"

Worst of all is the word "consistent", a word in (unfortunately) common use by forensic scientists, pathologists and lawyers. To a scientist, and to a dictionary, "consistent with" is simply the opposite of "inconsistent with". The definition of "inconsistent" is precise and narrow. Two events are inconsistent with one another if they cannot possibly occur together. Thus, a person cannot be in two different places at the same instant and so evidence that he was in New York at a particular instant is inconsistent with the proposition that he was in London at the same instant. Anything which is not inconsistent is consistent. Thus, the proposition "several murders were committed in New York today" is quite consistent with the proposition "it rained in London today", although it may be irrelevant.

Unfortunately for clear communication, Craddock, Lamb and Moffat found that lawyers usually interpret "consistent with" as meaning "reasonably strongly supporting", while scientists use it in its strict logical and neutral meaning. When a pathologist says that certain injuries are "consistent" with a road accident there is no implication about whether or not there has been a road accident. It is possible that the injuries could occur given the circumstances that have been described. It is therefore perfectly sensible to say that something is "consistent but unlikely". If there is some genuine dispute about the cause of the injuries what would the pathologist be able to say? He might say that the injuries were consistent with either an assault or a road accident but are more likely to have occurred if there had been an assault than if there had been a road accident. If they are equally consistent with both then they do not help us decide which of them occurred.

Standardising word meanings

Clearly, if verbal presentation of scientific evidence is to work, we must be careful to ensure that experts use the same forms of words to express the same values for evidence. It is certainly necessary that whenever a word is used within a trial it should mean the same thing each time and it would also be a help if words were used to mean the same thing in different trials. Lawyers and jurors should also be able to understand the precise weight of what the expert is trying to convey. To ensure this, we must adopt conventions about the form of words to be used.

A number of scales have been proposed to describe the effect of different likelihood ratios. Evett suggested the following scale:[6]

---

[5] Craddock, JG, Lamb, P and Moffat, AC, "Problems of Written Communication: Understanding and Misunderstanding" [1992] HOFSS Technical Note and see *R* v *Lucas* [1992] 2 VR 109, 118 where Hampel J quoted from the Splatt Royal Commission Report and concluded, "I think that there is in this case the danger that consistency could assume the colour of identity, or at least of probability".

[6] Evett, I "Interpretation: a Personal Odyssey", pp. 9–22, in Aitken, CGG and Stoney, DA (eds) *The Use of Statistics in Forensic Science* (Ellis Horwood, Chichester, 1991).

Likelihood ratio in the range of	Evidence strength
1–33	weak
33–100	fair
100–330	good
330–1,000	strong
1,000+	very strong

Therefore, a piece of evidence with a likelihood ratio of 500 would be said to be "strong support" for the hypothesis. The scale correctly refers to the strength of the evidence and not to the probability of the hypothesis.

This scale is drawn up by a forensic scientist used to dealing with relatively high likelihood ratios. Most of the "ordinary" evidence which courts are content to regard as strong evidence contributing to a conviction probably weighs in with likelihood ratios in the 10 to 50 region, which, according to this scale, would make them only "fairly strong" evidence.

Thinking through the implications of using such a table, however, one will see that there may be no escaping the use of figures in the end because:

• The defence can always ask "what is meant by the expression 'strongly supports'?".

• If the jury is to understand the evidence correctly it will have to have the table explained to it, complete with the numerical equivalents.

• If we need to distinguish between the weights of two pieces of evidence in the same category, the table will have to be refined. Refinement, however, is simply a process of making words more and more like numbers.

• Words become inadequate for evidence that is more strong than "very strong" but less than certainty.

• Numbers have the overwhelming advantage that they can be combined rationally, whereas words cannot. What do two pieces of "good" evidence make?

It appears that the only way to express the relative strength of pieces of evidence that is not open to misinterpretation is to use numbers, perhaps followed by some verbal gloss. The best approach is probably the method employed in _Pengelly_ in which the expert stated the likelihood ratio and then said that the evidence "strongly supported the hypothesis that the blood came from Pengelly". (Using the list in the table above the evidence would have "very strongly supported" the hypothesis.)

These verbal conventions may be helpful in that they proceed a step further than a mere likelihood ratio. By saying that the evidence supports or strongly supports an hypothesis some minimal guidance is given as to how to combine the evidence with the remainder of the evidence on that issue. Thus, the verbal conventions are, crudely speaking, the equivalents not just of the likelihood ratio but also of how to use it to update the prior odds.

4.3 Problems with the likelihood ratio

For some evidence it is difficult to determine a likelihood ratio. This occurs when it is hard to calculate the probability of getting the evidence given the alternative hypothesis, often described as "obtaining a match by chance". This would give the denominator of the likelihood ratio. Sometimes that probability is so small that it may not matter what the values of the other probabilities are. In this case we refer to being practically (or morally) certain that the match could not have occurred unless the prosecution hypothesis was true.

Probability models

In order to determine the likelihood ratio, and in particular the denominator (the probability of getting the evidence supposing the alternative hypothesis), we need some way of calculating the probability given the assumptions and the particular situation. One method is to use a mathematical probability model. For example, where the evidence is a blood type and the alternative hypothesis is that "the perpetrator is some unknown person from the population" we would calculate the probability from the known proportion of that blood type in the population. This is a very simple probability model.

Attempts to create agreed probability models of fingerprints and handwriting have so far failed. Likewise, it seems impossible to create probability models for traces left by rifle barrels and photocopiers which may change characteristics over time. This is due not only to the number and complexity of the factors to be considered.

A probability model assumes that there is some answer to questions such as "what is the total possible number of fingerprints?". The principle of individuality, however, tells us that no two fingerprints are identical. The question, rather, is how confident are we of our ability to distinguish between them? The differences between the various models (discussed later in chapter 8) merely reflect the varying degrees of confidence of the modellers that they can distinguish between one feature and another and one position and another in two impressions.

Apart from this, no two impressions of the same fingerprint and no two bullets fired from the same rifle will be identical in any case. Impressions depend on the pressure used in making them; rifles wear and accumulate more flaws. The question for the expert is whether there is sufficient information to decide that two (non-identical) impressions have the same origin.

The professions affected by this problem, such as fingerprint identification, handwriting analysis and firearms examination, have, in consequence, developed a reliance upon, and have even built a mystique around, "experience". Frequently, these matters are dealt with by police or by non-scientist employees of the police. The approach has tended to become highly technical and rule-bound. In some jurisdictions, experts will not testify at all unless they are prepared to say categorically that the two impressions had the same origin.

With fingerprints this approach is almost universal, as we will see. The extent to which the experts see their credibility resting on rules rather than on their own judgment can be seen by the unfavourable reaction in the British Fingerprint Society's journal to a report which recommended a move away from the rule-bound approach.[7] In other areas it may depend upon whether the analysis is the responsibility of police or scientists – the latter being more prepared to give qualified testimony.

In these cases it seems that the expert is giving evidence of identity when, and only when, in his judgment the probability of getting the evidence assuming the alternative hypothesis is so small that it does not matter what the numerator or even the prior are. At what point this is reached seems to be a matter of judgment and experience and there most writers on expert evidence are content to let the matter rest. This may have had the unfortunate effect of removing the incentive to carry out the basic research necessary to build appropriate models.

Intellectually, this is unsatisfactory and further work is required in order to understand the processes involved in making these decisions.

In the meantime the proposal that all forms of scientific evidence be given in the form of a likelihood ratio is a counsel of perfection.

The expert's utterance as evidence

An alternative approach is to regard the fact that the expert holds a particular opinion as the "evidence" from which the probandum may be inferred. Although the opinion may be framed in terms of the question the court is trying to decide, it can treat the fact that the expert has uttered the opinion like any other evidence. That is to say it should ask itself the questions "what is the probability of this evidence given identity" (for example) and "what is the probability of the evidence given non-identity?".

It might be possible to assess these probabilities. One factor would be the expert's record in previous blind testing. Fingerprints or handwriting known to have the same, or different, origin could be included covertly in the expert's caseload. In the event of a misidentification a thorough debrief should be held. Experience suggests that the problem revealed would invariably be a failure to identify impressions as matches, rather than wrong identifications[8] although even if misidentifications do occur they cannot be used crudely to construct a likelihood ratio for the expert's opinion. Experts, not being machines, will improve with experience and, in particular, will learn by studying instances of misidentification.

It would also be necessary to test with a range of impressions of different quality since the likelihood ratio would depend very much on their completeness and clearness. If blind testing was conducted with impressions of marginal quality the bare result would have to be adjusted if the impressions in a particular case were

[7] Luff, K, "The 16-point Standard" (1990) 15 *Fingerprint Whorld* 73.
[8] This impression would be supported by Evett, IW and Williams, RL, *A Review of the Sixteen Points Fingerprint Standard in England and Wales* (British Crown Copyright, 1989).

of good quality (and vice versa). In more overt testing the quality of print could be driven down to the point where experts either were not willing to express an opinion or (improbably) gave a wrong identification.

Practical certainty

A statement by an expert that two samples or impressions have a common origin is described as a judgment of "moral" or "practical" certainty. Where statistics and models exist, experts agonise over the question of what size of likelihood ratio represents evidence so overwhelming that a conclusion can be expressed that the samples come from the same source. Where there is no such data witnesses seem to be much more confident in expressing such a conclusion. It must be that in these cases the probability of getting the evidence under the alternative hypothesis is believed (subconsciously) to be so low, and the likelihood ratio, therefore, so high, that it does not matter what the other figures in question are. But how high a likelihood ratio is high enough?

Probably expressions of "practical certainty" are currently being given at levels of likelihood ratio far lower than those afforded by readily quantifiable evidence, such as DNA analysis. The effect of quantification in the latter cases is to call attention to a very small doubt which could otherwise be glossed over with few qualms. This phenomenon has been noted before.[9] The explanation is probably psychological rather than rational.

Although they have listened to fingerprint identification for decades courts seem unwilling to allow witnesses giving evidence of DNA analyses to express certainty that the samples came from the same person or to say that they believe it "beyond reasonable doubt". Where a DNA analysis yields a likelihood ratio of one billion or more, how can an expert express in words the strength of this evidence?

One suggestion, which both stresses the overwhelming strength of the evidence in such a case and reminds the court that the question of whether a particular person left a particular mark must also be considered in the light of all the evidence, might be to say:

> "... it should require an enormous amount of other evidence (such as an absolutely unshakeable alibi) to make one believe that these two samples did not come from the same person."

4.4 The ultimate issue rule

Definition

Historically, it was the rule at common law that a witness could not express an opinion on the question which the court had to decide – the so-called *ultimate*

---

[9] Robertson, B and Vignaux, G, "Extending the conversation about Bayes" (1991) 13 Cardozo LR 629–646. For an example of the argument that a "quantifiable doubt" is a "reasonable doubt", however small it may be, see *R* v *Chedzey* (1987) 30 A Crim R 451, 464 per Olney J.

issue rule.[10] The strongest modern statement of the rule was by Neville J in the English High Court in *Joseph Crosfield & Sons Ltd* v *Techno-Chemical Laboratories Ltd*:[11]

> "It is not competent in any action for witnesses to express their opinions upon any of the issues, whether of law or fact, which the Court or a jury has to determine."[12]

During this century courts have become increasingly accustomed to hearing evidence in the form of "these two impressions were both made by the same finger" or in the form of a "probability of paternity". In the face of this the courts have retreated and the rule has become eroded. Rule 704(a) of the US Federal Rules of Evidence, for example, provides (subject to exception):

> "Testimony in the form of an opinion or inference otherwise admissible is not objectionable because it embraces an ultimate issue to be decided by the trier of fact."

The Civil Evidence Act 1972 (UK), section 3 provides:

> "(1) Subject to any rules of court made in pursuance of Part I of the Civil Evidence Act 1968 or this Act, where a person is called as a witness in any civil proceedings, his opinion on any relevant matter in which he is qualified to give expert evidence shall be admissible in evidence."

Where the Rule is said still to exist it has always been difficult to state authoritatively. Even the *Joseph Crosfield* formulation is of uncertain application because it is difficult to separate the class of issues "which the jury has to determine" from other factual questions in the case. *Phipson on Evidence* suggests that:

> "(a) where the issue involves other elements besides the purely scientific, the expert must confine himself to the latter, and must not give his opinion upon the legal or general merits of the case; (b) where the issue is substantially one of science or skill merely, the expert may, if he himself observed the facts, be asked the very question which the jury have to decide."[13]

Rationale

There appear to be two main fears motivating the rule. One is that the expert will take on the role of the advocate. The case most often cited in this regard is *Clark* v *Ryan*[14] in which the expert witness expressed a view as to how a road accident had happened. The court was concerned that the expert had been used to "argue the plaintiff's case and present it more cogently and vividly before the jury".[15]

---

[10] *R* v *Wright* (1821) Russ & Ry 456, 168 ER 895 is often cited as an early example, although it is very weak authority for any particular proposition.
[11] (1913) 29 TLR 378.
[12] (1913) 29 TLR 378, 379.
[13] *Phipson on Evidence*, MN Howard *et al* (eds) 14th ed (Sweet & Maxwell, London, 1990), p 811.
[14] [1960] CLR 486, [1960] ALR 524.
[15] *Per* Dixon CJ [1960] CLR 486, 489.

The second fear is that an expert might usurp the role of the jury, and this is given as a reason for excluding evidence in several cases. In fact it seems to be enough if the evidence went "some distance towards usurping the jury's function".[16] Formally this fear can be argued to be unfounded on two grounds.

- Any jury can simply reject the expert evidence.

"[The expert cannot usurp the function of the jury because] the jury may still reject his testimony and accept his opponent's, and no legal power, not even the judge's order, can compel them to accept the witness' statement against their will."[17]

A notorious and vivid example is the paternity case in which the jury found against Charlie Chaplin despite a blood analysis which, they were told, clearly excluded Chaplin from being the father of the child.

- It is rare that any witness will be asked "the very question which the jury has to decide". Guilt or liability will usually depend upon a number of issues and the expert will usually only be giving evidence on one.

In practice, however, many trials do come to hinge around a single issue. If there is a substantial body of expert evidence on that issue the testimony of experts may well appear to dispose of the issue and hence of the case.

Experts must not give evidence on legal concepts

The sticking point is that courts insist that an expert witness should not give evidence which involves interpreting and applying a legal concept. Thus in *R* v *Kemp*[18] Devlin J (presiding at trial) held that what was a "disease of the mind" was a legal concept for the judge to define. The medical witness could not therefore state whether the accused was suffering from a disease of the mind. The role of the witness was to make a medical diagnosis and explain to the court the ramifications of that diagnosis. The judge would then decide whether the condition could amount to a "disease of the mind".[19] Some courts now appear to restrict the operation of the rule to this kind of question. In the Australian case *R* v *Palmer*, Glass J stated:

"The true rule, in my opinion, is that no evidence can be received upon any question, the answer to which involves the application of a legal standard. It is not possible, for example, to tender evidence that a defendant was negligent, that a deceased lacked testamentary capacity or that the accused was provoked. These are questions, the answers to which can only be given by the jury after the judge has instructed them upon the rule of law which they must apply."[20]

---

[16] *R* v *S* [1989] 1 NZLR 714.
[17] Wigmore, *Evidence in Trials at Common Law Vol 2*, Chadbourn Revision 1979 (Little Brown & Co, Boston), p 936.
[18] [1957] 1 QB 399. *Cf* the troubling case of *Charlson* [1955] 1 WLR 317, [1955] 1 All ER 859, where Barry J allowed a witness to say that the accused was not suffering from a disease of the mind and was sane.
[19] [1957] 1 QB 399, 406.
[20] [1981] 1 NSWLR 209, 214.

The ultimate issue rule therefore seems to have narrowed considerably in scope. Almost unanimously[21], commentators seem to approve of its abolition so far as it pertains to purely factual issues. It is regarded as obsolescent[22], redundant[23], or alleged to lead experts into "expressing their opinions on crucial aspects of the proceedings in indirect and allusive terms, rather than using the terminology that they customarily employ."[24]

The rule and logical inference

It may be, however, that the rhetoric of the rule is preventing us seeing the real problem. When we examine cases in which expert evidence has been challenged on the ground that it was an opinion on the ultimate issue, we find that the problems are often caused by the expert giving evidence in a form which conflicted in some way with the analysis in the previous chapters.

● *Probability of the issue.*   First, and most obviously, the expert may express a probability as to the issue. This is habitual in paternity cases where the courts seem to raise no objection. As explained later in chapter 6 this involves arbitrarily assigning a prior probability without reference to the facts of the case. A notorious instance occurred in the New Zealand case of *McKay.*[25]

In that case the accused allowed himself to be interviewed about the facts of the case while under the influence of a "truth drug". Two psychiatrists testified that they believed that what he said then was true on balance of probability. The Court of Appeal ruled this evidence inadmissible. Leaving aside any question of the efficacy of the truth drug (which is where argument should have been centred) it is obvious that the psychiatrists could not testify to the truth or otherwise of what the accused said. What they should have told the court was how much more likely the truth drug made it that the accused was telling the truth. It appears that their experience was that 70% of questions asked under its influence were answered truthfully. This bare frequency, however, tells us very little. The level of truth-telling must surely depend upon the question asked. If one conducted a random survey and asked thousands of people under the influence of a truth drug whether they were guilty of murder the overwhelming majority would truthfully deny it.

We also need to consider the probability that this defendant would say what he did under the drug although it was not true. *Ex hypothesi* an appropriate survey will not be available as we cannot *know* whether any accused murderer's denial is true. The factors to be considered are the strength of character of the subject and the seriousness of his situation. As

---

[21] For one exception see Friedman, RD, *The Elements of Evidence* (West, 1991), pp 83–85.
[22] Hodgkinson, *Expert Evidence: Law and Practice* (Sweet and Maxwell, London, 1990), p 150.
[23] Jackson, JD, "The Ultimate Issue Rule – One Rule Too Many" [1984] Crim LR 75.
[24] Freckelton, I, *The Trial of the Expert* (Oxford University Press, Melbourne, 1987), p 75.
[25] [1967] NZLR 139.

so often, one of the judges hinted at the correct approach[26] but, because of the way the psychiatrists gave their evidence, the result was a ruling which set back rational analysis of these problems.

- *Transposing the conditional*   The second problem found whenever the expert appears to be usurping the role of the jury is that the expert may either have inverted the conditional or given evidence which invites the listener to do so. This is, in fact, what happened in *R* v *S* (see **2.4**). There may or may not be an intention to usurp the role of the jury, but what actually happens is that the jury is misled. The fallacy of transposing the conditional is discussed more fully in chapter 6.

- *The expert's own alternative hypotheses.*   Finally, there are cases such as *Clark* v *Ryan* in which the evidence was based upon assumptions, some of which related to disputed facts. In other words the expert's evidence was based upon hypothetical questions. As discussed in chapter 3 this should cause no problem provided that the chosen hypothesis is stated, that there is some reasonable prior probability for the hypothesis and the extent to which the opinion rests upon these assumptions is made clear.

Valuation evidence

It would seem that the most difficult evidence to reconcile with the ultimate issue rule is that of experts such as property valuers whose evidence must obviously be in the form of an opinion on the issue for the court, namely the value of the property. The court will decide how much "weight" to put on that opinion by examining the valuer's qualification and experience and analysing the factors taken into account when coming to an evaluation. This can be analysed in likelihood ratio terms if we regard the valuer's *utterance* as the evidence and ask questions like:

What is the probability that this valuer would state a value of, say, one million dollars if:

- the value were one million dollars or less
- the value were more than one million?

This leads one to the same sorts of questions as the more traditional approach but also enables one to combine the valuation with other evidence such as that of a different valuer who may have different experience and assess a different value.

The rule is correct

Our discussion shows that the rule is, after all, correct. It is in fact required by logic. The expert should be able to tell the court what effect his evidence ought to

[26] Turner J "[the witnesses] are quite unable to say that, by the administration of the drugs, more is done than to render it less likely than before that the patient may tell lies" (at p 150). The evidence foundered on the rule that self-serving out-of-court statements by the accused are not admissible. Such statements yield very low likelihood ratios. Administration of a truth drug presumably increases that likelihood ratio, but by a speculative amount.

have in the court's decision-making – in other words to give a likelihood ratio for the evidence. This is not the same as expressing an opinion about the matters to which his evidence relates – in other words giving a probability for an hypothesis. This applies not only to the ultimate issue but to any question to which the expert evidence relates. In order to assess a posterior probability for the ultimate issue, or for any question, the expert would have to assume a prior probability and we have already seen in chapter 2 why this should not be done. Not only can the expert not express an opinion on the ultimate issue but, ideally, the expert should not even express an opinion as to the matter to which his evidence relates.

We therefore defend the ultimate issue rule on the following grounds.

- In some cases the "ultimate issue" is a matter of legal categorisation and not of scientific expertise. An example of this is the definition of "insanity".

- Where the issue is whether or not something occurred, the scientist should usually only testify as to the strength of the scientific evidence. To express an opinion on the ultimate issue is to assume prior odds.

In fact, an expert should only express an opinion on any issue under the same circumstances as an ordinary witness, namely when the opinion is "a compendious mode of summarising a sequence of inference based upon perceived facts".[27]

4.5 Summary

- Forensic scientific evidence which has likelihood ratio, R, is best presented in the following form: "This evidence is R times more probable if the accused left the mark than if someone else did. This evidence therefore [very] [strongly] supports the proposition that the accused left the mark".

- As an alternative to the second sentence above, the witness could say: "Whatever odds you assess that the accused was present on the basis of other evidence, my evidence multiplies those odds by R".

- A scientific witness should only express the strength of a particular piece of evidence and not give an opinion on the issue. The exception to this is when it is impossible to analyse all the factors on which a judgment is based, as when a fingerprint or handwriting expert gives evidence that two samples have a common origin.

[27] Landon, PA, Book review (1944) 60 LQR 201.

Chapter 5

THE CASE AS A WHOLE

Chapter 5

THE CASE AS A WHOLE

Once we know how to interpret a single piece of scientific evidence we must consider how to combine it with the rest of the evidence in the case. Of course, this is the task of the judge or jury and not the scientific witness, but it will help them if scientists understand how the evidence is to be combined, and present it to make that possible.

Scientific evidence is often regarded as standing alone and as somehow of a different character to other evidence. There are a number of reasons for this. One is the lawyers' expectation that scientific witnesses can give definite answers: yes or no, identity or non-identity. We suspect that the way in which fingerprint evidence, in particular, has been given has contributed to this view. Another is that scientific evidence may be quantifiable and there seems to be a view that probability theory only applies to such evidence. A third may be that the evidence is being given by professional people about whom some of the usual doubts about witnesses ought not to arise.

It is clear, however, from our argument that scientific evidence on an issue must be rationally combined with other evidence on the same issue. In this chapter we shall show how that is to be done.

5.1 Combining evidence

We can begin by looking at a case with two pieces of scientific evidence. At the scene of a murder a bloodstain is found which is not the victim's. Two different blood tests are carried out: one to determine the blood group and the other to obtain a DNA profile. The blood grouping tests reveal characteristics shared by only 1% of the population. We would therefore assess a probability of 0.01 for the hypothesis that a "randomly selected" person's blood would match these characteristics. In the DNA test only 1 out of the 4 DNA probes[1] used is successful and

---

[1] See Chapter 8.

reveals characteristics shared by only 0.5% of the population. A man is arrested, his blood is tested and found to share both of these characteristics. Call this evidence E_1 for the blood test and E_2 for the DNA test. The prosecution hypothesis is that the accused left the blood and is therefore guilty (H_1). If he is guilty then clearly both tests would match the bloodstain. (It is certain, for example, that we would get evidence E_1 for the blood test, $P(E_1|H_1) = 1$ in symbols.) The defence is only that someone else was the murderer (H_2). Supposing this hypothesis is true, the probability of getting the blood match is only 1% ($P(E_1|H_2) = 0.01$).

The blood group evidence by itself (E_1) gives us a likelihood ratio of 100 (that is, $P(E_1|H_1)/P(E_1|H_2) = 1/0.01 = 100$) so that whatever the odds in favour of guilt before we consider the blood or the DNA evidence, those odds can be multiplied by 100 after we consider the blood evidence alone. If we started with odds in favour of H_1 of 1 to 1,000, say (that is 1,000 to 1 *against* guilt) we would end up with odds of 1 to 10 in favour of H_1 after noting the blood group evidence.

Now we can consider the DNA evidence E_2 in the light of the blood group results. We first have to consider whether these pieces of evidence are *independent* of one another. Two pieces of evidence are independent if the truth or falsity of one would not affect our assessment of the probability of the other. Suppose, for example, evidence against a suspect for robbery consisted of a matching blood sample and the presence of a large quantity of banknotes under his mattress. There is no reason to suppose that people with any particular blood group are more likely to hoard cash than people with any other blood group and so these two pieces of evidence can certainly be regarded as independent.

In reality there are only a few useful sets of propositions which are genuinely independent of one another. Nearly all propositions will exhibit some degree of dependence upon one another and that degree of dependence will change if the conditioning factors are changed. There are not, therefore, really two separate categories, dependent and independent evidence. There is a sliding scale of degrees of dependence. However, in many cases the degree of dependence will be so small that it will make little practical difference to our calculations and such evidence can, for practical purposes, be regarded as independent. With that *caveat* in mind we shall look at the treatment of independent and non-independent evidence.

Independent evidence

If two pieces of evidence are independent their likelihood ratios can be calculated separately. The combined strength of the evidence is found by applying the likelihood ratios one after the other. Alternatively, the combined effect can be found by multiplying the likelihood ratios to give a combined likelihood ratio which can then be applied itself.[2]

---

[2] Because in this case the probabilities just multiply. The denominator of the combination is $P(E_1 \text{ and } E_2|H_2) = P(E_1|H_2) P(E_2|H_2)$.

The probability of getting the DNA evidence (E_2) given the prosecution hypothesis that the accused left the blood is $P(E_2|H_1) = 1$ since the DNA would then match. The probability of the evidence if it was someone else is $P(E_2|H_2) = 0.05$. The likelihood ratio of the DNA evidence by itself is, therefore, $1/(0.05) = 200$.

There is ample research to attest to the fact that the characteristics revealed by the DNA probes used in forensic science are independent of the characteristics revealed by the blood grouping tests. That is to say our probability of a reading from a particular DNA probe is not affected by knowing that a person is group A, B, O or whatever.

That being the case, we can apply the ratios of the two pieces of evidence one after the other to the prior odds. If the odds before the evidence were 1 to 1000, as we assumed above, the blood group evidence (E_1) with a likelihood ratio of 100 gives posterior odds of $(1/1000)(100) = 1/10$, odds of 1 to 10 in favour of the prosecution hypothesis. Now bring in the (independent) DNA evidence (E_2) with a likelihood ratio of 200 to give posterior odds of $(1/10)(200) = 20/1$ or 20 to 1 in favour of the prosecution hypothesis.

Alternatively, we can combine the likelihood ratios into one. For example, if the expert on blood tests was giving evidence on both tests the joint effect could be found by multiplying the two likelihood ratios to give a combined likelihood ratio of $(100)(200) = 20,000$.[3] This is applied to the prior odds in the normal way: if the prior odds are 1 to 1000 as assumed, the posterior odds would be $(1/1000)(20,000) = 20/1$ or 20 to 1 in favour of H_1.

Non-independent evidence

In contrast, the population frequencies of different blood groups are known to be different for different races. If we have a matching blood group and eyewitness evidence that the offender was of a particular race these pieces of evidence will not be independent. If it has become more likely that the offender was of a particular race then our assessed probability of finding particular blood groups in the scene sample will be different. This will be true even if we are not wholly convinced by the eyewitness evidence. Because of this, race and blood-grouping are said not to be independent.

In these circumstances the combined likelihood ratio for the two items of evidence, race and blood group, cannot be obtained simply by multiplying together the raw likelihood ratios in the way we did before. The likelihood ratio for the second item of evidence must take into account not only the hypotheses but also the first item of evidence.[4]

---

[3] In fact the blood-grouping evidence itself consists of likelihood ratios from a number of characteristics combined in exactly this way.

[4] In fact, calculations can and perhaps should always be presented in this way. However, when E_2 is "independent" of E_1 then $P(E_2|E_1\ H_1) = P(E_2\ |H_1)$ and the inclusion of E_1 makes no difference to the calculation.

It has been said that the product rule does not apply in these circumstances.[5] This argument implies that "the product rule" is that special case which only applies when the two items of evidence are independent. Properly, however, the general statement of the *Product rule* takes dependence into account. This is explained more fully in the Appendix.

It is sometimes asserted that analysis of scientific evidence makes unjustified assumptions of independence and that in our calculations we should allow for undiscovered dependencies. The concept of conditional independence makes this less complicated than it seems. If we have good eyewitness evidence that the perpetrator was of Vietnamese appearance (as in *Tran*[6]) then the hypothesis that the offender was of any other race becomes, at least for the present, not worthy of serious consideration. From then on the hypotheses to be compared are that the offender was the accused and that the offender was some other Vietnamese and we are only concerned with the frequency of the DNA profile in that population. If we also have blood-group evidence then, again, we are only concerned with the frequency of the blood group in the Vietnamese population. Although each of these pieces of evidence does depend on race, once we restrict ourselves to databases of Vietnamese, knowing the blood group will not affect our assessment of the DNA profile. The blood and DNA evidence are then said to be "conditionally independent" of each other, that is, they can be treated as independent as long as we are only considering Vietnamese suspects.

Hypothesis refinement

An alternative way of viewing the process of examining evidence in court is to recognise that as we work our way through the evidence we refine our hypotheses, exactly as investigators do.[7] We are then concerned, not with the dependencies between various items of evidence, but with the relative probabilities of evidence given two specific hypotheses.

As each item of evidence is considered, the effect is not only to change the odds but also to make more specific and detailed the hypotheses being considered. A number of hypotheses may require consideration and the evidence will be of greater or lesser power in discriminating between them. Thus, on the basis of eyewitness evidence we might have three hypotheses in *Tran*: that the offender was the accused (H_1), that the offender was some other Vietnamese (H_2), and that the offender was someone, of some other race (H_3). We then introduce DNA evidence, (E). The likelihood ratios for each of the pairs of hypotheses might be:

$$\frac{P(E|H_1)}{P(E|H_2)} = 50, \quad \frac{P(E|H_1)}{P(E|H_3)} = 500, \quad \frac{P(E|H_2)}{P(E|H_3)} = 10$$

[5] *R* v *Hammond*, unreported 7 December 1992 , CCC920108.
[6] *R* v *Van Hung Tran* (1990) 50 A Crim R 233.
[7] Schum, D and Tillers, P, "Marshalling evidence for adversary litigation" (1991) 13 Cardozo LR 657.

The first of these is the likelihood ratio of the evidence in the light of the two hypotheses, H_1 (the perpetrator is Tran) and H_2 (the perpetrator is some other Vietnamese) and shows how much the evidence E distinguishes between them. The evidence is 50 times more probable under hypothesis H_1 than under hypothesis H_2.

The second term shows that the evidence is even more probable under hypothesis H_1 than under the hypothesis that the offender was neither Tran nor some other Vietnamese, H_3 (since the blood test would reveal Vietnamese-like characteristics).

The "degree of dependency" is expressed by the third likelihood ratio, but it is irrelevant to the question which the court has to determine, which is to compare H_1 versus H_2.

A further example can be provided by a case involving firearms. A victim has been shot. At first all that is known is that a firearm has been used and that a suspect has been arrested nearby in possession of a rifle. Examination then reveals that the bullet is a .762 rifle bullet with five lands and a right-hand twist. The suspect's rifle is a .762 assault rifle and can be seen by the untrained eye to have a right-hand twist with five lands. By the time the examiner's microscopic comparison of the bullets is undertaken the hypotheses to be compared are that the bullet came from the accused's weapon or that it came from some other .762 rifle with a right-hand twist and five lands.

Two things have happened. One is that the hypothesis that some other type of weapon was involved has become of such low probability that it is not considered for the present. (One can imagine cases where, for example, only a bullet fragment is recovered and other hypotheses might remain credible.) The other is that the hypotheses to be compared have become more refined. This is true of both the alternative and the prosecution hypotheses. This point may be concealed by talking constantly of the probability of the evidence, given that the shot was fired from the accused's rifle, as if the probability assessment was determined by the physical characteristics of the rifle. In fact, of course, the probability assessment is affected by what *we know* about the accused's rifle, so that it is only by the time the microscopic examination is undertaken that the prosecution hypothesis becomes that the bullet was fired from the accused's .762 right-hand twist five-landed barrel.

This sequence of hypothesis refinement means that the problem of the interdependencies of a large number of pieces of evidence is much less of a practical problem than might at first be thought.

5.2 Combinations of uncertain evidence

Can a proposition be more probable than any of the pieces of evidence used to prove it? This question has troubled courts and commentators with reference to evidence generally and not just to scientific evidence. In the famous Australian "Dingo baby" case, *R* v *Chamberlain*[8], Brennan J said:

> "First the primary facts from which the inference of guilt is to be drawn must be proved beyond reasonable doubt. No greater cogency can be attributed to an inference based upon particular facts than the cogency that can be attributed to each of those facts."[9]

Further, Gibbs CJ and Mason J approved the statement in *R* v *Van Beelen*[10] that it is:

> ". . . an obvious proposition in logic that you cannot be satisfied beyond reasonable doubt of the truth of an inference drawn from facts about the existence of which you are in doubt."[11]

The counter argument was presented by Deane J that:

> ". . . [if] the case against an accused is contingent upon each of four matters being proved against him, it is obvious that each of those matters must be proved beyond reasonable doubt. . . . On the other hand, if . . . a particular inference against an accused could be drawn from the existence of any one of 200 different matters, each of which had been proved on balance of probabilities, it would be absurd to require that a jury should disregard each of them unless satisfied . . . that any particular one of those matters had been proved beyond reasonable doubt."[12]

This was considered subsequently by Roden J in *R* v *Shepherd*[13] who identified two different situations – one where each piece of evidence was logically necessary to prove the point and the other where the effect of each piece of evidence was to increase the probability of the hypothesis. Roden J was upheld on appeal by the High Court of Australia when it reinterpreted *Chamberlain*.[14]

In fact we are not primarily concerned with whether the evidence is true but whether the evidence increases or decreases the probability that the hypothesis is true, *i.e.* its probative value. Bearing that in mind we can see that Deane and Roden JJ are on the right track but have themselves been distracted by the question of the probability that the evidence is true.[15]

Numerous commentators have pointed out that it is not clear what are "primary facts" and what is "evidence" that must be proved beyond reasonable doubt. As Roden J said in *Shepherd*:

[8] *Chamberlain* v *R* (1984) 51 ALR 225.
[9] (1984) 51 ALR 225, 291.
[10] (1973) 4 SASR 353, 379.
[11] (1984) 51 ALR 225, 260.
[12] *Ibid*, 313.
[13] *R* v *Shepherd (No 3)* (1988) 39 A Crim R 266 CCA (NSW).
[14] *The Queen* v *Shepherd* (1990) 170 ALR 573.
[15] Robertson and Vignaux, "Inferring Beyond Reasonable Doubt", (1991) 11 OJLS 431.

". . . any matter which was the subject of evidence could be reduced to a level at which the jury could be said to be satisfied beyond reasonable doubt, even if it be at as basic a level as that the witness said what is recorded in the transcript."[16]

This is the key point. Suppose a witness says "X is true" and X is something from which some other fact of importance to the case is to be inferred. We are not directly concerned with whether X is true or not. The evidence that we consider is that the witness has said this. The relevant questions are "what is the probability of the witness uttering this given H_1 or given H_2?". All the factors that make X potentially uncertain, for example the witness may be dishonest or mistaken, go to reduce the likelihood ratio by making it more probable that the witness would say this even if it was untrue. The relevant question is not "how probable is it that X is true?" but "what is the likelihood ratio of the statement made?" in the light of the alternative hypotheses being considered by the court.

For example, if, as is assumed in a number of logical puzzles, a witness is equally likely to tell the truth or to lie, the likelihood ratio for any statement made by that witness would be 1 and therefore irrelevant. In real life, people lie for reasons and so proper likelihood ratios can be constructed by considering the incentives a particular witness has, to tell a particular lie at a particular time.

In a typical case we might have three or four pieces of evidence, each tending to prove that the accused was the perpetrator. There might be an eyewitness identification, an alleged confession, and a blood sample. Each of these pieces of evidence may yield a likelihood ratio which increases the odds that the accused was the perpetrator. The combined effect is obtained by multiplying their likelihood ratios together (assuming that the pieces of evidence are independent). Provided each likelihood ratio is over 1 the effect will be to increase the odds in favour of the accused being the perpetrator. Removing one of them only reduces those odds, it does not demolish the case. The odds, given two of the pieces of evidence, will be greater than given just one of them. They are increased again by a third piece. If enough evidence is accumulated these odds can easily rise above the odds in favour of the truth of any of the pieces of evidence.[17]

On the other hand there are some situations where a proposition can only be true if two other matters are both true. For example, the proposition "the accused was fishing within US waters" can only be true if the accused was fishing *and* the accused was within US waters.[18] The proposition to be proved is a logical conjunction of the other two. Here, the probability of that combined proposition cannot be greater than the probability of either of the two component propositions. On the other hand this logical structure is seldom met when we are reasoning about individual facts. In a criminal case it occurs at the final stage of the reasoning. The defendant can only be found guilty of a charge if each

[16] *R* v *Shepherd* (No 3) (1988) 39 A Crim R 266, 272 (CA).
[17] See the discussion of the extension of the conversation in the Appendix.
[18] A New Zealand example is in *Takeuchi* v *Ministry of Agriculture and Fisheries*, unreported, Ongley J, 5 June 1985, High Court, Wellington, M 43/85 and M 42/85.

element is proved, as in the fishing case above, since the charge consists of the conjunction of all the elements.

It is even possible for items of evidence which, individually, would be regarded with great scepticism to prove an hypothesis in combination. Eggleston shows how evidence from apparently unreliable witnesses can combine to produce good evidence.[19]

For example, suppose you had two friends who were great practical jokers but who did not know each other. If one telephoned you to tell you that he had just seen the Prime Minister drunk in the street, would you believe him? What if, quite independently (remember the friends do not know each other) the other phoned to tell you the same thing. Would this increase the probability in your mind that the Prime Minister was drunk?

5.3 Issues in the case

In discussions of scientific evidence it is common to refer to the "probability of evidence given guilt". It goes without saying, however, that guilt may hinge on issues which scientific evidence has nothing to say about. For example, in a rape case where identity is evidenced by DNA analysis, the defence may be a claim of consent; in a case in which presence is proved by fibre evidence the accused may claim to have rendered first aid to a victim after an assault, and so on.

An expert on glass may have nothing to say about whether a person was acting under duress, but there will be more marginal matters where scientists could be of greater help to the court than they may traditionally have been. Consider the following series of pairs of hypotheses:

(i) H_1 = the accused had glass on his clothing;
      H_2 = the accused had no glass on his clothing.

(ii) H_1 = the glass on the accused's clothing was of similar refractive index to the glass of the broken window;
      H_2 = the glass on the accused's clothing was not of similar refractive index to the glass of the broken window.

(iii) H_1 = the glass on the accused came from the window;
      H_2 = the glass on the accused did not come from the window.

(iv) H_1 = the accused was close to the window when it was broken;
      H_2 = the accused was not close to the window when it was broken.

(v) H_1 = the accused broke the window;
      H_2 = the accused did not break the window.

Classically, the forensic scientist's technical expertise would have provided evidence on the first two pairs of hypotheses and the scientist would provide statistical evidence which would help to distinguish between the third pair of hypotheses. Should the witness be working further forward along the chain of reasoning?

The answer is surely yes, as long as the expert speaks in terms of likelihood ratios and does not purport to assess a probability for the ultimate issue. In order

---

[19] Eggleston, R, "The mathematics of corroboration" [1985] Crim LR 640.

to reason from one proposition to another some background knowledge is required. Most of us do not know how close one has to stand to a breaking window to acquire a large quantity of microscopic glass fragments and whether the person breaking the window can be distinguished from other close bystanders. Forensic scientists have a responsibility to acquire such knowledge and to pass it on to jurors.

Likewise, there are occasions when scientific evidence will itself raise the possibility of alternative hypotheses which might have to be eliminated by ordinary police investigation. An obvious example is the possibility that a sibling of the accused might have left a mark with a particular DNA profile at the scene of a crime.

We will see in chapter 6 that these kinds of questions would never have been pursued had classical statistical methods remained the dominant method of assessing forensic scientific evidence. In the classical approach the technician is given two samples of glass to see if they "match". The technician knows nothing about the circumstances of the offence and need not consider the probabilities of transfer and persistence.

Only once we start to ask questions like "what is the probability of the evidence given such and such an hypothesis?" are we made to realise that all these factors must be explored. Once these issues are explored forensic scientists will become even more helpful in structuring the argument in a case than they have been up to now.

5.4 The standard of proof and the cost of errors

Strictly speaking, a section on the standard of proof does not belong in a book on expert scientific evidence, because it is the case as a whole and not any particular part of it, or any particular fact within it, that must be proved to the required standard.

As we have seen, scientific evidence should be admissible whenever it tends to favour one material hypothesis over another, unless it falls foul of some exclusionary rule of evidence. Unfortunately, this is not how the matter is always seen. Hodgkinson[20] suggests that expert evidence must have "high probative value" in order to be admissible. He cites no authority for this proposition and never tells us how high is "high". In any case, until the technical tools described here were available, there was no way of measuring the probative value of evidence. Magnusson and Selinger[21] refer to the requirement that "the expert's conclusion is reliable beyond reasonable doubt" in criminal cases and Byrne refers to the ability of mental health professionals to "form an opinion on the balance of

---

[20] Hodgkinson, T, *Expert Evidence* (Sweet and Maxwell, London, 1990), p 4.
[21] Magnusson, E, and Selinger, B, "Jury Comprehension of Complex Scientific Evidence: The Inference Chart Concept" (1990) 14 Crim LJ 389.

probabilities, the standard to which expert witnesses are expected to adhere in providing opinion evidence in civil litigation".[22]

On the contrary, we emphasise that there is no reason of principle why these standards, which do not apply to any other items of evidence, should apply particularly to scientific evidence. Indeed, these statements seem to assume that the expert is providing an opinion on an issue. However, we have seen that an expert should not decide whether he is justified, by a given standard of proof, in expressing an opinion that something is the case. Instead, he should explain how much the scientific evidence increases the probability of the hypothesis concerned. The standard of proof is a matter for the court, not for the expert.

The role of the tribunal of fact is twofold. First, it must assess the probability (or the odds) that the plaintiff's or prosecution's case is true. This should be done rationally, considering all the evidence in the manner we have described. Evidence should not be left out of account just because it fails to meet a test imposed by the scientist. Having assessed this probability the tribunal must make a decision. The decision is whether to find the defendant liable or, in a criminal case, "guilty". If decisions are to be made consistently we need rules about what sort of probability assessments justify a finding of liability.

Civil cases

The standard civil case concerns a loss which has actually been suffered in the real world and the decision in the case will simply determine on whose shoulders the loss is to fall. There is no reason to favour plaintiffs or defendants and so the standard of proof chosen is "balance of probabilities". This means that the tribunal must find that the probability that the plaintiff's case is true is greater than 0.5. This standard of proof will lead to the greatest number of correct decisions and the smallest number of wrong decisions.

If the consequences of a wrong decision are more serious for the defendant than for the plaintiff then the obvious course is to require a higher assessment of probability before finding the defendant liable. This means that although, inevitably, the total number of mistakes will increase, one is less likely to make the more serious error. This problem arises not only in child sex-abuse cases but also where the decision in a civil case may result both in financial loss and in a party being labelled fraudulent or criminal.[23] It can be summed up by the two questions "what are the odds and what are the stakes?".

Criminal cases

The extreme situation is a criminal prosecution. It is regarded as most important that we avoid convicting the innocent even at the cost of acquitting the guilty. This is summed up by the adage "It is better that 10 guilty persons escape than

---

[22] Byrne, "Allegations of Child Sexual Abuse in Family Law Matters" in Freckelton and Selby (eds) *Expert Evidence* (Law Book Company, 1993).
[23] See Robertson, BWN, "Criminal allegations in civil cases" (1991) 107 LQR 194 and cases referred to therein.

one innocent suffer".[24] The standard of proof required is therefore "beyond reasonable doubt". This standard cannot be quantified in the same way as "balance of probabilities", since it embodies both stages – the probability assessment and the decision to convict. The standard will therefore be different for different cases since the costs of a mistake depend on the case and the seriousness of the charge.

Child sex-abuse cases

The role of the standard of proof can be seen most sharply in child sex-abuse cases. A wrong decision can have serious consequences for the child. On the one hand the child may be exposed to further danger; on the other it may be needlessly removed from its family. If these two costs were considered equally serious then a decision would be made on balance of probabilities. Much of the dispute about the appropriate standard of proof in such cases depends on the value put on family life. If one believes that removal from the family gravely damages a child one will require a high probability of continuing danger before taking this course. If one does not believe this, one would remove the child on the mere suspicion of abuse.

Is a quantifiable doubt a reasonable doubt?

A particular problem may arise with scientific evidence expressed in probabilistic terms. Some argue that if a doubt is quantifiable it is a "reasonable" doubt. In one sense this is true, but we cannot conclude that evidence which can be quantified gives rise automatically to a reasonable doubt in the sense that it should lead to an acquittal.[25] This would not be a rational response since it would lead to the surprising conclusion that types of evidence which were thoroughly researched and understood would always lead to acquittals, while we carried on convicting people on the basis of less well-understood evidence such as handwriting analysis. If this argument were to be followed through then, if we ever achieved quantification of all forms of evidence, conviction would become impossible. In some cases a quantified likelihood ratio might be far greater than we would find if we could analyse handwriting comparison fully. Once we admit, as the legal system does, that we can never be certain then, surely, the mere fact that we can quantify our uncertainty should make no difference to the decision, except to make it more solid.

The common law itself developed this structure, "What are the odds and what are the stakes?" over the last three centuries and it is now reinforced by modern decision theory. We do not intend to go any further into this point here. We just re-emphasise that what standard of proof is required is a matter of policy for the court and not something that expert witnesses need concern themselves with. Furthermore, the standard of proof applies to the case as a whole, whereas scientific evidence is directed to particular issues.

[24] Sir William Blackstone, "Commentary on The Laws of England", Book IV Ch 27.
[25] As Olney J concluded in *R* v *Chedzey* (1987) 30 A Crim R 451 (CA).

What if the scientific evidence is the only evidence?

It may be objected that where scientific evidence is the "only evidence" it must prove the case beyond reasonable doubt. Certainly, in a particular case the only contested issue may be identity and the only evidence relating to that identity may be scientific, so that the scientific evidence would indeed have to prove the issue "beyond reasonable doubt". However, such cases are extremely unusual and this question usually arises from a failure to realise what else acts as evidence of identity.

The question may be clarified by considering:

- the following question: what do you mean by "only evidence of identity"? Do you mean that prior to hearing this evidence the perpetrator could have been anyone in the world?

- the following statement: the only case in which forensic scientific evidence is the only evidence of identity is a case in which we start to screen the entire population and stop when we find the first "match". The flaws in such a procedure are obvious.

In practice there are nearly always other factors tending to identify the accused as the perpetrator, such as a relationship with the victim, the fact that the accused lives in the same small town or the fact that the accused cannot produce an alibi for the occasion. In general, scientific evidence is always to be combined with other evidence relevant to the same issues and does not stand alone. Courts have recognised this fact even where the issue is presence and the evidence is a fingerprint.[26]

In the United States nearly all the notorious contested cases in which DNA evidence has been excluded have, nonetheless, resulted in the conviction of the accused. Elsewhere, where there appears to be no evidence other than the DNA evidence this may be because the prosecuting attorney has decided not to use other evidence, believing that the DNA evidence alone would secure a conviction.[27] The solution is for prosecutors to realise that forensic scientific evidence must be combined with other evidence.

A set of facts that might be envisaged is where a sample taken from a suspect in respect of one crime provides evidence of his involvement in another, but investigation fails to reveal further evidence relating to that offence. Even here, the DNA evidence cannot be considered in isolation but must be considered alongside questions such as whether evidence in respect of one of these offences is admissible in respect of the other.[28] In the end, argument may come down to the question of the appropriate population to provide the prior odds to which the likelihood ratio is to be applied. The standard of proof applies to the posterior odds and not to the scientific evidence alone.

---

[26] *R* v *Buisson* [1990] 2 NZLR 542, 548.
[27] *R* v *Hammond*, unreported, 7 December 1992 (London) CCC 920108.
[28] Which itself is entirely a matter of relevance: *DPP* v *P* [1991] 2 AC 447 (HL).

5.5 Assessing priors

How are the prior odds to be assessed? First, note that "prior" does not mean "prior in time". "Prior odds" refers to the odds assessed on the basis of all the evidence that the jury has considered before it turns its mind to the scientific evidence.

There is no difference in principle between prior odds (or probabilities) and any other odds. It is just a matter of applying our reasoning process to all that other evidence. Much of this evidence will be in a form that is not easily quantifiable, but if a juror believes that the evidence is helpful it must be because it appears to be more probable under one hypothesis than another and therefore helps to distinguish between them.

This is not the place to consider the argument in the legal literature about whether "ordinary evidence" can be assessed in a probabilistic fashion. The relevant point here is simply that the prior odds depend upon the other evidence in the case. Experts should therefore neither assume priors nor, worse, conceal an assumed prior by giving evidence in the form of a probability of the matter to be proved.

5.6 The defence hypothesis and the prior odds

We have seen that the defence can affect the power of any particular piece of evidence by its choice of alternative hypothesis. This does not mean, however, that all the defence has to do is to choose the alternative hypothesis which most reduces the likelihood ratio. This is because the choice of defence hypothesis will also affect the prior probability ratio. As an extreme example, consider a case in which a Pitcairn Islander is accused of a murder in New York and his DNA analysis resembles that of stains left at the scene. If the defence insists that the accused's analysis be compared with that of other Pitcairn Islanders then that is tantamount to an admission that the offence was committed by a Pitcairn Islander. In that case the prior odds are not several million to one against but perhaps a few dozen to one.

Thus, in the Australian case, *Tran*[29], the defence effectively admitted that the offence was committed by a Vietnamese. Any evidence relating to opportunity, for example, now becomes more powerful. This is because evidence relating to opportunity usually implicates a large number of people who can be shown to have been in a particular area at a particular time. Of those people we are now only concerned with those that are Vietnamese.

We have seen that a likelihood ratio of one million or more if the alternative offender was a randomly selected person can be reduced to a few hundred if the alternative hypothesis were that the perpetrator were the accused's brother.

---

[29] *R* v *Van Hung Tran* (1990) 50 A Crim R 233.

However, the prior odds of the hypothesis of guilt would have risen from odds of 1 to millions, up to 1 to two or three. The fall in the value of the evidence can be overwhelmed by the rise in the prior.

Thus, it may even be counter-productive for the defence to insist on such a line. What the defence cannot do, although some courts have not been astute enough to grasp this, is to insist on an alternative hypothesis that the offender was someone genetically closely resembling the offender and then, when considering other evidence, revert to an alternative hypothesis that the offender could have been anyone else equally implicated by evidence of opportunity, motive and so on.

5.7 Case studies

We consider four cases which further illustrate the general method. In *Chedzey* (below) there was discussion of how the so-called statistical evidence should be used in the case; we revisit *Pengelly* to combine conventional blood-testing evidence with the DNA evidence; we look at a case of "back-calculation" and, finally, another paternity case.

A bomb-hoax call

The Australian case *Chedzey*[30] is one of several which are cited as examples of the limitations of statistical evidence. The case is discussed at some length in this light by Bates[31] and is cited as an example by Tapper.[32] In the case itself, Kennedy J referred to writing on mathematics and probability in legal cases, but said (at p 458) there appeared to have been:

> "... an undue emphasis upon this aspect of the evidence to the exclusion of the other evidence [which] led to a failure on the part of the learned trial judge to emphasise to the jury that, in a case substantially dependent on circumstantial evidence, it is essential that all the facts be considered together."

What the court failed to do was to provide a detailed rational explanation of how this was to be done.

Chedzey was accused of making a bomb-hoax call. The call was made to Perth police station and the only evidence against Chedzey which the court was prepared to consider was that the call was traced to the accused's home by means of the telephone company tracing equipment. Chedzey consistently denied having made the call although he did change his account of his movements on the evening concerned.

Evidence was given that the equipment had been tested by some 12,700 calls being made from known numbers of which only five were subject to error. No

[30] *R v Chedzey* (1987) 30 A Crim R 451.
[31] Bates, F, "Describing the Indescribable – Evaluating the Standard of Proof in Criminal Cases" [1989] Crim LJ 331–342.
[32] Tapper, *Cross on Evidence*, 7th ed (Butterworths, London, 1990), p 159.

information was given about these errors and whether they shared any common features. From this the expert concluded, and both courts accepted, that the tracing equipment was "99.96% accurate". The trial judge directed the jury in a way capable of being interpreted as meaning that it could find that this probability of 99.96% was proof beyond reasonable doubt. Chedzey was convicted and appealed. The Western Australian Court of Criminal Appeal quashed the conviction on the ground that it was unsafe and unsatisfactory. In particular Kennedy J and Olney J were concerned that the judge's summing up would have led the jury into basing its verdict entirely upon the tracing evidence and ignoring the remainder of the evidence in the case.

Let the two alternate hypotheses to be considered at trial be:

H_1 = the hoax call was made from Chedzey's telephone;
H_2 = the hoax call was made from another of the telephones in Perth.

We will use the symbol N to represent the number of telephones in Perth.

The evidence considered at the trial was:

E = the tracing equipment indicates Chedzey's telephone.

The test referred to by the expert was aimed at determining the probability of a correct trace, that is that the tracer would correctly identify the telephone from which a call was made. This is $P(E|H_1)$ in our notation. This would be 1 if the tracer always operated perfectly. The test consisted of making 12,700 calls from known numbers and seeing whether the tracing equipment correctly identified them. In fact there were five errors found. Of the 12,700 calls, 12,695 were correctly traced. Thus, the probability of tracing a call to Chedzey's telephone, if Chedzey had, in fact, made the call, is $P(E|H_1)$ = 12,695/12,700 = 0.9996.

To determine $P(E|H_2)$ we need to know why the equipment fails when it does so, what it will do when it is in error and, in particular, the probability that it will wrongly trace a particular telephone, in this case, Chedzey's.

We can consider two extreme examples of behaviour. Suppose that whenever the equipment is in error it does not report a number wrongly but instead indicates "no trace". In that case although there would be 5/12,700 (that is, 0.04%) errors (*i.e.* "no traces") it would not indicate a telephone number on those occasions. Whenever it did give an indication it would always be correct. The probability of obtaining the evidence, E, if the call was not made from Chedzey's telephone would be zero because it would have said "no trace": $P(E|H_2)$ = 0. The likelihood ratio is therefore 0.9996/0. It would be infinitely large, which means no matter what the prior odds were, we are *certain* the call came from the indicated number and no amount of evidence could alter that belief.

At the other extreme we can imagine (absurdly) that whenever the equipment makes an error it always indicates Chedzey's number and never another. If Chedzey made the call there would be a $P(E|H_1)$ = 0.9996 probability of the equipment indicating so and if he did not make the call there would be a $P(E|H_2)$ = 0.0004 probability of it doing so (*i.e.* all the errors). The likelihood ratio is

0.9996/0.0004 = 2,499. This is a powerful piece of evidence – despite the malfunction which might be thought to make it useless – but unless there is other evidence it will not be enough. We still have to consider the prior odds.

The prior odds, $P(H_1)/P(H_2)$, we shall take as $1/N$ since without any other evidence, any telephone in the Perth area could have been the source of the hoax call. Assuming the number of telephones in Perth, N = 1 million, then the prior odds would be 1,000,000 to 1 against the call coming from Chedzey's telephone. The odds in favour of H_1 before receiving any evidence are 1 to 1,000,000.

The call tracing evidence multiplies these odds by the likelihood ratio of 2,499 to give odds of about 1 to 400 that the call came from Chedzey's telephone:

$$\frac{1}{1,000,000}(2499) = \text{about}\frac{1}{400}$$

Thus, on the evidence of the tracing system alone it is unlikely that the call came from Chedzey's number, even in the absurd case that his telephone gets all the mistakes.

Suppose, instead, that when it makes a mistake the tracer chooses a telephone at random in the Perth area. The probability of a mistake is 0.0004. Given a mistake, the probability of it choosing any particular phone is $1/N$, where N is the number of telephones in the area. Thus, the probability of the tracer wrongly choosing any particular telephone, $P(E|H_2)$ is 0.0004/N. We already have $P(E|H_1)$ = 0.9996. The likelihood ratio is therefore

$$\frac{P(E|H_1)}{P(E|H_2)} = \frac{0.9996}{0.0004/N} = 2499N$$

For N = 1,000,000 this gives an enormous likelihood ratio of about 2.5 billion. Again, we assume prior odds of $1/N$. (If the tracing evidence is considered before other evidence and if we regard the prior only as the number of telephone lines available, then it does not matter what N is since the Ns will cancel out.[33]) The posterior odds are the product of the prior odds and the likelihood ratio: $(1/N)(2499N)$ = 2499. Thus, the odds that the call came from Chedzey's telephone (before other evidence had been considered) are 2499 to 1.

Had the expert adopted the logical approach, attention would have been directed towards the proper questions, of which the two major ones were:

- what did the tracing equipment do on the occasions when it made an error? and

- why did the equipment fail when it did, were there any features common to the test calls which resulted in error (*e.g.* were they shorter than others) and did those features apply to the call in this case?

---

[33] The order in which we consider evidence will not, of course, affect the outcome but can make the arithmetic easier or more difficult.

Assuming that nothing pertinent emerged from those questions the evidence could have been explained to the court as producing posterior odds of 2499 to 1 in favour of the hypothesis that the call was made from Chedzey's telephone. The way in which this figure was arrived at would have to be fully explained. The evidence of Chedzey's denials and the changing story could then be considered not, as Kennedy J put it, to determine whether this was one of the exceptional errors, but to produce new posterior odds by applying their likelihood ratios. It might be thought that very powerful evidence would be needed to reduce odds of 2499 to 1 below a level of "beyond reasonable doubt".

The important point is that, far from being over-emphasised, Bayes' Rule, properly applied, would have shown the jury precisely how to do what Kennedy J was concerned that they should do: to consider all the facts together.

Pengelly[34]

Returning to this New Zealand case[35], the bloodstains found at the scene of the crime were analysed using both conventional blood tests and DNA tests. The DNA tests had a likelihood ratio of 12,450 for the two hypotheses that Pengelly left the stains or that some unknown person left them. It had been stated by another witness that the blood characteristics found could be found in approximately 3.01% of the local population. The likelihood ratio for the blood test is, therefore, about $1/0.0301 = 33.17$.

The forensic scientist stated that:

> "On combining the DNA results and other results I concluded that 1 in at least 413,000 people, including Pengelly, could have produced the results pertaining to the bloodstain."

The two likelihood ratios were multiplied to produce a single likelihood ratio of $(33.17)(12450) = 413,000$. It was not expressed as such since the New Zealand Department of Scientific and Industrial Research (now the Institute for Environmental Health and Forensic Sciences) had not at that stage moved to expressing conventional blood test results in likelihood ratio terms.

Gumbley v *Cunningham*; *Gould* v *Castle*

In these cases[36] two defendants in separate incidents were investigated for allegedly driving when they had had too much to drink. One was found at the scene vomiting, obviously ill and had to be taken to hospital. He was not tested until about four hours later. The other was found at his home about four hours after an accident involving his car. He displayed no obvious signs of having been drinking. Both gave samples of blood which proved to have alcohol concentrations somewhat below the prescribed limit.

---

[34] See the earlier discussions of this case in chapters 2 and 4.
[35] *R* v *Pengelly* [1992] 1 NZLR 545 (CA).
[36] [1988] 2 QB 171.

The Crown adduced scientific evidence based on "back-calculation", *i.e.* an extrapolation from the blood alcohol sample at four hours after driving, to estimate the blood/alcohol concentration at the time of driving. The expert stated that the first defendant would have been over the limit and that the second was "likely" to have been over the limit. The issue on appeal was whether such evidence was admissible. The court decided that it was, but suggested that future courts be very careful to ensure that such back-calculation evidence is easily understood and highly persuasive of an illegal concentration.

Accordingly, the appeal of the first appellant was dismissed, while the appeal of the second appellant was allowed.

Let in each case:

H_1 = "the defendant's blood/alcohol concentration at the time of driving was over the prescribed limit".
H_2 = "the defendant's blood/alcohol concentration at the time of driving was below the prescribed limit".

E = "the observed blood/alcohol concentration when measured".

$P(E|H_1)$ and $P(E|H_2)$ in each case will depend on factors such as the time delay since stopped, the rate at which alcohol was consumed, the rate at which it was metabolised and the defendant's physical state, body weight, tiredness, hunger, etc. In practice, experiments may have to be done to estimate the effects of these factors.

By saying that one defendant *would* have been over the limit and that the other was *likely* to have been over the limit, the expert was stating $P(H_1|E)$ in vague terms. To do so required assessing the prior. Presumably, a neutral 1 to 1 prior was assumed without reference to the facts of the cases.

The court, however, did have some prior information in each case. It upheld the conviction in the case where the evidence indicated a high prior probability, while allowing the appeal in the case where the circumstances suggested that a prior of 1 to 1 or less may have been appropriate. In the latter case the likelihood ratio was also evidently lower and the resulting probability assessment of "likely" did not meet the required standard of proof.

Argument in the case focussed on the admissibility and "persuasiveness" of the "back-calculation" technique, but the decision of the Court of Appeal can be satisfactorily explained in terms of the overall strength of each case. The "back-calculation" is simply a matter of inference from available evidence, as with any calculation, and there is no reason in principle why it should not be admissible. In the mind of the court in one of these cases a high likelihood ratio was applied to a fairly high prior odds, and in the other a low likelihood ratio was applied to low prior odds. The witness's failure to express the evidence in Bayesian terms, however, focussed attention on the witness's conclusions and increased the doubts of counsel and court about their validity. The real question about the evidence is whether the factors taken into account in calculating $P(E|H_1)$ and $P(E|H_2)$ were the correct ones and were correctly handled.

Loveridge v Adlam

In this New Zealand paternity case[37] the scientific evidence produced a very high likelihood ratio in favour of paternity. Unfortunately the witness then concluded his evidence with a statement of the "probability of paternity". Remarkably, he gave two such probabilities: "using conventional tests the probability of paternity was calculated to be 99.9%, and by DNA 99.5%". The paternity index (*i.e.* the likelihood ratio) based on the conventional tests was given as 9,222. If we assume that the likelihood ratio from the DNA was 198, this gives a combined likelihood ratio of 1,825,956, say 1.8 million. This assumes that the two pieces of evidence are independent.

If there were, say, 1,000 other equally possible fathers, the prior odds that the respondent was the father would be 1 to 1,000. Multiplying this by the scientific evidence's likelihood ratio of 1.8 million we get posterior odds that the respondent was the father of 1,800 to 1. (This corresponds to a probability of 1,800/1,801 = 99.94%.)

The respondent denied having had intercourse with the applicant at the appropriate time and the applicant's evidence on the subject was not very convincing. The judge said:

> "Naturally I have reflected carefully whether the statistical assessment of the likelihood of the respondent's paternity should cause me to alter the view I had formed on the applicant's credibility. I think, in the circumstances of this case, that to take that approach would be tantamount to saying that the statistical assessment on its own, without any other evidence at all connecting the respondent with the applicant at the relevant time, amounts to sufficient proof of paternity. .... As already indicated, it is of no evidential value at all unless there is a credible foundation in the other evidence in the case which makes it relevant. ... As it is, there is no credible evidence that the respondent had intercourse with the applicant at the time when the child was conceived ..."

The judge had earlier commented:

> "If, for instance, it proved impossible for the putative father to have had intercourse with the mother at the time when the child must have been conceived, any statistical assessment of the probability of his paternity must be invalid and irrelevant in relation to the particular facts."

The judge also referred to the possibility that another male could have had an equally high "probability of paternity". These remarks were astute, but because the judge had been led to believe that the interpretation of such evidence was a matter within the expertise of a biochemist, rather than a matter of logic, he evidently felt unable to question the validity of the form in which the evidence was expressed.

If it was impossible for the two to have had intercourse then the prior odds in favour of the respondent's paternity would have been infinitely low, and no

[37] *Loveridge* v *Adlam* [1991] NZFLR 267.

likelihood ratio given by DNA or any other technique, no matter how high, could alter that. However, such odds could only be achieved by unimpeachable evidence that the respondent was away from the applicant for every minute of the period in question. (Even then the problem of artificial insemination arises!)

The way in which the evidence was given prevented the judge from seeing how he could combine the scientific evidence that the child was the child of the respondent with the equivocal evidence relating to whether the two had had intercourse. It was certainly not proved beyond doubt that they could not have had intercourse. Suppose that after hearing the evidence about whether the two might have had intercourse during the relevant period the judge decided that this was unlikely. Suppose that he assessed the odds of the defendant's paternity after that evidence as 1 to 10 (*i.e.* 10 to 1 against). Applying the likelihood ratio of 1.8 million to those prior odds would give posterior odds of 180,000 to 1 in favour of the respondent's paternity.

Had the evidence been given in the way we recommend in this book the judge would have seen how it was to be combined with the other evidence in the case.

5.8 Summary

- Forensic scientific evidence should not be considered in isolation but should be combined with other evidence on the same issue.

- Items of scientific evidence are not required to be able to prove any issue to any particular standard on their own.

- If the items of evidence are independent, the weight of each item of evidence is given by its likelihood ratio.

- Bayes' Rule gives the correct logical method for combining pieces of evidence on an issue.

Chapter 6

ERRORS OF THINKING

Chapter 6

ERRORS OF THINKING

Although the approach explained here is clear and logical, the analysis of forensic scientific evidence has usually followed different methods. As a result, readers may already have come across methods of explaining scientific evidence different from those in this book. Some of these methods of presenting evidence are not as helpful as they might be, but some are quite fallacious. In this chapter and in chapter 7 we will consider some problems which commonly crop up in cases.

In chapter 7 we will look at problems in the way in which forensic scientific evidence has been presented; in this chapter we concentrate on problems that lawyers and courts have had in interpreting even correctly presented evidence.

6.1 A brace of lawyers' fallacies

Two fallacious arguments are commonly used in court when evidence in the form of a likelihood ratio is given. These relate to the way the evidence is to be handled and can arise even when the witness has given the evidence perfectly correctly. Thomson and Schumann have called these the prosecutor's and the defence attorney's fallacy.[1]

The prosecutor's fallacy

We referred to the prosecutor's fallacy in chapter 2 when dealing with the breath-testing device. It occurs when someone *transposes the conditional*, that is, claims (or implies) that $P(E|H)$ is the same as $P(H|E)$.

This illustrative example was suggested by Ian Evett. Let us take H = "this animal is a cow" and E = "this animal has four legs". Then $P(E|H) = 1$, which is

---

[1] Thompson, WC and Schumann, EL, "Interpretation of Statistical Evidence in Criminal Trials: The Prosecutor's Fallacy and the Defense Attorney's Fallacy" (1987) 11 *Law and Human Behaviour* 167.

to say: it is certain that this animal has four legs given that it is a cow. This is not the same as P(H|E) which is the probability that this animal is a cow given that it has four legs. Thus, the two are not the same. To pretend or imply so is a fallacy.

The most expert of witnesses can occasionally commit a slip of the tongue, especially when responding to badly worded questions from counsel. Counsel and judges summing up to the jury may commit this fallacy even when evidence has been correctly given and, of course, the fallacy may be being committed behind the closed doors of the jury room.

There are two conditionals which are in danger of being transposed. The first is in the numerator of the likelihood ratio, the second in the denominator.

The numerator of the likelihood ratio tells us the probability of the evidence given the prosecution hypothesis. You cannot assume that this is the same as the probability of the hypothesis given the evidence. For example, in *R* v *B* a psychologist testified that the alleged victim reported a dream of a sort "frequently experienced by sexually abused young people" (see 2.4). From this and other observations, she appeared to conclude that the child had been abused. In order to consider the value of the evidence, however, we need to know how frequently non-abused children have these dreams. To the extent that non-abused children have these dreams the evidence will be reduced in value. This logical trap is regrettably common; indeed Thompson and Schumann found that 90% of doctors whom they surveyed committed this error in considering diagnostic tests. In other words, they believed that if a sign or symptom occurred in 99% of cases of "drizzling fever"[2] then there was a probability of 99% that a patient with this sign had the disease. One only has to remember our example of the sexually abused, but breathing child, to see that this is not so.

A stark example of transposition occurred in the "Birmingham Six" case in which the witness reported that he was "99% certain that the men had handled explosive".[3] The witness had carried out a standard statistical significance test which failed to consider any specific alternative explanation for the test results. The probability of getting the test result, assuming that the men had handled explosives, was over 99%. The high probability of the result given the hypothesis became, in the witness's mind, a high probability for the hypothesis, given the result.

The second form of this fallacy is transposing the denominator of the likelihood ratio. The denominator will often be the probability of getting the evidence assuming the alternative hypothesis, a "match by chance". The fallacy is to believe that this transposes into the odds in favour of guilt. Therefore, if the odds against a match by chance are one million to one, we might leap to the conclusion that it is a million to one on that the stain came from the accused, or

[2] Also known as Ward Edward's Syndrome after its discoverer; Edwards, W, "Influence diagrams, Bayesian imperialism, and the Collins case: an appeal to reason", (1991) 13 Cardozo LR 1025, 1048.
[3] Mills, H, "The Birmingham Six Case – Vital Scientific Evidence Kept From Defence" *The Independent*, 28 March 1991.

that there is only one chance in a million that it came from anyone else.[4] This forgets the fact that the numerator might not be as high as 1. It also ignores the prior, the potential effect of which was demonstrated by the HIV test example in chapter 3. Regrettably, examples of this error in logic can often be found in the Law Reports. One example is provided by the Lord Chief Justice of England, who said in *R* v *Cannan*:

> "So far as the DNA evidence was concerned it seems that the chances of anyone else having been responsible for this semen found on the knickers was something like 260 million to one against."[5]

Obviously, the witness who gave the evidence cannot have assessed the odds against anyone else being responsible for the mark and must have intended to testify that the characteristics found were shared by only one in 260 million people. If the suspect pool was the entire male population of the world then there would be roughly 10 men who would share these characteristics, so the posterior odds would actually be 9 to 1 against any particular one of them (until further evidence, such as the date and place of the offence, is considered).

When discussing *Pengelly* in chapter 2 we saw that the characteristics found were only shared by 1 in 12,450 of the population. Clearly, we cannot infer from this that the odds were 12,450 to 1 in favour of guilt. The role of this evidence is to tell us by how much to change our prior odds. These will have been determined by the number of possible suspects and other evidence. Only by combining the new evidence with the previous evidence (by multiplying the prior odds by the likelihood ratio) can we arrive at odds in favour of guilt.

The use of the paternity index is an example of transposition of the conditional becoming institutionalised. This process can lead to the bizarre result that each of two non-excluded candidates for paternity can be said to have a probability of paternity in excess of 99%. The correct structure of reasoning in paternity cases was explained in 3.3.

The defence attorney's fallacy

In the preliminary hearings in the OJ Simpson case in California the prosecution gave evidence that the blood at the scene of the crime had been analysed by conventional blood-grouping techniques and matched that of the accused. These characteristics were shared, it was said, by 1 in 400 people. The defence argued that an entire football stadium full of Los Angelenos would also match *and that this evidence was therefore useless.* This is a classic example of the defence attorney's

[4] This has also been called the "coincidence fallacy". Evett, I, "Interpretation: a Personal Odyssey" pp 9–22 in Aitken, CGG and Stoney, DA, (eds) *The Use of Statistics in Forensic Science* (Ellis Horwood, Chichester, 1991).
[5] (1991) 92 Cr App R 16, 18 (CA). The English Court of Appeal recognised the fallacy when it had been explained (*R* v *Deen*, unreported, 21 December 1993), but the Cook Islands Court of Appeal did not (*Police Department of Rarotonga* v *Amoa Amoa* SPLR (to be reported)). Other examples of instant transposition by people given correct information include Alldridge, P, "Recognising Novel Scientific Techniques: DNA as a test case" [1992] Crim LR 687, 690 and chapter 6 of Grubb, A and Pearl, DS, *Blood Testing, AIDS and DNA Profiling; Law and Policy* (Jordan Publishing, Bristol, 1990), *passim*.

fallacy. The fallacy lies in the last half-sentence. If the evidence had to stand alone, the calculated odds would be correct, but the value of the evidence lies in its effect on the remainder of the case and it should not be considered in isolation.

This can be seen by examining the HIV test considered in chapter 2. Although a positive test was far from conclusive it did shorten the odds against a particular person being infected from 10,000 to 1 down to 100 to 1. It is therefore very powerful evidence which should not be ignored. Whenever a test proved positive the person would be given a second, more expensive and more sensitive test. The combined result could lead to a correct diagnosis. Obviously, if the person was already displaying signs of the infection we might even regard the first test as sufficient indication to enable diagnosis.

The defence attorney's fallacy is frequently met; indeed, it was institutionalised in the common law rule in paternity cases that blood-grouping was only admissible to exclude a person and could not be used to support the hypothesis that a particular person was the father. This rule arose in the days when only the A, B, and O groups could be distinguished. One of these groups might be shared by up to 40% of the population. Nonetheless, if there was other evidence implicating the defendant and his blood was of the appropriate group, the blood group evidence should not have been rejected, it should have been seen as multiplying the odds in favour of paternity by $(1/0.4)$, *i.e.* 2.5.

The defence attorney's fallacy depends upon persuading the court to consider a single piece of evidence in isolation from the remainder of the case. Where "ordinary" evidence is concerned, the courts have always said that all the evidence on an issue must be considered together. As we argued in chapter 5, there is no reason why scientific evidence should be treated differently or separately just because it is capable of easy quantification.

This fallacy also springs from the idea that the quantified scientific evidence should be applied only to a quantified prior such as that derived from the size of the local population. However, probability is the tool for the efficient handling of information in individual cases. The likelihood ratio provided by the evidence can just as well be applied to prior odds which are the odds in favour of the accused's guilt after all the other evidence in the case is considered.

The defence attorney's fallacy is contrary to logic and established legal principle, and has frequently been exposed as such in the literature. Nonetheless, television viewers round the world were treated to an example of its use by a trained lawyer in the early stages of the OJ Simpson case.

The balanced approach

The prosecutor's fallacy is an argument that evidence should be given more weight than it deserves. The defence attorney's fallacy is an argument that evidence that is actually of value should be ignored. The balanced approach[6], as

[6] Evett, IW, "Interpretation: A Personal Odyssey" in Aitken, CGG and Stoney, DA *The Use of Statistics in Forensic Science* (Ellis Horwood, Chichester, 1991), p 13; Evett, IW, "Bayesian Inference and Forensic Science: Problems and Perspectives" (1987) 36 *The Statistician* 99–105.

shown in this book, is to compare the probabilities of the evidence given both the prosecution and defence stories. This gives a likelihood ratio which tells you the value of the evidence and the impact that it should have on the case as a whole.

6.2 Double-counting evidence?

Each piece of evidence must be considered only once in relation to each issue, otherwise its effect is unjustifiably doubled.[7] However, this does not mean that once an item of evidence has been used by one decision-maker for one purpose it cannot be used by another decision-maker for another purpose. Thus, the fact that the police have used an item of evidence to identify a suspect does not mean that the court cannot use it to determine guilt. Of course, the court must not use the fact that the accused is in the dock as evidence of guilt and then also consider the evidence produced, since to do so would be to double-count the evidence which led to the arrest and which is also used in court. Wigmore cautioned jurors "to put away from their minds all the suspicion that arises from the arrest, the indictment and the arraignment".[8]

Fear of double-counting evidence has misled some about the weight of the evidence which caused the suspect to come under suspicion. A man might be stopped in the street because he is wearing a bloodstained shirt and we are now considering the value of the evidence of the shirt. It has been suggested that because this was the reason for selecting this particular suspect we should change the way the evidence should be thought about, that it is less useful than if the suspect was arrested on the basis of other evidence.[9]

This is not correct. The power of the evidence is still determined by the ratio of the two probabilities of the accused having a bloodstained shirt if guilty and if not guilty. It is just that there happens to be less evidence in one case than the other. When the suspect is stopped because of a bloodstained shirt there may be no other evidence. When the suspect is arrested on the basis of other evidence and then found to have a bloodstained shirt, the likelihood ratio for the bloodstained shirt is to be combined with a prior which has already been raised by the other evidence. Once again the power of an item of evidence is being confused with the strength of the evidence as a whole.

6.3 The accuracy and reliability of scientific evidence

The lawyers' first instinct is to question the "accuracy" and "reliability" of scientific evidence, but it should be evident that the major problem raised by

---

[7] In fact, if double-counting was done properly it would not matter; the second likelihood ratio would be conditioned on the first and have no effect, since $P(A|A) = 1$.

[8] *IX Wigmore on Evidence*, para 2511 (Chadbourne Revision, Little, Brown and Co, 1981).

[9] Stoney, DA, "Transfer Evidence", pp 134–135 in Aitken, CGG and Stoney, DA, *The Use of Statistics in Forensic Science* (Ellis Horwood, Chichester, 1991).

scientific evidence is how it is to be interpreted. A concentration on technical problems is a consequence of the widely held view that the witness can make definitive assertions about the origin of a sample. The apparent belief is that if experiments and testing procedures were only done correctly, the scientist would produce the "right" answer. It follows that the only attack that can be made on such evidence is that an error in procedure has been made or information suppressed. Since such an attack impugns either the competence or the integrity of the witness it is guaranteed to generate confrontation.

The classical statistical analysis, discussed in chapter 7, leads one to ask whether a technique is sufficiently "reliable" for one to be able to draw inferences from it. The problem of knowing exactly what "reliable" means was raised at the beginning of the book (where we said that we would not use the word), but analysis suggests that this is in any case a wrong approach. If evidence is reported in likelihood ratio terms then all the possibilities for error should be incorporated into the likelihood ratio. The more carefully procedures are conducted the stronger the evidence should be one way or the other. If there are many possibilities for error the result may be likelihood ratios so low that the evidence may not be worth introducing.

In many cases this will not be so. Evett *et al* conducted empirical tests of the application of these inferential techniques to the Metropolitan Police database of DNA samples.[10] These tests involved taking repeat samples from prisoners which were compared with their original samples and also comparing all the samples in the database with each other. The results showed satisfactorily that when two samples from the same person are compared, high likelihood ratios in favour of identity are usually obtained and that when two samples from different people are compared likelihood ratios well below 1 are almost invariably obtained, reducing the probability of the hypothesis of common origin. These tests, since they were comparisons of actual samples, will automatically incorporate the effects that critics have identified as sources of possible error, such as variations in experimental conditions, or the fact that members of the database are related without knowing it. This obviates the need for laboratories to quote a likelihood ratio based on an error rate detected in blind testing.[11] The likelihood ratios produced take into account any factors which might affect the outcome, including ones we have not identified.

The emphasis throughout, therefore, should be on using all the available information to assess the likelihood ratio for the evidence in relation to the hypotheses. The attempt to create categories of "reliable and unreliable" evidence is a diversion.

The cases and the legal literature discussing expert evidence tend to concentrate overwhelmingly on measurement accuracy, quality control and on the

---

[10] Evett, IW, Scranage, J and Pinchin, R, "An Illustration of the advantages of efficient statistical methods for RFLP analysis in forensic science" (1993) 52 Am J Hum Gen 498.

[11] As argued in Lempert, R, "Some caveats concerning DNA as criminal identification evidence; with thanks to the Reverend Bayes" (1991) 132 Cardozo LR 303.

possibility that unfavourable results may have been withheld. We now consider these matters and the extent to which they are real problems.

Accuracy

Testing procedures vary in their ability to discriminate between individual sources. At one time, for example, it was only possible to distinguish the A, B, AB, O and Rhesus factors in blood. The legal system therefore would not then consider blood-grouping in support of paternity (we have made this point above when discussing the defence attorney's fallacy). However, it is a mistake to regard a test which cannot distinguish all individuals as being in some way "unreliable". The accuracy and sensitivity of the testing procedure will certainly affect the denominator of the likelihood ratio – that is to say, the cruder the test the higher the probability of obtaining the evidence although the suspect is not guilty and, hence, the lower the value of the evidence. This is a matter that affects the weight of the evidence, however, and should not determine its admissibility.

Any testing or measuring system may also suffer from bias. We have noticed that our bathroom scales appear consistently to add a few pounds to our "true" weight. Provided that they do this consistently, comparisons can be made over time or between people. Bias in forensic scientific testing can be avoided in the same way by ensuring that the same procedures and equipment are used to test both the control and the trace. This, of course, potentially conflicts with the requirement that the two samples should not be allowed to contaminate one another. The most obvious example is in DNA testing where the samples may even be tested simultaneously on the same gel. This ensures, as far as possible, that the two samples are tested under identical conditions, but means that great care must be taken to avoid cross-contamination. This is why there is some debate about whether the trace and suspect sample should be run in adjacent lanes or whether they should be separated by independent check samples of known profile.

Honest reporting

The conventional model of scientific testing leads to the idea that the test may produce results, some of which are favourable to the prosecution and some of which are favourable to the defence. There may then be a problem in ensuring that the results favourable to the defence are reported by a scientist who works for law enforcement agencies. This is frequently the reason why the defence will retain an independent expert.

Although this problem has arisen in a small number of headline-grabbing cases[12] it is much more likely that the difficulty in a particular case is how to interpret the results. A former Home Office forensic scientist, now working as a consultant for defence counsel, has written:

---

[12] *R v Ward* [1993] 1 WLR 619, [1993] 2 All ER 577 (CA).

"The questions defending counsel needs to have answered do not usually hinge on whether the results of my separate and independent analysis agree with those produced by the prosecution's scientist but often on the significance of his reported findings. To miss that point is to miss the greater part of why one was instructed in the first place."[13]

It is not only defence counsel who miss this point but also courts. In many cases where the problems relate to the interpretation of the evidence the courts in their comments revert to the idea of concealing results favourable to the other side.

For example, the New Zealand Court of Appeal in *R* v *Tihi* said that forensic scientific evidence:

"... must be carefully presented so that it is an accurate account of the result of any analysis of exhibits in the case and fairly presented. It must give a complete picture including results favourable to an accused as well as those favourable to the Crown."[14]

It can be seen from the examination of *Tihi* later in this chapter that the one thing that was not controversial was the test result. The witness reported having obtained a positive reaction and there is no suggestion that she had suppressed any contrary results. The question was how the result was to be interpreted. Nonetheless, the court, in its comments, reverts to the true/false model of scientific examination.

Often, two scientists draw different inferences from the same test result because their assessments of the prior probabilities are different. There are two ways of dealing with this. The hard way is to examine the two witnesses exhaustively to identify the factors that lead them to assess the prior differently. The easy way is to restrict the witnesses to giving the likelihood ratio yielded by the evidence. If there is still a difference between the witnesses this will often be because they are assuming different alternative hypotheses. Examination of the witnesses and careful consideration of the structure of the case will reveal which hypothesis is the more appropriate.

Preece v *HM Advocate*, discussed at the end of chapter 3, is sometimes quoted as a case in which evidence was suppressed. Even this did not involve the results of tests, some of which were revealed and some concealed. The result, said to be concealed, was actually in the expert's written report. It was that the test on a sample taken from the victim showed that she shared the characteristics found in the sample at the scene of the crime. This may have made the fact that the accused shared those characteristics irrelevant but it did so by altering the alternative hypothesis. The witness concentrated on the alternative hypothesis mandated by the classical statistical method, namely that the data occurred by chance. The most obvious alternative hypothesis in a case such as this should be that the blood was the victim's. In this situation the blood group evidence is equally likely

---

[13] Stockdale, R, "Running with the hounds" (1991) 141 NLJ 772.
[14] [1990] 1 NZLR 540, 548.

whether the perpetrator were the accused or anyone else. In other words, it does not help us to choose between these last two hypotheses.

There remains the possibility that a forensic scientist will deliberately record results other than those actually observed. Unfortunately, this is not unknown in the scientific world generally and there have been some notorious scandals.[15] It is very difficult, however, to find firm allegations of this sort in the law reports. In *Preece* v *HM Advocate*[16] it was alleged that the witness made unsupportable claims on behalf of the testing procedures, and this is just the sort of assertion which, once made, can be tested by normal scientific methods.

Apart from the Judith Ward case,[17] the closest to an allegation of misreporting in the United Kingdom would the Birmingham Six case[18] in which it appears that the forensic scientist may have recorded the strength of the testing solution incorrectly and was subsequently unwilling to admit that an error had been made. Even here it was not alleged that the scientist had falsified the result of the test. What the expert may have done was to increase the probability of obtaining a positive result from certain other chemicals by using a solution at such a strength that it would react with other substances. However, the scientist interpreted the results using a significance test, in other words his "alternative hypothesis" was that the data occurred "by chance" rather than the explanation put forward by the defence. Once again it was the interpretation that was in question, not the experimental result.

Quality control

The legal literature often expresses concern about the standards of care exercised in handling and analysing samples. A sample found at the crime scene may already be contaminated or degraded. It should be handled in such a way that no further contamination or degradation occurs and it is also vitally important to be able to prove that the sample analysed is indeed the sample taken from the crime scene. Continuity is assured by a variety of processes, including heat-sealed numbered sample bags and un-openable numbered seals.

It is common for the defence to devote considerable energy to a detailed examination of the testing process in the hope of uncovering some failure of procedure which might cast doubt on the accuracy of the evidence. In *Pengelly*[19], for example, the transcript of the evidence of the prosecution expert contains several pages of cross-examination on testing procedures. It was left to the judge to ask the really significant questions about interpretation. In the event the grounds of appeal rested on interpretation, not quality assurance, and this is much more likely to be where the real problems lie, for a number of reasons.

[15] Broad, W and Wade, N, *Betrayers of the Truth* (OUP, 1982).
[16] *Preece* v *HM Advocate* [1981] Crim LR 783.
[17] *R* v *Ward* [1993] 1 WLR 619, [1993] 2 All ER 577 (CA).
[18] See Heather Mills, "The Birmingham Six Judgement – Vital Scientific Evidence Kept From Defence", *The Independent*, London, 28 March 1991, p 47. We have also been told of alleged deliberate fraudulent reporting in other jurisdictions, but the point remains that such problems are rare compared to the interpretational problems which commonly arise.
[19] *R* v *Pengelly* [1992] 1 NZLR 545.

Of course, any profession should strive to maintain and develop its standards. In science the most important measure of quality assurance is the constant susceptibility to peer review. This demands the publication of results in refereed journals and the independent replication of experiments. In forensic science there may be some problems in following these procedures. Many forensic scientists are government employees and may be subject to some control over what they may publish. Furthermore, whereas it is normal in general scientific literature for controversial articles to be published and generate debate the publication of a controversial article on forensic science may have an immediate impact in the court room – hence the controversy over the articles in *Science*[20] at the end of 1991 and the allegation that pressure had been exerted on the editors not to publish the paper originally submitted until a rebuttal could be published alongside it.

However, it is not possible to subject test results in an individual case to this sort of multiple-peer review before trial. At best, the defence may retain an expert or two, within the limits of its budget, and the prosecution forensic science agency will have internal verification procedures, although, again, these have cost implications.

Furthermore, it may not be possible to re-test samples found at a crime scene owing to their small size or poor condition. Whenever possible, for example when blood samples are taken from a driver suspected of having had too much to drink, samples are divided so that independent analyses can be made. Usually one would be able to obtain a new sample from the source of the "control" and that may be important, as we shall see.

Nonetheless, reputable forensic science agencies strive constantly to improve their quality standards. Laboratories will routinely refuse to analyse samples which are not properly packaged. Internal procedures are scrutinised and papers are published which are devoted entirely to the question of quality control.[21] In practice, however, while it is obviously right that quality control should be closely scrutinised, it should create few problems in court. It seems to be over-emphasised in litigation as compared with problems of interpretation, perhaps partly because counsel find it easier to deal with and partly because of the idea discussed above that if the scientist carried out the right procedure they would produce the "right" answers.

One obvious reason why quality control should not be a problem in court is that the effect of any contamination or degradation of the sample will almost invariably be to make a trace sample look different from a control although in fact they had the same origin. This means that its effect will usually be that a person will be wrongly eliminated as a suspect and will never appear in court, rather than that someone will be wrongly charged and convicted. It is extremely unlikely that

[20] Lewontin, RC and Hartl, DL, "Population Genetics in Forensic DNA Typing" (1991) 254 *Science* 1745, and Chakraborty, R and Kidd, KK, "The Utility of DNA typing in Forensic work" (1991) 254 *Science* 1735.

[21] Kubic, TA and Buscaglia, J "Quality Assurance in the Forensic Laboratory", in *The Use of Statistics in Forensic Science* (Ellis Horwood, Chichester 1991).

contamination of a trace sample will, by coincidence, make it resemble a control. The two samples could only be made to resemble one another falsely if one contaminated the other or if they were both affected by a common source of contamination.

If it is suspected that the control has been contaminated by the scene sample or that both have been contaminated by an outside source this can be checked by obtaining an independent control sample. Legal powers may not be provided for the taking of repeat samples, which creates the possibility that the defence could allege that contamination has occurred while withholding the evidence that would enable this to be checked. The most difficult circumstance is the contamination of the trace sample by the control because the trace sample may be incapable of being re-tested, and procedures must be rigorously followed to try to avoid this.

Laboratory error rate

An alternative to thoroughly scrutinising the history of the relevant samples is to argue that the value of the evidence is limited by the possibility of error by the laboratory. The argument runs that if DNA frequencies in millions or even billions are being quoted, it is highly likely that the chance of an error by the laboratory is greater than the frequency of the characteristics. H_2 is composed of two parts:

H_{2a} = the suspect was not the perpetrator but happens to have the same profile as the perpetrator;

H_{2b} = the suspect was not the perpetrator and the control sample was double-loaded into the gel or the scene sample was contaminated by the control sample.

$$P(E|H_2) = P(E|H_{2a})P(H_{2a}|H_2) + P(E|H_{2b})P(H_{2b}|H_2).$$

Thus, the probability that the laboratory made an error is indeed a relevant consideration.

At this point the argument goes astray because it is then said that the probability that the laboratory made an error is measured by its "error rate" in past testing. Several blind and open tests have been conducted in the United States and stories have appeared in the media about the number of errors detected.[22]

The question that should be asked is "what is the probability that the laboratory obtained this evidence on this occasion because it made a mistake in handling the samples?". The error rate will not provide an appropriate answer to this question for several reasons:

- Frequency figures of this sort are only appropriate when we reach the limits of our knowledge. A laboratory is not a "black box". Any errors in

---

[22] For discussion of the tests and results, see Roeder, K, "DNA Fingerprinting: A Review of the Controversy" (1994) 9 *Statistical Science* 222. For examples of the argument that the error rate should be taken as the limit on a DNA likelihood ratio, see the defence submission re DNA evidence in the OJ Simpson case.

earlier tests should have been debriefed and improvements made. The details of the history of the particular sample will also be available.

- The conditions of the previous tests may not reflect conditions in forensic scientific case-work. Indeed, some of the US tests seem to have been designed to encourage error. In one such test, laboratories were required to load 50 samples onto one gel in 50 neighbouring tracks. This kind of procedure would not be followed in case-work.

- The circumstances of cases vary. In some cases a sample may be tested and the test result recorded at a time when there is no suspect. Some months later a sample from a suspect or a person arrested for another offence may be tested and the results found to correspond with the record of the scene sample test. In such circumstances it is difficult to see how a relevant error could possibly be made.[23]

It is correct, therefore, to say that the possibility of error by a laboratory is a relevant consideration. It is wrong, however, to argue that the possibility of error in a given case is measured by the past error rate. The question is what the chance of error was on this occasion, and when the circumstances are examined, the answer may well be virtually nil.

6.4 Case studies

We now look at a series of case studies that illustrate further features of the method. We look at the defence of the Earl of Ferrers in 1760, at a murder case where the existence of blood as evidence was under question, and at a case of broken glass.

The mad Earl of Ferrers

Lawrence, Earl of Ferrers was tried for murder in 1760.[24] The Earl, conducting his own defence before his peers, pleaded insanity. He called a doctor whom he asked, amongst other things, the following questions (at col 943):

> "Whether spitting in the looking-glass, clenching the fist, and making mouths is a symptom of lunacy? – I have frequently seen such in lunatic persons.
> Whether walking in the room, talking to himself, and making odd gestures, are symptoms of lunacy? – Very common ones.
> Whether drinking coffee hot out of the spout of the pot is a symptom of lunacy? – I should think it one in the present case; it is not a general one."

How is this evidence to be interpreted?

The issue was whether the noble Earl was insane. The evidence offered was his unusual behaviour. The House had to assess the probability of insanity given the

---

[23] *R v Hammond*, unreported, 7 December 1992, CCC920108 was an example of such a case.
[24] (1760) 19 State Trials 885.

behaviour. In the first two instances the doctor is clearly giving evidence of the probability of the behaviour given insanity. He says that such behaviour is frequently encountered in insane people. There may, of course, be other explanations for such behaviour, that is to say there will be some probability of obtaining the evidence if various alternative hypotheses, such as a violent temper, were true. Furthermore, not all lunatics will display such symptoms.

The value of the evidence will thus be the probability of finding the evidence if the accused was insane, divided by the probability of finding the evidence if the accused had some other condition such as a violent temper. The expert has not really been very helpful. He has not provided the information necessary to compare these probabilities; if we believe, as seems sensible, that the House could form their own judgments as to whether this behaviour is more commonly met in insane people than in sane people, then there was no need for an expert witness at all.

The third answer is problematic. The classical approach might be to establish how many lunatics drink coffee hot from the spout of a pot. If we find that very few do so then we would reject the hypothesis that a person doing so was a lunatic. We know, however, from experience that almost no normal person drinks coffee hot from the spout of a pot. The doctor doubtless meant that while the incidence of such behaviour amongst lunatics is low, amongst normal people it is minute. However rare this behaviour might be amongst lunatics it was even rarer amongst non-lunatics. The value of the evidence therefore depends upon its likelihood ratio, not upon its probability under the hypothesis we are trying to prove. It is the ratio rather than the absolute numbers which determines the likelihood ratio and, hence, the power of the evidence. Thus, if only one in a thousand insane people might do this act, but only one in a million normal people would do it, the behaviour is a strong indicator of insanity with a likelihood ratio of one thousand.

The blood on the belt

In this New Zealand case, Tihi and another were accused of murder.[25] There was good evidence that a belt had been used to beat the deceased and Tihi's accomplice was found carrying a belt a short distance away soon afterwards. The belt was not obviously bloodstained and was submitted for forensic examination. The scientist said that "positive results were obtained in a non-specific test for blood . . . insufficient material was present to confirm the presence of blood". She explained that a "non-specific test" was one where a positive result could also be obtained from some plant material and some oxidising agents present in paints, bleaches, etc.

The judge admitted the evidence but described it as "inconclusive or neutral and not prejudicial". On appeal, the Court of Appeal said that "To simply say . . . that the tests were inconclusive would leave the jury wondering what that meant. Juries are entitled to know the nature of the test and its result so that they

---

[25] *R v Tihi* [1990] 1 NZLR 540.

understand the evidence".[26] The court was satisfied, however, that, after the explanation of what "non-specific test" meant, the jury would have understood the true significance of the evidence.

The major question was to determine if the belt was used in the assault. To find this we will need the probability that there was blood on it.

Define the following prosecution and defence hypotheses:

H_1 = the belt was used in the assault;
H_2 = the belt was not used in the assault.

The evidence is that:

E = there was a positive reaction to the non-specific test.

To aid our discussion, define the subsidiary hypothesis:

B = there was blood on the belt;

for which we will also need its negation:

not-B = there was no blood on the belt.

(1) Was there blood on the belt?

The first question is, what is the probability that we will get a positive reaction if there is blood on the belt, $P(E|B)$? The witness should have been able to tell us this and should have been questioned about it. It appears to have been assumed to be 1.

The next question is, what is the probability of a positive result from the test if there was no blood on the belt, $P(E|\text{not-B})$? Neglecting any incorrect chemical reactions, this will be the probability that the belt carried other substances that yield a positive test result. If the only such substances were highly toxic, for example, we might assess that probability as very low since it is not likely that a person would be wandering around innocently with such substances on their belt. However, this test is sensitive to everyday items, such as paints, bleaches and, apparently, even some plant material. Assessment of $P(E|\text{not-B})$ requires a population profile and evidence about the accused's lifestyle. (Notice that this is an example of a mark on the accused.) If, for example, the accused was a painter then paint would very probably be on the belt and $P(E|\text{not-B})$ might be close to 1.

Since, on the information given, we have no reason to differentiate the value of $P(E|\text{not-B})$ from $P(E|B)$, we must assess the likelihood ratio as 1. In other words the evidence as it stood was useless. Contrary to the Court of Appeal's statement the jury was given absolutely no guidance about what the evidence meant.

The judge admitted the evidence as "inconclusive or neutral". "Inconclusive" cannot mean that it does not by itself prove the case, since conclusiveness is neither a requirement nor a disqualification for admission. "Neutral" appears to mean yielding a likelihood ratio of 1, and hence irrelevant.

[26] [1990] 1 NZLR 540, 548.

(2) Was the belt used in the assault?

The purpose of showing that there was blood on the belt (finding the probability of B given E) is to lead to the inference that it had been used in the assault (H$_1$) and, hence, that its holder was involved. One question that arises is whether a belt used in this particular assault would have such a small amount of blood on it that it would need sophisticated analysis to detect it. No evidence is reported about the amount of blood shed during this very serious assault. If there was a lot of blood P(B|H$_1$) would be large unless there had been the opportunity to clean it.

The expert witness should have considered the two hypotheses B and not-B. She would then have identified the true value of her test result. She might also have indicated what evidence the investigators also needed, such as Tihi's occupation and lifestyle. On the basis of the information contained in the Law Report we suspect that this would have identified the evidence as irrelevant.

The parties and the court in *Tihi* clearly regarded the scientific evidence as a puzzle. We can see that the problems were entirely a matter of how to interpret the evidence. Despite this, the court, in its frequently cited closing comments (quoted above), focussed entirely on the need for accurate reporting of test results. While this cannot be disputed this exhortation unfortunately perpetuates the idea that the most difficult aspect of scientific evidence is getting an accurate account of the analysis. It also assumes that certain results can, in themselves, "favour the accused" or "favour the Crown" when their value will depend upon the hypotheses being considered. These concluding comments were entirely irrelevant to this particular case.

Broken glass

In this English case, Abadom[27] was charged with robbery. The case rested on evidence that a window had been broken during the robbery and that fragments of glass found on Abadom's shoes had come from the window. An expert witness testified that the refractive indices of the window glass and the fragments were identical. The witness also testified that this refractive index occurred in only 4% of all glass samples in the Home Office collection. He then said (p 366) "considering that only 4% of controlled glass samples actually have this refractive index, I consider there is very strong evidence that the glass from the shoes ... originated from the window". On the other hand a defence expert said that 4% of the annual manufacture of glass in Britain was between 20,000 and 40,000 tons, and that window glass having this refractive index was therefore not uncommon.

In this last statement we have a classic example of the defence attorney's fallacy. The argument clearly is that there is so much of this sort of glass about that this evidence does not mean much.

The prosecution expert has not himself fallen into the prosecutor's fallacy but his reasoning is extremely compressed. The juxtaposition of the 4% figure and

---

[27] *R* v *Abadom* [1983] 1 WLR 126, [1983] 1 All ER 364.

the phrase "very strong evidence" invites the conclusion that there is a 96% chance that the glass on the shoes came from the window in question.

The only point on appeal was not relevant to our discussion here – it was whether the 4% figure was admissible given that the Home Office records were hearsay. The flaws in the expert evidence were not detected by the courts nor, apparently, by counsel.

A lot more information is required in order to assess this evidence. We need to know whether it is usual to have any glass on one's shoes. If it is unusual then this evidence is increased in value unless there is an alternative explanation for the glass.

Let us analyse the problem as much as we can with the information available to us.

Let H_1 = the accused broke the window;
H_2 = someone else broke the window;
E = the accused has a group of glass fragments, matching that from the window, on his shoes.

We will also need some other propositions:

C = the accused has a group of glass fragments on his shoes;
F = a piece of glass matches the window glass;
G = the accused has a group of matching glass fragments on his shoes acquired from another source;
T = the perpetrator will have a group of glass fragments transferred to and retained on his/her shoes.

If Abadom broke the window The probability that the accused would have matching glass on his shoes if he broke the window ($P(E|H_1)$ is the probability that glass from the window would be transferred to his shoes and stay there to be observed. This is called the transfer probability, for which we will use the symbol $P(T|H_1)$[28] where T is defined in the list above and the hypothesis H_1 also describes the way in which the window was broken. There is surprisingly little research on this probability. The implicit assumption appears to have been that it is 1.0, which is somewhat disadvantageous to the accused. The assessment of the probability will depend mainly upon the details of the incident. If there were eyewitnesses, as there were in *Abadom*, they need to be asked whether the perpetrator kicked the window in or broke it with a long pole, whether he walked over the shattered glass subsequently, and so forth. In this way the scientist can identify the relevant factors and make some assessment of $P(T|H_1)$. A computer program, CAGE, has been developed to guide the scientist in doing this. It is described briefly in chapter 8. In *Abadom* it appears to be assumed that $P(T|H_1)$ was 1. Suppose, for the sake of argument in this case, that it was highly probable that the accused would have acquired glass fragments from the window if he broke it, and assume

---

[28] For simplicity we are combining the transfer probability with the probability of persistence, that is the probability, given that glass is transferred to the clothing or shoes, that it would stay there.

that $P(T|H_1) = 0.95$. Of course, if the glass came from the window the sample and the window's characteristics would match.

If Abadom did not break the window Since this is a case where material alleged to have come from the scene is found on the accused, the question now is what is the probability that the accused would have this matching glass on his shoes notwithstanding that he was not the perpetrator, that is, $P(B|H_2)$? To calculate this we need to know the probability of having a group of glass on one's shoes and the probability that it matched this particular window, although one did not break it.[29] We can assume that these are independent, so we can multiply the probabilities directly.

The emphasis is now on the accused, not on a randomly selected member of the population. Perhaps there is no reason to regard the accused differently from a randomly selected member of the population, but this will depend upon information about the accused from the prosecution and from the accused himself. If he were a demolition worker his shoes might be filled with glass of all sorts. If there is no special reason why the accused might have such glass on his shoes then the best the jury can do is to regard him, at least so far as glass on his shoes is concerned, as a randomly selected member of the population.

In that case the probability that he would have matching glass on his shoes, although he was not the perpetrator, $P(B|H_2)$, is the probability that he would have any glass on his shoes at all, $P(C|H_2)$, multiplied by the frequency of occurrence of glass of that refractive index, typically found on shoes, $P(F|H_2)$.

The witness did not consider $P(C|H_2)$ at all. Survey evidence is needed to assess this. Surveys conducted both before and after *Abadom* are discussed in chapter 8. In short, they indicate that it is exceedingly unusual to have any large amount of window glass on your shoes. So $P(C|H_2)$ is very small; certainly very much less than 1. Let us conservatively assume that the probability of having a group of glass fragments on your shoes is, say, 0.5.

$P(F|H_2)$, the probability of glass picked up at random in the street, matching the window glass can be taken as 0.04.

The way the expert gave evidence embodied various assumptions, so that $P(E|H_2) = P(C|H_2) P(F|H_2) = (1) (0.04) = 0.04$ This should have resulted in a likelihood ratio:

$$\frac{P(E|H_1)}{P(E|H_2)} = \frac{P(C|H_1)P(F|H_1)}{P(C|H_2)P(F|H_2)} = \frac{(1)(0.95)}{(0.5)(0.04)} = 47.5$$

where we have substituted all the values. In other words, whatever the odds in favour of Abadom breaking the window based upon the other evidence the glass evidence makes them about 47 times higher.

If Abadom had an occupation that made it almost certain that he would have glass fragments on his shoes, $P(C|H_2)$ would be 1 and the likelihood ratio would

---

[29] This is P(matching glass on shoes|H_2) = P(glass on shoes|H_2)P(matching glass|glass on shoes,H_2).

fall to 23 or so. If the probability of a random person having glass fragments on his shoes is much less than 0.5, the evidence against Abadom would have been strengthened considerably. Taking the Belfast survey's data[30], which is for glass found on clothing, we might assume this probability to be around 0.03, since Abadom actually had several fragments of similar glass on his shoes (see **8.2** below). The likelihood ratio would then be about 792.

The questions the defence should have asked were:

- Did the accused's lifestyle make it more probable that he would have glass fragments on his shoes than a randomly selected person? (Whatever assessment resulted from information about the accused would be the appropriate figure to use rather than any survey data.)

- Was there more than one group of glass fragments found on Abadom's shoes? (This is extremely unusual, but if several different types of glass were found on the accused's shoes we have a version of the multiple bloodstain problem and the value of the evidence correspondingly decreases.)

The defence expert's evidence about how many tons of such glass is produced was quite irrelevant and was, as we said, a flagrant example of the defence attorney's fallacy. The likelihood ratio depends upon the proportion of that particular glass, $P(F)$, not upon the absolute quantities.

It is interesting to note that $P(C|H_2)$, the probability that an ordinary person would have glass on his shoes, is simply a population profile. Courts occasionally reject DNA evidence for lack of a such a profile[31], although they have for years readily admitted evidence of glass fragments without such information. The difference, of course, is that in the case of glass it is advantageous to the accused to pretend that everyone has glass on their shoes or in their clothing. Increasing understanding of the relevant factors in such a case makes us realise that the evidence is much more convincing than originally thought.

Had the prosecution expert considered the probability that the glass would have been found had the accused committed the offence and contrasted that with the probability that the glass would have been found had the accused not committed the offence he would have directed his own mind and the minds of the investigators to the relevant issues. He would also have given clear guidance to the court as to how to combine the evidence with the other evidence in the case and directed attention within his department to the need to collect further information.

[30] McQuillan, J and Edgar, K, "A survey of the distribution of glass on clothing" (1992) 32 JFSS 333.
[31] See the discussion of DNA in chapter 9.

6.5 Summary

- Evidence must be considered in the light of the prior odds and the other evidence and not in isolation. Failure to do this leads one to either the prosecutor's or defence attorney's fallacy.

- Evidence must not be double-counted, that is it should not be used more than once in relation to any one issue but it can be used for more than one purpose. In any case, its weight is given by its likelihood ratio.

- While quality control and accuracy in reporting results are essential if evidence is to be useful, problems in any particular case are much more likely to be raised by problems of the interpretation of the evidence.

Chapter 7

CLASSICAL STATISTICS AND DATABASE MATCHING

Chapter 7

CLASSICAL STATISTICS AND DATABASE MATCHING

This chapter is more technical than most and can be by-passed, at least on first reading, without disturbing the flow of our argument. It steps aside to look at the difficulties relating to the orthodox statistical approach when dealing with forensic evidence, and tries to show why these problems occur. It also examines problems with searching for a match in databases of forensic information, such as those containing DNA profiles.

The method of analysing evidence outlined in this book has only recently returned to favour. Previously, the method known as the frequentist or classical method was used. This was based upon the methods recommended by statisticians for use in analysing the results of agricultural and scientific experiments. It stems from statistical models developed since the mid-nineteenth century, but it is coming under increasing attack even within the physical sciences[1] and is certainly inappropriate in an investigation of a single situation where diverse kinds of evidence must be combined. It has also built up unrealistic expectations of forensic science because lawyers have become used to being told that something is either so or not so (as with fingerprints) and have not realised that some evidence is being ignored for reasons of policy rather than science.

These orthodox methods are still met in some forensic scientific writing and many lawyers, if they have been exposed to the subject at all, will have been taught frequentist approaches at school. We therefore consider it worthwhile to set out an explanation of the problems which such methods may have caused in forensic science and our response to the orthodox frequentist arguments.

---

[1] As discussed by Loredo, TJ, "From Laplace to Supernova SN 1987 A: Bayesian Inference in Astrophysics", in Fougère, PF (ed) *Maximum Entropy and Bayesian Methods* (Kluwer Academic Publishers, Dordecht, 1990); Jaynes, ET, "Probability Theory as Logic", in Fougère, PF (ed) *Maximum Entropy and Bayesian Methods* (1989); in scientific methods generally, Colin Howson and Peter Urbach, *Scientific reasoning: the Bayesian approach* (Open Court, La Salle, Ill, 1989).

7.1 The classical statistical approach

Throughout this book we treat probability as a measure of strength of belief and the rules of probability as rules for rationally and efficiently handling information. This is sometimes called the "Bayesian" approach, although we prefer the term "logical" since the method is essentially a generalisation of ordinary logic.[2] The classical statistical definition of probability is quite different; it is that probability refers only to the frequency of an event in a long-run series of trials. This is usually known (by Bayesians) as the "frequentist" definition of probability.

One important difference is that a Bayesian is willing to discuss the probability of a hypothesis, while frequentists will only discuss the probability of data. For example, a Bayesian would be prepared to discuss the probability that it will rain tomorrow and in doing so will take into account not only meteorological data and whether the sky at sunset was red, but also other sources of information. A frequentist statistician, seeking to retain objectivity, might only consider the proportion of days that it rained at this time of year in the historical records. If the data were available he could tell you how frequently it had rained on days following red skies at sunset. In an instance such as this, where our judgment is heavily dependent on recorded data, the difference between the two schools of thought may be small but where, as in a court case, one is trying to combine different sorts of evidence to make a judgment about an individual incident, the difference between the two approaches becomes vital.

The orthodox methods, which together make up "statistical inference", set out to test a single hypothesis. In effect, they compare that hypothesis with the so-called null-hypothesis that "the data occurred by chance". They find the probability that such extreme data which were observed would have occurred under the statistical model representing pure chance. If that probability is very small then the null-hypothesis can be rejected and the result is regarded as supporting the hypothesis being tested. In contrast, we have argued throughout this book that hypotheses can only usefully be compared when they are both specifically and positively expressed and that evidence is useful whenever it is more probable under one hypothesis than under the other.

Application of orthodox methods to forensic science

Consider a forensic scientist comparing an evidence sample with a control sample. For example, he may have been given some glass fragments found on a suspect accused of breaking a window (the *evidence* sample) and will be given or extract samples of glass from the window for comparison (the *control* sample). In the classical approach the scientist will take three steps.

(i)   Consider if the two samples "match".

---

[2] We introduce this point and indicate references to its development in the Appendix.

(ii)   If there is a match, consider the probability of such a match occurring by chance (the null-hypothesis).

(iii)   Form and express a conclusion as to whether the two samples have the same origin.

Each of these steps raises problems and we shall examine them in turn, in the context of the glass example just introduced.

(i) *Matching*   At this stage of the process the scientist carries out tests, such as microscopic examination and chemical reactions, on the two samples. The result will always be some difference between the two samples, even where the samples come from the same source, because the material varies in characteristics with position in the window and because the measurement techniques ultimately have some element of uncertainty in the limit. The scientist will then consider the statistical significance of the difference; that is to say, he will estimate how probable it is that this difference would be obtained if the two samples had the same origin. This latter condition is known as the null hypothesis.

This probability is calculated using a mathematical probability model which uses the measured or assumed variation in the physical characteristics of the origin material and in the measurement process. The variations are described by a "probability distribution" which displays the probability of observing different values of the measurements. When we reach the limits of our knowledge of the factors which can affect an outcome, we often use a "normal" or "Gaussian" distribution. This bell-shaped distribution assumes that the unknown factors may affect the outcome in either direction and are therefore likely to cancel each other out to some extent. The most likely value should therefore be nearer our estimate rather than further from it. This distribution is also mathematically easy to work with. Its peak (which is also its mean or average) is at the average value of the control sample with smaller and smaller probabilities of getting values further and further away from the centre. Thus, in *Figure 7.1*, which shows the probability of getting a fragment of glass of different refractive indices from a window, the average refractive index is at the centre point, but it is still possible to get samples from the window which differ in value from the average. One would be very unlikely to get samples with values very far from the centre.

The *standard deviation* of the control distribution is a way of measuring its range of variability. For data that fits a Gaussian (or normal) distribution, the total range is about three standard deviations as shown in *Figure 7.1*. In fact, 99.9% of measured values should be within about three standard deviations (actually 3.05) of the mean; 99% within about 2.6; and 95% within about two standard deviations (actually 1.96).[3]

The scientist measures the evidence sample of glass and marks its average at the appropriate point on the horizontal axis of the graph. If the trace sample came from the same window as the control we would expect this to be near the centre.

---

[3] We are using the large sample approximations here. When we have small samples, as is typical in forensic work, a different, but similarly shaped distribution is used.

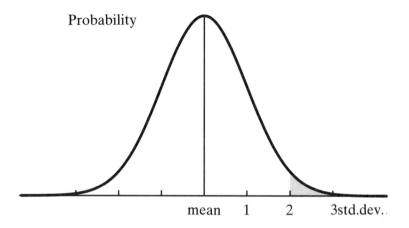

Figure 7.1 *The Normal or Gaussian Distribution for a refractive index measurement of glass from a window. The height of the curve is proportional to the probability of getting that particular value of index, but the probability of obtaining a particular value or more (or less) is represented by the area under that segment of the curve, not the height. The highest probability is associated with the average index at the centre of the curve. Variation from the average becomes less and less probable as the difference from the centre increases. The marks along the bottom axis show steps of 1, 2 and 3 standard deviations from the mean. The shaded area is the probability of getting a value of 2 or more standard deviations larger than the mean value. That probability is about 0.025. (The total area under the graph, being the probability of getting some value of index, is 1.0.)*

Locations far away from the centre are much less probable. As we saw above, values of 2.6 standard deviations or more away from the centre have a probability of less than 1%.

Suppose we have a policy that we declare that all trace samples within 2.6 standard deviations of the centre "match". Then we will state a match on 99% of the occasions when the samples actually come from the same source. We would be wrong on 1% of those occasions. If the difference between the samples is less than 2.6 standard deviations there is said to be a "match" – otherwise not. If the trace is considered not to be a match that is the end of the test. Any such limits are quite arbitrary but are usually 95% or a 5% "level of significance"[4] (given by limits of 1.96 standard deviations), 99% (2.6 standard deviations), or 99.9% (3.05 standard deviations).

If the scientist has to decide whether two samples are different, rather than the same, the question is "is this result statistically significant?". This means, are the differences so great that we are unlikely to have found them by chance in two samples which are really the same? If the difference falls outside the range of 2.6

_____
[4] Statistical significance is discussed below.

standard deviations then it would occur in fewer than 1% of pairs of the samples from the same source and is said to be "significant at the 1% level", in other words there was a probability of 99% of obtaining a smaller difference if the two samples were really the same.

(ii) *"Odds against a match by chance"*   Once it has been decided that the two samples "match", the evidence is regarded as "associative". That is, it associates the suspect with the crime. The question now becomes, how strongly associative is it? In this stage of the classical procedure the scientist will consider the odds against obtaining the result by chance if it did not come from the control. This means considering how likely it is that we would find the result if we chose a piece of the appropriate material (glass, DNA or whatever) at random from anywhere *other* than the source of the control. This requires collection of data to enable an assessment of the frequencies of, for example, different types of glass.

(iii) *Formation and expression of a conclusion*   At this stage the scientist assesses a probability that the two samples have common origin. This will depend only on the odds against a match by chance, since if a match has been declared at stage (i) the probability of obtaining the evidence is assumed to be 1. In some cases, such as with fingerprints, an arbitrary threshold is adopted, above which the witness will assert that the samples have a common origin, and below which will refuse to give evidence. In other cases (*e.g. Abadom*[5]) the witness will say "it is probable", "highly probable", or even (in paternity cases) give a quantified probability for the hypothesis.

As we have said in earlier chapters, we and others object to this procedure because it involves the scientist assuming both a prior and an alternative hypothesis. The choice of this prior will not be determined by the facts of the particular case, but will be based on some convention. This problem has already been discussed in a variety of contexts.[6] Its origin is in the tenet that the data must be allowed to "speak for itself" and that other information should not intrude into the problem. In particular, orthodox statisticians are unwilling to admit that quantifiable probability assessments can be made on the basis of the type of information that courts are commonly offered.[7] As a result the orthodox approach to any particular piece of quantifiable evidence implicitly assumes a so-called "uninformative prior", *i.e.* that each of the possible explanations is equally probable.[8] This is the root of the distinction from the approach in this book. The logical (or Bayesian) approach recognises that all information or evidence can only be interpreted against a background of knowledge derived from other sources, and this is described by the prior.

Moreover, the consideration of odds against a match by chance amounts to a tacit assumption of a standardised alternative hypothesis, which may not be

[5] *R* v *Abadom* [1983] 1 WLR 126, [1983] 1 All ER 364.
[6] In chapters 2 and 3.
[7] A clear example of this argument is to be found in Harmon, RP, "DNA Evidence" (1993) 253 *Science* 261.
[8] Describing the orthodox procedure in Bayesian terms. In fact, orthodox statisticians would not accept the need for a prior at all, relying only on the data itself.

appropriate to a particular case. This standard assumption has led to the belief amongst lawyers that an item of evidence has some intrinsic value as support for a party's case. As we have seen, however, the value of an item of evidence depends strongly upon the alternative hypotheses being considered. The same piece of evidence can yield likelihood ratios of one million (very valuable evidence) or 1 (valueless evidence) if we choose different alternative hypotheses.

Problems of significance testing

There are a number of problems with significance testing. The major objection to significance testing is that it is not based on any logical principles following from the axioms of probability. A fatal objection to the technique's use in forensic science is that the result of a significance test cannot be combined in any rational way either with the results of other significance tests or with evidence expressed in other ways.

There are also a number of detailed flaws in this procedure.

- *The "fall off the cliff" effect*   It is clearly illogical to say that a difference of 2.5 standard deviations is evidence of common origin, and a difference of 2.7 standard deviations is inconclusive or should lead to rejection of the hypothesis of common origin. This sudden change in decision due to crossing a particular line is likened to falling off a cliff, one moment you are safe, the next dead. In fact, rather than a cliff we have merely a steep slope. Other things being equal, the more similar the samples the stronger the evidence that they had a common origin, and the less similar the samples the stronger the evidence that they came from different sources.[9]

- *The proper match criteria*   The operation of "matching" has diverted attention from the crucial question of interpretation. Great energy is wasted on the question of what the criterion for a match ought to be in a given case. This question has vigorously exercised courts[10], commentators and even legislators in the United States. In comment on *Castro*, Lander criticised Lifecodes Corporation because although their criterion for a match was three standard deviations they declared as matching samples those that differed by 3.06 and 3.66 standard deviations respectively.[11]

  Concern has also been expressed that different laboratories may have different criteria for a match.[12] There is no answer to the question "what is an appropriate significance level?". The 99% and 95% thresholds are commonly used in scientific work but are entirely arbitrary. There is no rational basis for choosing precisely these levels; they are merely conventional common sense values used in ordinary scientific work.

[9] Evett, I, "Interpretation: a Personal Odyssey", pp 9–22, in Aitken, CGG and Stoney, DA, (eds) *The Use of Statistics in Forensic Science* (Ellis Horwood, Chichester, 1991).
[10] *E.g., People* v *Castro* (1989) 545 NY Supp 985 (SC,NY).
[11] Lander, E, "DNA fingerprinting on trial" (1989) 339 *Nature* 501.
[12] "Letting the 'Cops' make the Rules for DNA Fingerprints" (1991) 254 *Science* 1603. *R* v *Lucas* [1992] 2 VR 109.

Results may be obtained outside these levels even though the samples have common origins.

- *Evidence may be rejected even though it favours the hypothesis*   Take an extreme example and imagine that someone had broken the only window in the world made from some particular glass with a refractive index very different from any other glass and with only small variations. If we found a fragment of glass with a refractive index in the same general range but different by more than three standard deviations from its mean a sensible observer would still assess a high probability that the fragment came from the window. The significance test could take no account of this situation and would reject that hypothesis out of hand.

  A less contrived example may be where band positions in a DNA analysis differ by more than three standard deviations but bands in that general range are extremely unusual. Suppose that the probability of obtaining the difference observed if both samples came from the same source was 0.5%. Thus, $P(E|H_1)$ = 0.005. Suppose, also, that DNA bandweights observed in the scene sample were exhibited by only 1 in 10,000 of the population. Thus, the probability of getting the evidence if it came from some unknown person is $P(E|H_2)$ = 0.0001. The evidence would be 50 times more probable if both samples came from the accused than if the scene sample came from someone else. This is clearly useful evidence, but the classical approach ignores the question of how rare these characteristics are in the general population, concentrating only on the difference between the two samples. The orthodox approach would simply reject the hypothesis that they came from the same source.

  Another example is provided by the *Ferrers* case introduced earlier. Here an expert was asked whether "drinking coffee hot from the spout of the pot was a sign of insanity?". Such behaviour may be quite unusual even amongst the insane, but because it is even more unusual for a sane person it tends to support the hypothesis that the person is insane.

  The correct purpose of the probability model should be to calculate the probability that one would obtain the result given a common origin.[13] This probability should simply be recorded and compared with the probability of the evidence under the alternative hypothesis.

- *Evidence is overvalued*   Conversely, this approach leads to an overestimation of the strength of the evidence because once a sample has survived a significance test the probability of obtaining the evidence given the hypothesis is then treated as 1. However, as we have argued above, regard should be had to the probability of obtaining the evidence. This will almost always be less than 1 and even on the classical approach may be quite low. Since we are going to divide this number by the denominator to

---

[13] The significance test does not tell us this; it tells us the probability that the variation would be the variation observed *or greater* in the long run.

produce the likelihood ratio, the effect is arbitrarily to inflate the power of the evidence.[14]

- *Conceptual confusion* In fact we do not need the concept of a match at all. Confusion is caused by considering the fact of a match as the evidence, whereas the evidence is equivalently and correctly stated as the combination of two propositions:

E_1 = the sample from the scene has profile A;
E_2 = the sample from the accused has profile B.

These can be used to analyse the evidence in any situation, whereas the concept of a match is designed for those cases in which a characteristic is either present or absent and can only be stretched with difficulty to characteristics which are continuously variable or which involve measurement problems. Where we are dealing with a characteristic which can be changed by time or deliberately, like hair length or colour, these two propositions will emphasise the relevant considerations when the match/no-match approach cannot cope at all.

- *Transposition of the conditional* The match/no-match approach invites the listener to transpose the conditional. In particular, the significance test may easily trap one into thinking that if the evidence is highly probable given the hypothesis, the hypothesis must be highly probable. We looked at this problem in chapter 6.

- *Odds against a match by chance* The use of the alternative hypothesis that the data "occurred by chance" has two unfortunate consequences. The first is that it diverts attention from the relevant issues in the case. It may well be that occurrence by chance is not at all the appropriate alternative hypothesis in a particular case. This will be true whenever there is other evidence tending to identify the perpetrator (or father, in a paternity case). The second is in its effects on the non-scientific mind. Two opposing attitudes are visible. One is the belief that a piece of forensic scientific evidence has some intrinsic value determined this way, whereas, as we have seen, its value is determined by the context. The second, countervailing effect, is the belief that scientific and statistical evidence cannot cope with the realities of legal cases since it ignores much of relevance to the particular case. As a criticism of the orthodox approach, this is correct.

What is a confidence interval?

It is common for scientific witnesses to qualify frequencies used in determining the odds against a match by chance by giving a range about the estimated

---

[14] Evett, IW, Scranage, J and Pinchin, R, "An Illustration of the advantages of efficient statistical methods for RFLP analysis in forensic science" (1993) 52 Am J Hum Gen 498 showing that this approach actually increased the number of false inculpations.

frequency based on a "level of confidence".[15] These are based on the classical statistical concept of the confidence interval.

Suppose we have surveyed a sample of 1,000 people from the population and discovered that 23 of them have blood type V. Sensibly, we would infer from this that our best estimate is that 2.3% of the population were blood type V. Based on this information we would say that there is a probability of 0.023 that any person "randomly selected" from this population would have that blood type.

However, if we were to take many more similar samples of 1,000, in some there would be more than 23 people with type V, suggesting a larger proportion in the population, and in other samples there would be fewer, suggesting a smaller proportion. Most samples would contain around 23 type Vs.

To determine a confidence interval we first decide on a *confidence level.* Conventional confidence levels are 95% or 99%. Suppose we decide to use a 99% confidence level. We then calculate a range within which we would expect that 99% of such estimates of proportion (from many samples of 1,000) would fall. This is called a *99% confidence interval.* If we are then asked to make an estimate of the proportion in the population we could quote the 2.3% and give a 99% confidence interval about that value as a measure of our uncertainty in the estimate. This confidence interval can be calculated from a probability model of the sampling process and the characteristic itself.

For example, assume that there are truly 2.3% of Vs in the population and we take many samples of 1,000. A probability model would predict that 99% *of these samples* would have proportions of Vs falling between 1.07 and 3.53%.[16] This is the 99% confidence interval.

Orthodox statisticians are very careful to emphasise that this is very different from saying that there is a probability of 99% that the true proportion lies between 1.07 and 3.53% (this is akin to inverting the conditional). The correct interpretation is that, in the long run, if in each case one said that the proportion is within those boundaries, one would be correct 99% of times.

However, we do not have a collection of samples like this. We have a single sample with 23 type Vs out of 1,000. Somehow we must use this information to determine the likelihood ratio. We want to calculate the denominator, that is, the probability that some person, picked "at random" from the population of possible perpetrators, would have blood type V. When we do this we are not interested in how many samples of 1,000 might contain 5 or 50 or 23 blood type V people. We are not interested in which group of 1,000 our random person might have been in if we had surveyed the population in this way. We are only interested in what we know about the frequency of type V in the whole population given the single sample we have. If someone asked us what the proportion is we

---

[15] *R* v *Elliott* 70154/89, unreported, 1 SC NSW 1990. *R* v *Tran* (1990) 50 A Crim R 233.
[16] [Technical note] We assume a normal approximation to binomial sampling. This gives an estimated variance of the number of Vs as Npq where p is the "true" proportion, q = 1–p, and N is the size of the sample. In this example the variance is 22.47 and the standard deviation is the square root of this, 4.74. Thus, by dividing by 1,000 we would quote the estimated proportion as 2.3 ± 1.23% (that is 1.07 to 3.53%) where the range is ± 2.6 standard deviations.

would, of course, be uncertain about the true value; we would have to quote a range of uncertainty, and there is also a Bayesian way of doing this (although the logical interpretation is different from the orthodox one).

If we have 23 Vs in our sample it could be that the true frequency is 0.0005 or 0.05, but getting 23 in each of those cases is very improbable (the probability of getting the evidence E = 23 given a real frequency of f = 0.0005 is very small. A Bayesian would state a range within which there is a certain probability of the true frequency lying. We could choose this probability to be 99%, just as in the orthodox method, and get a Bayesian interval corresponding to it.

However, these calculations are only important if, for some reason, we are trying to estimate the frequency of a characteristic in the population. We are not usually interested in this in a case. What we want to do is to estimate the probability that a particular person would have this characteristic. The evidence on which we should condition our probability assessment should be the data we actually have, namely the sample survey, and not an "estimate" of the frequency in the population.

Thus, suppose H_2 is the alternative hypothesis that the stain of type V was left by some unknown person from the population and S is the result of the sample survey (the observation of 23 out of 1,000 sampled). Then $P(E|H_2S)$, which is the denominator of the likelihood ratio, can only be the proportion found in the survey unless we have some other additional and relevant information. There is no uncertainty in the assessment of $P(E|H_2S)$, provided we are clear that the condition is the sample survey and not an "estimator". There is, therefore, no uncertainty in the likelihood ratio which uses this probability.

This still leaves the question of how confident we can be that our sample, which gave 23 type Vs, is representative of the population as a whole. The larger the sample we have taken the happier we will be that it is giving us an answer close to what we would find if we surveyed the entire population. If we have reason to suspect that the survey is biased one way or the other then we should use all the information we have to come to a better assessment. If we have no such reason, there is no reason to use any figure other than that given by the survey itself.

7.2 Databases

Suppose that we screen a large number of potential suspects or consult a database to find a suspect by matching the perpetrator's fingerprint, blood type or DNA profile.

It is commonly claimed that the evidential value of such a "match" is affected by the number of comparisons one has made. In other words if one has found a "match" by searching a large database, or by conducting a large-scale survey, the match is less valuable as evidence. This argument is applied to fingerprints, DNA profiles, glass-refractive indices or any other scientific evidence based upon a series of comparisons, one of which is called a "match". Stoney and Thornton, for example, state, "The value of any fingerprint for identification is inversely proportional to the chance of false association. This chance depends on the number of comparisons which are attempted".[17] They come to this conclusion because (citing Amy) "each person in the suspect population represents a set of trials and each trial carries with it a chance of false association".[18] They go on to define the chance of false association as the frequency of incidence of the fingerprint multiplied by the number of comparisons made.[19]

This latter figure is actually the expected number of associations, that is to say the expected number of matches found in the course of an investigation. Such a "match" may be true or false. What Stoney and Thornton are concerned with is the probability of obtaining a match from a database. They then conclude that if there is a high probability of obtaining a match from a database, any match so obtained is less valuable as evidence.

Certainly, the larger the database the more likely we are to find a match. If the proportion of characteristic V is 1 in 1,000 and we consult a database of size 10,000, then we would expect about 10 matches in the database. It is almost certain that we would get at least one match in this case. The probability of one or more matches is $1-(1-f)^N$, where f is the frequency of the characteristic in the population and N is the size of the database. If the characteristic is rare and the database small (so that Nf is very much smaller than 1) the probability of a match is about the same as the expected number of matches, the size of the database multiplied by the proportion of the characteristic, Nf.

The fact that the probability of a match increases as the database gets larger leads to the erroneous conclusion that the larger the database the weaker the evidence. This, in turn, leads to recommendations about dealing with evidence from database searches, usually aimed at arbitrarily reducing the strength of the evidence. The NRC Report, for example, recommends that the DNA factors in the database should be ignored for the purpose of assessing the value of a "match" and only those DNA tests using other probes should be taken into account in assessing the value of the evidence.[20]

What matters is not how probable finding a match is, but the evidential value of a match once one has been found. What will usually be in question will be the probability of finding the evidence if the suspect was not the perpetrator. Does the size of the database affect this assessment? There are two cases: when we already know the frequency of the characteristic in the population and when we do not.

When we know the frequency

The probability of obtaining the evidence if someone else left the mark is just given by the frequency of the characteristic in the population. For example,

[17] Stoney, DA and Thornton, JI, "A Critical Analysis Of Quantitative Fingerprint Individuality Models" [1986] 31 JFS 1187, 1214.
[18] *Ibid* at 1202. This view also appears to be held by the National Research Council Committee on DNA, see *DNA Technology in Forensic Science* (National Academy Press, 1992).
[19] Stoney, DA and Thornton, JI, "A Critical Analysis Of Quantitative Fingerprint Individuality Models" [1986] 31 JFS 1187, 1209.
[20] National Research Council, *DNA Technology in Forensic Science* (National Academy Press, 1992).

suppose the pool of possible suspects was all adult males in the United Kingdom (approximately 20 million) and the characteristic observed was eyes of two different colours. The medical literature might tell us that 1 in 10,000 people have eyes of two different colours.[21] We therefore estimate that about 2,000 adult males in the United Kingdom have eyes of two different colours and the odds that any particular one was the perpetrator are 1,999 to 1 against.

If we now searched a database of one million adult males (from the same total pool of 20 million) we would expect to find 100 "matches" and we would expect (since we know the frequency) around another 1,900 matching individuals from the remaining 19 million outside the database. If we searched a database of five million we would expect to find 500 "matches" in the database and expect another 1,500 from the remaining 15 million outside. In each case the posterior odds are always the same, 1,999 to 1 against the hypothesis that the suspect is the perpetrator. Where we know the frequencies, the size of the database makes no difference.

When we do not know the frequency

Of course, there are cases where we do not know the frequency in the population. For example, suppose we have an unidentified body with eyes of two colours and there is no information in the medical literature about the frequency of this characteristic. We search through all available databases, one of which will be the criminal records, in order to find "matches" and we find one. If we have no probability model derived from other studies then the best estimate we can make is that this characteristic is shared by a proportion of 1 over the database size. Thus, if the database has 10,000 entries and we have exactly one match then we estimate that 1 in 10,000 people share this characteristic. If we found only one match after 100,000 comparisons we would believe that the characteristic was much rarer, only occurring in about 1 in 100,000 people. In other words, if we have found one "match" (in fact for any given number of matches found) the larger the number of comparisons we have carried out, the stronger the "match" is as evidence.

To see that this is correct, consider a database which contains the entire population, such as a car-registration system in Hawaii. This contains descriptions of all cars in circulation in Hawaii (including visitors' vehicles). A car involved in a crime is photographed and is identifiable as a black Rolls Royce. The database is searched and only one black Rolls Royce is found. We believe that there are no others unregistered. This "match" is extremely powerful evidence, whereas, without the database, if we had simply found a black Rolls Royce in an avenue with 100 parked cars, we would have to consider that there may be other such cars in the state.

Searching a database, therefore, can serve two purposes: first, it actually identifies possible suspects; secondly, we may use it to estimate the proportion of the population who have this characteristic. Where more than one "match" is

---

[21] This information would have been gathered from surveys.

found we simply divide the number of "matches" by the number of comparisons to estimate the frequency.

Randomisation of samples

It is sometimes argued that it is important that the samples we use to calculate our frequencies are "random samples". A random sample of people is one in which each person has an equal chance of being selected. Many DNA databases are made up of samples from criminals and it may be argued that this is not a properly "randomised" sample.[22]

What we are really concerned about is that the database should be "representative" of the relevant population. What should concern us is not so much that each person has an equal chance of being selected but that each factor has a chance of being selected, determined by its frequency in the relevant population.

In fact, such a database from samples from criminals can be used safely for our purpose. There either is a genetic disposition to crime or there is not.

- If there is no genetic disposition to crime then there is no reason to suppose that the distribution of factors will be different in a population of criminals than from the general population. A database of criminals is therefore as likely to be representative as any professionally "randomised" sample.

- If, on the other hand, there is a genetic disposition to crime, then the alternative hypothesis in a case must be that the perpetrator was another violent criminal. A database composed of samples from violent criminals is then the correct database to use.

Where there is some obvious reason why the sample may not be representative then the results may be biased in one direction and allowance should be made for this. If there is no obvious reason why the sample is not representative then, certainly, any sample may not precisely reflect the make up of the population as a whole, but it is the best information we have and there is no reason to use any other figure.

What happens if no one in our database matches the trace from the scene? We know that there is at least one such person, the perpetrator. Perhaps we have a suspect who matches. What can we infer from the fact that no other matches were found in the database? The larger the database the less probable it is that there is another such person. Even in this case, techniques are available to calculate the probability that there are people outside the database who might "match".

Using this evidence

The frequency calculated in one of these ways provides the denominator for the likelihood ratio given by the evidence. As we have seen, for any given number of

---

[22] *E.g. R* v *Lucas* [1992] 2 VR 109, 115.

"matches", far from devaluing the evidence, a larger database increases the probability that one of the "matches" is the perpetrator. If there is only one "match", the larger the database, the more probable it is that the suspect is the perpetrator.

However, the nature of the database will affect the prior odds to which the likelihood ratio is applied. Whenever a database is searched the alternative hypothesis being investigated is that the perpetrator could have been any member of the population from which the database is chosen. If the database is drawn from the whole of New Zealand (population 3.5 million) (for example, DNA samples taken from convicted criminals throughout the country) then the prior odds (prior even to eliminating the very elderly, young and infirm) are 3.5 million to 1 against the suspect's guilt. A DNA analysis giving a likelihood ratio of one million reduces those odds to 3.5 to 1 against. In other words, we expect there to be three or four people in New Zealand who would "match" those characteristics and more evidence is required to determine which of them is the guilty party. As long as we have strong information about the frequency it does not matter how many "matches" we find in the database itself. If there were two "matches" in this case we would still expect there to be one or two more possible "matches" in the population not included in the database. Each of the three or four people who "match" are equally likely to be guilty (based, of course, on this evidence alone) regardless of whether they are in the database.

Traps with databases

Why, then, is there so much concern about the use of evidence derived from databases? The answer is that it is possible to fall into the sort of logical traps we have already explained in this book. These are mainly the concern of investigators rather than of courts assessing the value of the evidence.

- Finding a "match" in a database does not necessarily mean that we have found the perpetrator. We would expect the possible suspect pool to contain a number of "matches" equal to the size of the pool multiplied by the frequency of the characteristic. Not all these potential "matches" will be in the database. Without other evidence a person with the relevant characteristics outside the database is just as likely to be the perpetrator as a "match" within the database.[23]

- A search of a database should not stop when one "match" is found. To stop at that point is to lose information. This is less likely to occur today when searching is done by computer. If for some reason a search has to be stopped then the frequency of the characteristic (if not already known) can be estimated by dividing the number of "matches" found by the number of comparisons actually made.

[23] Which raises the vexed question whether presence in the database is itself evidence – i.e. similar fact evidence.

- Where a match is found by searching a database then the overall evidence against that person may be less than when someone is arrested for other reasons and then found to match the perpetrator's characteristic. The other reasons for arrest, themselves, provide evidence.

- If a database is drawn from the whole country then, at this point, the pool of possible suspects must be regarded as being the whole country. National criminal records should be regarded as a database drawn from the whole country.

- The probability of obtaining a match by conducting some procedure is of interest to investigators who have to decide how to allocate resources. Many standard statistical procedures analyse a problem from a standpoint prior to obtaining any evidence. The court, however, is in a different position. It has evidence in hand and wants to know how strongly that evidence supports the alternative hypotheses. Some of the confusion over the value of database evidence stems from a failure to separate the standpoints of the investigator and the court.

What the discussion does emphasise is a need for care when searching databases (such as collections of DNA profiles), or making large-scale searches or surveys. Such a search might reveal a high likelihood ratio for a particular person as compared with a randomly selected person. If, at that stage, there is no other evidence to identify the perpetrator then we must remember to estimate how many other such suspects there might be who are not on the database. Other things being equal, all would be equally worth investigating. It would be a classical mistake to transpose the conditional – to believe that the likelihood ratio represented the odds in favour of guilt and go looking for evidence to support the hypothesis of guilt.[24]

What is particularly dangerous is for scientists to take it upon themselves to doctor the evidence to allow for the possibility of these errors on the part of others. These logical traps are simply acute examples of problems general to rational investigation. They are obscured rather than illuminated by instructions to ignore or doctor data such as those in the National Research Council Report.[25]

7.3 The right questions and the wrong questions

How is it that these orthodox methods of giving forensic scientific evidence have survived for so long and still appear in court? We believe it is because, in certain simple cases, asking the wrong question seems to lead to the right answer. When we ask the wrong questions in the wrong situations, however, we may go seriously astray.

[24] Chamberlin, TC, "The Method of Multiple Working Hypotheses" (1890) 15 *Science* 92.
[25] See n 20 and accompanying text.

The question the court wants the scientist to answer is the post-data question, "How much does the evidence from the mark at the scene increase the probability that it was the accused who left it?". The frequency reported in the classical approach answers a different question, namely the pre-data question, "What is the probability of obtaining this match by carrying out this procedure?". Forensic scientists have long been able to give evidence in this way because, in certain simple cases, the wrong question appears to produce a helpful and correct answer.

Consider a simple case where a bloodstain is found at the scene of a crime. The blood is analysed by techniques which identify factors which are either present or absent, such as the ABO factors. The blood of any suspect will also be analysed, and if it matches the mark at the scene the scientist will report that the two samples "could have come from the same person" and that blood of this type occurs in $x\%$ of the population. This may be expressed in the forms of "odds against a match by chance".

For example, if the frequency of the characteristics of the mark at the scene was 1% then the scientist would classically report that value and, perhaps, add that the odds against a match by chance were 99 to 1.

If, in contrast, we ask the questions posed in this book, the two conditional probabilities we need are $P(E|H_1) = 1$ and $P(E|H_2) = 0.01$, equivalent to the frequency of the characteristic. Thus, the likelihood ratio $P(E|H_1)/P(E|H_2) = 100$ and, whatever the court previously assessed the odds in favour of the accused's guilt as being, it should now multiply those odds by 100.

The classical method has survived because, in this simple case, the correct likelihood ratio can be derived intuitively from the 1% frequency that the forensic scientist reports. Indeed, giving odds against a match has been defended by Magnusson[26] precisely on the ground that "it will be ready for use in a Bayesian argument".

When the wrong questions give the right answers

Four conditions have to be satisfied so that asking the wrong question will give the right answer:

- the test must be for a characteristic which is either present or absent, such as an ABO factor; in other words, the sample must either match or not match. We call this the match/no-match approach;

- there must be only one mark, for example one bloodstain or one group of glass fragments;

- the population from which the frequency of a match by chance is derived must contain both the accused and the perpetrator and not contain special subgroups with different frequencies;

- comparison is made only with one person – the accused.

[26] Magnusson, E, *Incomprehension and Miscomprehension of Statistical Evidence: An Experimental Study* (Australian Institute of Criminology Conference on Law, Medicine and Criminal Justice, 1993).

Only if all the above conditions are satisfied will asking the wrong question give the right answer. In any other case they will give the wrong answer. Let us see why.

The factors measured must either match or not match

The first problem is that the probability of the evidence if the prosecution case was true, $P(E|H_1)$, may not be 1. Blood tests detect factors which are either present or absent (although even then there may be false positives and negatives). With glass measurements, however, there may be continuous variations in the refractive index over one window; two samples from the same window may not have precisely the same refractive index. Lindley[27] pointed out the problem in 1977, but because the solution proposed was "Bayesian" and, hence, controversial, most scientists failed to change their practices.

The advent of DNA evidence made the problem acute. If two DNA profiles from the same person are analysed, slight differences in observed band positions may occur under the best of conditions – and forensic scientists work frequently with degraded and contaminated samples. The problem is to decide whether two bands are "really" the same or not.

In order to carry on giving evidence in the classical way a stratagem was adopted. This was to define a "match" using significance tests leading to all the problems explained above. The match/no-match procedure, because it may reject evidence which actually favours the hypothesis, leads to an increase in false exclusions. It is often argued that this is acceptable since it errs in favour of the accused; in other words, it is a conservative procedure. However, work by Evett and others shows that the number of occasions on which falsely inculpatory evidence is obtained is also increased.[28] Arbitrary adjustments to evidence, motivated by conservativeness, cannot be guaranteed invariably to be conservative.

Only a single mark must be tested[29]

Where a single bloodstain, thought to belong to the perpetrator, is found at the scene, its value as evidence depends on the frequency of that blood group in the relevant population (f). The likelihood ratio will be $1/f$ if the alternative hypothesis is that it came from some unknown member of the population. The smaller the frequency, the greater the likelihood ratio. A stain of a blood group that occurs in 2% of the population ($f = 0.02$) has a likelihood ratio of 50.

A more difficult question arises when there is more than one trace at the scene of a crime. Suppose, for example, that there are two different bloodstains and the accused is found to match one. What is the value of this evidence?

---

[27] Lindley, DV, "A problem in forensic science" (1977) 64 *Biometrika* 207.
[28] Evett, IW, Scranage, J and Pinchin, R, "An Illustration of the advantages of efficient statistical methods for RFLP analysis in forensic science" (1993) 52 Am J Hum Gen 498.
[29] The concept and working in this section are based upon Evett, I, "On meaningful questions: a two-trace transfer problem" (1987) 27 JFSS 375.

Orthodox analysis of the two-trace problem

The orthodox approach to this two-trace problem is to consider the probability that the suspect would match one of the two samples left at the scene, given only the characteristics of the suspect. In order to obtain this we must first consider the probability that the suspect would match either stain and then add the probabilities together, since if he does not match one he might match the other. Assume that the frequencies of type 1 and type 2 in the population are, respectively, f_1 and f_2. The probability of matching either one stain or the other is (f_1+f_2). (The assumption, then, is that the value of the evidence is the reciprocal of this, that is $1/(f_1+f_2)$.)[30]

For concreteness, assume stain 1 is of blood type 1 with proportion in the population 0.5, and stain 2 is of type 2 with proportion 0.01; the probability of a match by chance is 0.5+0.01 = 0.51. We would then say that this matching could easily occur by chance and reject the evidence.

This must be wrong, since the evidence against the suspect must be much stronger if he matches the rare blood group than if he matches the common one. The orthodox approach gives the same answer no matter what the accused's blood group.

It is answering the wrong question. A court is not concerned with the probability that a person plucked from the street at random would match one of these two bloodstains. The court wishes to know what is the value as evidence of the fact that the suspect *does* match one of the stains. While in the most straightforward case, where there is only one stain and one suspect, the orthodox method happens to give the correct answer; in the more complex case this approach breaks down and gives a wrong answer.

When the correct answer to the two-stain problem is worked through it turns out that only the suspect's blood group matters, and that the evidence is worth half of what it would have been had there been only one stain (*i.e.* $1/2f$). We might expect this result intuitively, since once we have arrested a suspect there are two chances of one of the stains matching his blood. The value of the evidence is determined by the rarity of the suspect's blood type and the number of stains. The rarer the suspect's blood type, the stronger the evidence. If there are three bloodstains the value of the blood group match would be one-third what it would have been had there been only one bloodstain and so on. At first thought it is surprising that the rarity of the second, non-matching bloodstain does not matter.

When a mixed bloodstain is tested by conventional blood-typing the presence of two different types is clearly revealed. When such a stain is tested by a DNA probe the calculation is more complicated, but the principle remains the same.[31]

---

[30] National Research Council, *DNA Technology in Forensic Science* (National Academy Press, 1992), chapter 2.

[31] Evett, I *et al*, "A guide to interpreting single locus profiles of DNA mixtures in forensic cases" (1991) 31 JFSS 41.

We can conclude that the orthodox method and the logical method give similar answers when there is only one stain (although the logical method presents it in such a way that it can be combined with other evidence). If there is more than one stain, the strength of the reported evidence can be very different for the two methods.

The population must be homogenous

This requirement has caused much difficulty in court, particularly in cases where DNA tests have been used to establish identification. Defence experts often claim that the prosecution evidence was unreliable if the accused's population was not homogeneous, that is, it contained sub-populations with very different blood type or DNA characteristics. Technically, this claim is that the population was not in "Hardy-Weinberg" equilibrium, that is, not homogenous by way of random mating.

The reason for this is that if we ask the orthodox question, "What is the probability that the *accused* would match the stain at the scene before we analyse his blood?", we are immediately led to ask, "What do we know about the *accused* which might affect our assessment of this probability?". We know that the frequency of biological characteristics varies between races and between sub-groups of races. Thus, if the suspect is one-half American Indian, one-quarter French and one-quarter Italian then we may not feel that we can confidently assess the probability that he would match the stain at the scene without knowing the frequency of the characteristics amongst such people;[32] hence the argument that we should not use DNA evidence unless a particular database is available for the accused's sub-population.

On the other hand, the two questions in which the court is really interested are: "What is the probability that the stain at the scene would have these characteristics if the accused left it?" and "What is the probability that the stain at the scene would have these characteristics if someone else left it?". *The characteristics of the accused are not relevant to either of these questions.* Sub-populations are only a concern when there is some evidence that the *perpetrator* comes from a particular sub-population (whether the accused does or not). In this case we should use any data we have about the sub-population in our alternative hypothesis. We will seldom have information pointing to a very small population and, when we do, as explained in chapter 3 the effect on the prior odds may be so much greater than on the likelihood ratio of the new evidence that the evidence against the accused is actually strengthened.

It has been argued by some statisticians that the race of the accused is "in general" relevant to the probability that a perpetrator other than the accused would have had the relevant characteristics.[33] It is important to realise that "in general" in this context is a technical term which means essentially "in theory it is possible that" and does not mean "generally" or "usually". In fact, the race of

---

[32] *Commonwealth* v *Curnin* 565 NE2 d 440 (Mass 1991).
[33] Balding, DJ and Donnelly, P, "Inference in Forensic Identification" (1995) 158 JRSS A 21-53.

the accused will only affect the issue in one instance; that is, when the information used to calculate the probability that a member of a pool of suspects would have the characteristics is that the accused has the characteristic and that the other suspects have some genetic relationship with the accused (*e.g.* the accused's brothers and sisters).

A logical approach to the questions which the court wants answered, therefore, reveals that where a mark such as a bloodstain is found at the scene of a crime the race of the accused is usually irrelevant.

Comparison is made with one person only

The problems perceived with databases arose because the wrong question was being asked. If we are concerned with the probability of a match given a procedure, our assessment will climb as the database size increases. If we ask the different (but correct) question, "How much does the evidence increase the probability that it was the accused that left the mark?", we see that the size of the database is usually irrelevant. What is relevant is what we know of the frequency of the characteristic. Only if the frequency is measured from the database will the size of the database make any difference and then, as explained above, for any given number of matches the evidence becomes stronger as the database increases in size.

7.4 Case study

Here we have only one case which illustrates the dangers involved in using orthodox statistical methods where the standard alternative hypothesis of matching by chance is assumed.

The Birmingham Six

In this case a bomb explosion occurred in Birmingham.[34] Some hours later a group of Irishmen who were travelling to an IRA funeral were arrested as they were about to board the ferry for Ireland. Their hands were swabbed and the swabs tested positively for the presence of nitro-glycerine. As a result of the test results the scientist stated that he was "99% certain that the men had handled explosive".[35]

In this part of his evidence, at least, the forensic scientist, appears to have done all that he was trained at the time to do. He carried out a chemical reaction test and considered the single hypothesis that the suspects had nitro-glycerine on their hands. He decided that the hypothesis that the data had occurred by chance could be rejected at the 99% confidence level (although the statement he made clearly inverted the conditional).

---

[34] The detail of the evidence in this case is not reported. There are numerous secondary sources relating to this case. We quote sources for specific statements.

[35] Mills, H, "The Birmingham Six Case – Vital Scientific Evidence Kept From Defence" *The Independent*, 28 March 1991.

The chances of the swab results occurring by chance without contact with explosive were considered to be extremely low. The men claimed, however, that they had been playing cards on the train and there was some question as to whether cellulose from the playing cards could have caused the test result. By the time the case had been referred back to the Court of Appeal by the Home Secretary in 1991 experiments had shown that the particular test could obtain positive results even from soap.

Had the forensic scientist realised the necessity to consider alternative hypotheses related to the case he may have realised that the evidence of the test results could not distinguish between a number of possible innocent causes of reasonable prior probability.

7.5 Summary

- The court wishes to know by how much an item of evidence should cause it to change its belief in a hypothesis. Orthodox statistical techniques do not answer this question.

- Orthodox statistical methods may give wrong or misleading answers unless a range of conditions are satisfied. The logical approach can usually provide a usable answer even in other situations.

- If the factor being measured is not categorical, like blood types, the idea of a match can only be approximated by somewhat arbitrary criteria for what is meant by matching. This leads to serious difficulties like the fall-off-the-cliff effect, the rejection or, alternatively, the over-valuation of evidence, and the danger of transposing the conditional. The logical method does away with these difficulties.

- When there is more than one mark the orthodox method gets into difficulties.

- Since the alternative hypothesis will usually be that someone else, not the accused, was involved, the race (or sub-race) of the accused is not usually relevant to calculating its probability.

- The size of a database does not, of itself, affect the value of the evidence obtained by searching it. The value of the evidence is determined by the frequency of the characteristic in the relevant population.

Chapter 8

TRANSFER EVIDENCE

Chapter 8

TRANSFER EVIDENCE

The next three chapters describe different types of scientific evidence and suggest methods of interpretation. This chapter deals with fingerprints, glass, fibres and firearms. Chapter 9 examines blood evidence, including DNA profiling and chapter 10 investigates less tangible forms of evidence such as psychological characteristics and handwriting.

In the Introduction we referred to Locard's exchange principle – that every contact leaves a trace. Whenever a crime involving physical action is committed, traces from the perpetrator will be transferred to the victim or to the crime scene and traces from the victim and the crime scene will be transferred to the perpetrator.

Amongst the most obvious traces are fingerprints left at a crime scene by a perpetrator, broken glass which may collect on the perpetrator's clothing especially in burglary offences, fibres which may be transferred between perpetrator and victim, and bullets found at the scene bearing marks made by the barrel of the weapon. There are numerous other types of transfer evidence, such as tool-marks and hair, and the reader is referred to larger works on forensic science for more details. We shall consider the first four types of transfer evidence in the light of our method of reasoning.

8.1 Fingerprints

Although the uniqueness of fingerprints had been known for centuries[1] and had been studied by Francis Galton (1822–1911) and used by Henry Faulds and William Herschel, fingerprints only became a useful tool of forensic science when a workable method of classification was developed. This was done in Argentina by Juan Vucetich (1858–1925) and in England by Sir Edward Richard Henry

[1] "He seals up the hand of every man, that all men may know his work." *Book of Job*, chapter 37, verse 7.

(1850–1931) first as Inspector-General of Police in Bengal and then, successively, as Head of the CID and Commissioner of the London Metropolitan Police, where he set up the Central Fingerprints Branch in July 1902. In that year, 1722 suspects were identified. The previous *Bertillonage* system dropped out of use.

Nearly all countries now maintain fingerprint collections, either classified according to the Galton-Henry system, the Vucetich system[2], or computerised. Fingerprint collections serve two main purposes. The first is to identify arrested persons with a particular criminal record. This is important because prosecution and sentencing decisions may depend upon a person's previous convictions and the person may be wanted elsewhere. The second purpose is to enable the perpetrators of crimes to be identified by comparing marks left at the scene of a crime with marks in the collection.

Whenever a non-national is convicted of an offence the fingerprints taken are passed, via the International Criminal Police Organisation (INTERPOL), to the country of nationality. This means, in turn, that when a person is arrested, confirmation of identity may be obtained from the authorities in his country of nationality. Unfortunately, it is becoming increasingly easy to become the citizen of a number of countries, as well as to forge passports and other identity documents. Filing fingerprints with the country of nationality is not, therefore, a complete solution, but, pending the creation of an international database, it is the best available.

Such a database would be feasible if its purpose was limited to identifying people arrested with records. These comparisons are relatively easy. The fingerprint technician is provided with whole prints and, usually, a specific name and record with which to compare. The size of the database can be reduced by eliminating prints of little fingers, as in some US collections.

The second purpose – comparing marks at the scene with marks in the collection – is much more difficult and expensive. First, the mark from the scene may be partial and of poor quality and, secondly, there may not be a particular record with which to compare. There are three main ways such marks can be considered, and it is in this area that computerisation has had the greatest impact.

A suspect may have been arrested on the basis of other evidence. The fingerprint technician is then asked to compare the mark at the scene with an impression taken from the suspect under a power, such as that in section 61 of the Police and Criminal Evidence Act 1984. Secondly, a mark may be sent to the fingerprint office with a list of possible candidates for the crime. These may be local active criminals or persons with a particular, distinctive *modus operandi*. The fingerprint office can also resort to strategies such as including the place of residence or records of previous convictions among the search criteria. Thirdly, a mark may simply be put into the computer and the computer asked to come up with possible matches and to go on checking periodically so that the mark is

[2] Vucetich was an Argentinian of Croatian origin who developed a classification system in Buenos Aires and used it to solve a crime before the Henry system was implemented. For a readable history, see Thorwald, J, *The Marks of Cain* (Pan Books Ltd, London, 1965).

compared with all new additions to the collection. This last process has become very much more practicable with the advent of computerisation but, even so, it is demanding of computer time and is usually done outside peak periods.

Interpretation of fingerprints

Examining one's own fingers reveals that they are covered in fine lines, or "ridges" arranged in loops, whorls and arches. There are also frequent forks, breaks and other features. The basic patterns are genetically determined and vary in frequency from one race to another. The detailed features, however, must be due to processes of cell-division so numerous, so fine and so sensitive to outside influence that they are unpredictable. They can be shown not to be similar even for identical twins.

There have been numerous attempts to answer questions like, "How many different fingerprints could there be?", "How many similarities are required to enable a conclusion of identity to be drawn?", "What is the evidential value of a partial print with X similarities?". The review paper by Stoney and Thornton[3] describes the history of these attempts, starting with Francis Galton.[4] There is still no consensus model created to answer these problems and a little thought makes it obvious why.

Suppose fingerprints consisted of just one circle with one feature located somewhere around it. The question, "How many fingerprints are there?" would be the same question as, "How many points are there on a circle?". The answer, obviously, is an infinite number. The real question is, "How many can we distinguish between?". When considering this we must bear in mind that if we cannot orient the circle uniquely we will be able to distinguish fewer impressions. Also, two impressions made by the same finger may appear different because of variations in the amount and type of ink, the pressure used to take the impression and the surface on which the impressions are recorded.

Real fingerprints are, of course, vastly more complex than just a single circle. A whole print might have 30 circles or their equivalent in a number of shapes such as arches or whorls, and 70 clearly visible features. Furthermore, there are different types of feature.

Since there is an infinite variety of fingerprints, the models which have been proposed are of the identification process rather than of the fingerprint. Most models share two features. The first is that they classify fingerprints into basic patterns: the arch, the whorl, the loop, the compound and the scar. The latter classification is necessary, as a scar may conceal what type the inherited pattern is.

It is possible with some partial prints to be unable to identify the pattern even though quite a large area of print is visible. In particular, it may not be possible to tell whether one has part of a "loop" or an "arch".

---

[3] Stoney, DA and Thornton, JI, "A critical analysis of quantitative fingerprint individuality models" (1986) 31 JFS 1187.
[4] Galton, F, *Finger Prints* (MacMillan and Company Ltd, London, New York, 1892).

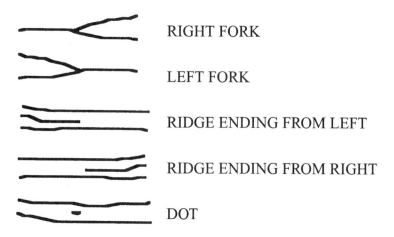

Figure 8.1 *Some basic recognisable ridge features in fingerprints.*

Figure 8.2 *More possible features: islands and trifurcations.*

The second common feature of fingerprint models is that they all make use of "ridge counts" between features. What is counted are actually the gaps between ridges. The advantage is that these cannot easily be altered by variations in the pressure with which the impression was made. Distances between features are therefore expressed in "ridges" rather than in normal units of length.

After those points of agreement, however, the models tend to diverge. Writers even vary in the number of different features they recognise. A basic list of features would include those in *Figure 8.1*.[5] This gives five different possibilities as to what a feature at any given position might be. Some writers have proposed other features such as the island (or lake) and the trifurcation (*Figure 8.2*).[6]

The features in *Figure 8.2* are essentially composites. A lake, for example, is a right fork followed by a left fork. The classification of these features is judgmental. How short does a lake have to be, for example, to avoid being classified as two forks? Is a trifurcation really two forks very close together? It seems better to stick to the minimum number of features requiring the minimum of judgment in their classification.

[5] Stoney, DA and Thornton, JI, "A Method for the Description of Minutia Pairs in Epidermal Ridge Patterns" (1986) 31 JFS 1217.
[6] Roxburgh, TJY, "On the Evidential Value of Finger Prints" (1933) 1 *Sankhya* 189; Gupta, SR, Statistical survey of ridge characteristics [1968] IC Pol R 130.

The other major difference between models is the extent to which they take the position of the features into account. The position can be altered by the pressure used to make the impression. Some models take into account the position of a feature relative to its core. This is done by dividing the print into four to 36 sectors and examining the features falling within each. The advantage of using sectors is that the absence of a feature can also be considered. If an area of each impression contains no features this is itself of evidential value. The disadvantage of position is that one has to be able to identify with certainty some reference point to start from, usually the "core" of a "whorl" or "loop". With a partial print this may not be possible.

Despite these difficulties scientists have studied fingerprints and tried to construct probability models. Roxburgh[7] describes the work done by Francis Galton, who cut up enlarged photographs of fingerprints and studied the statistics of the components. Another model was developed in 1911 by Balthazard.[8] He calculated that if a fingerprint contained 16 particular features, one would not expect to find another such in the world. A 16-point standard for identification is now regarded as extremely conservative and some elementary consideration shows why.

Consider a simple model similar to that proposed by Roxburgh. Suppose that a fingerprint consists of just 10 concentric circles corresponding to ridges. Number the circles from 0 to 9 and place 12 marks anywhere on these 10 circles. Each mark represents a feature, such as a ridge-ending or fork; for the moment it does not matter what (see Figure 8.3).

We select a corresponding reference point which appears on each print. It does not matter in principle where this is. All that matters is that we are able to select a particular point on one print and the corresponding point on the print with which we are comparing. The procedure will test the hypothesis that the reference point is the identical point from the identical fingerprint.

We orient the impressions in what appears to be the same direction about the reference points and draw a line vertically from the reference point in each print. In this case, since it is visible, we take the centre of the circles as the reference point. Now, the line is rotated clockwise until we meet a mark. The number of the circle on which the mark lies is recorded. We then rotate the line further until we meet another mark. We record the number of the circle on which that lies and so forth. In the end we will have a string of 12 digits.

Each of the 12 digits is a number from 0 to 9. If they are independent, that is to say that the fact that a mark is found on, for example, circle 3, does not help us predict where the next one will be found, then there are 10^{12} possible combinations, that is 10 million million. Since there are only approximately 50,000 million (5×10^9) fingers in the world we would not expect any one series of figures to appear more than once. If 16 points are used instead of 12, as is required in the

[7] Roxburgh, TJY, "Galton's work on the evidential value of finger prints" (1933) 1 *Sankhya* 50.
[8] Balthazard, V, "De l'Identification par les Empreintes Digitales" (1911) 152 *Comptes Rendus des Academies des Sciences* 1862.

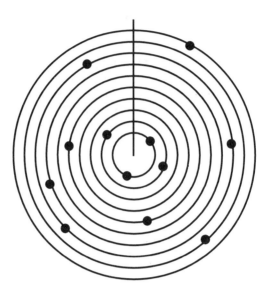

Figure 8.3 *Roxburgh's model of a fingerprint consisting of 10 concentric circular ridges, numbered from 0 to 9 from the innermost. The features are marked with a dot. The vertical line is rotated clockwise from the starting position. When a feature is encountered the circle number is noted. The line makes a complete rotation and the list of circle numbers gives the reading. In this case the reading would be 9, 0, 7, 1, 8, 4, 0, 7, 6, 4, 1, 7.*

United Kingdom, then there would be 10 thousand million million (10^{16}) combinations.

These patterns are only rough approximations to fingerprints, as Roxburgh noted: "Nature has not given to persons 10 concentric circles, but has given something very like it. She has not marked points as such, but the characteristics discussed in fingerprints are really such points."[9]

Does this calculation depend upon any unjustifiable assumptions? One assumption is that the positions of features are independent of one another. We do not know of evidence to the contrary, but testing this hypothesis is an example of the kind of research that could be carried out, now even more easily than ever before because of the greater use of computerised fingerprint systems.

If we had only eight points on our 10 circles then there would be 100 million combinations. Thus, the odds against a match by chance would be 100 million to

[9] Roxburgh, TJY, "On the evidential value of fingerprints" (1933) 1 *Sankhya* 189, 190.

1. It must be obvious, however, that even this is very powerful evidence and that the requirement that there be 12 points of comparison, let alone 16, errs considerably on the side of caution. This is especially true where the suspect has been arrested on the basis of other evidence or where more than one fingerprint is found. In some jurisdictions this is recognised by the application of a 12-point rule for single impressions or eight points on each of two or more impressions. Roxburgh was willing to identify on similarities that might be shared by 1 in 50,000 when the suspect had been arrested on other evidence but so far as we know no jurisdiction using a point counting rule differentiates between cases in this way.

It must always be borne in mind that using such conservative point-counting rules has a cost, namely that relevant and probative evidence is withheld from the prosecution and the court.

Are two features the same?

A fingerprint expert does not compare fingertips, but impressions. Each time an impression is taken of a fingerprint it will be slightly different owing to differences in pressure or the amount of ink used or other factors. Thus, features may appear differently in different prints of the same finger.

This means that the judgment that two features are the same may be just that – a judgment. One way of dealing with this problem is to allow a "match" where two features are consistent with each other. In *Figure 8.4* below, numbers 1 and 2 could be the same feature, but number 3 obviously could not be. It will be seen that the margins for error in the process are so great that this will not have any practical impact on the value of the evidence as it is presented at present. This problem, which Stoney and Thornton call *connective ambiguity* – that is, being unsure whether a connection is made in the ridge patterns – does, however, indicate that the judgment that there are "no significant differences" is not all that clear cut.[10]

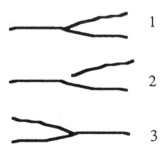

Figure 8.4 *Ambiguity in fingerprint ridges. Features 1 and 2 could easily be the same feature with a flaw in one of the prints but both are clearly different from feature 3.*

---

[10] Thornton, JI, "The one-dissimilarity doctrine in fingerprint identification" [1977] I C Pol R 89.

Point-counting rules

We have seen that there is neither consensus about the model of a fingerprint nor certainty in identifying features. Nonetheless, the search for a level at which an identification could be regarded as "certain" led to the various rules as to the number of points a fingerprint expert will require before giving evidence in court. These requirements varied from 17 in Paris (but 12 in the rest of France), 16 in the United Kingdom, 12 in the United States, Australia and New Zealand, and eight in parts of India. Why were these rules devised?

An outstanding feature of fingerprints is that (compared to DNA profiles or firearms) they are relatively cheap and easy to find, record and compare. These operations do not need staff with scientific training. They are, in fact, technicians, skilled in carrying out certain processes but not required to understand the theoretical basis for their work. Fingerprints are available, therefore, as evidence in a very large number of cases. If a forensic scientist had to be present in court to testify to the probabilistic effect of a fingerprint on each occasion their use would be enormously restricted. A rule was sought, therefore, which would dispense with any probabilistic argument.

This purpose is served by the rules as to the minimum number of points required for an identification. If the impressions contain this number of matching points the witness's statement that the impressions are from the same finger will be accepted without argument, and often without the witness having to appear in person. This is a position which the fingerprint technicians themselves are anxious to preserve. It certainly reduces the amount of argument about the evidence in court. The effect, however, is that much potentially useful evidence is never produced. The International Association for Identification (IAI), for example, prohibited the giving of testimony of the "possible, probable or likely friction ridge identification".[11] In fact there is, as the IAI had previously declared, no magic number of points which itself justifies a conclusion that two impressions came from the same finger.[12] The New Zealand Court of Appeal in *Buisson*[13] likewise ruled that there was no magic number of points required for admissibility in court and made two interesting observations. One was that much useful evidence was being kept out of court by decision of the technicians. The other was that the evidence of the fingerprint should (of course) be combined with other evidence to determine whether the accused had been present. These court rulings do not seem to have affected the working practices of fingerprint technicians so far.

The view is increasingly being expressed that point-counting is an irrelevance. It gives an impression of objectivity to the process which, as we can see from the discussion above, is quite false. In the United States the emphasis today is on maintaining standards of professionalism rather than on counting points. The

---

[11] International Association for Identification, "Resolution VII", *Identification News*, August 1979.
[12] Second interim report of the standardisation committee of the IAI, *Identification News*, November 1972.
[13] *R v Buisson* [1990] 2 NZLR 542 (CA). See Robertson, BWN, "Fingerprints, Relevance and Admissibility" [1990] NZ Rec Law R 252.

evidence given is a professional judgment that two impressions were made by the same finger. This judgment is supported not by a point-count but by the experience of the witness and his performance in the blind testing which is regularly carried out.

In other countries little or no such testing is carried out. One inquiry was initiated by the Home Office and the Association of Chief Police Officers in England and Wales.[14] This inquiry sent pairs of fingerprints from the same sources to fingerprint examiners all over the country. The examiners were asked to compare the prints, determine whether they were from the same source and indicate the number of points of comparison. There was also one "pair" of different prints, one of which was "doctored" to give it numerous points of similarity with the other. Not one examiner was taken in by the false pair, nor did any examiner misidentify the "best" pair of similar impressions from two different people that could be produced by any bureau in England and Wales. However, when examining and identifying genuine pairs of prints there was a wide variation in the number of points of comparison found. In the case of one print this varied from 11 to 40. In other words, some examiners would not have gone to court with this pair of impressions, although most would cheerfully have done so.

The fingerprint profession outside the United States has not been willing to accept the implications of this study.[15] For decades the profession has been used to justifying its identifications by reference to the number of points of comparison. This is to undermine its own professional status, however. Anyone with a reasonable magnifying glass can count points of similarity (Roxburgh and Galton did not complete five-year apprenticeships before publishing their work), but training is required to become a fingerprint expert.

In the field of eyewitness identification it is well known that recognition and description are two different processes and that people are better at recognition than description. So it is with fingerprints. What takes judgment and experience is the conclusion of common origin. An experienced professional would find it difficult to explain all the factors which cause one to come to that conclusion. The profession therefore avoids the issue by counting points of comparison. This is despite clear evidence that different experts will decide that prints are identical while disagreeing about the number of points of comparison and the evidence that experts will not misidentify impressions despite large numbers of points of comparison, any more than a mother will misidentify her twin children.

This suggests that the way forward, as Evett and Williams propose, is to concentrate on professional standards rather than on rules about numbers of points. Before any print is taken to court it should be agreed by at least two, if not three, examiners, at least one of whom is qualified to give evidence. The workload of experts should contain blind tests, *i.e.* pairs of impressions known to have come

---

[14] Evett, IW and Williams, RL, "A Review of the Sixteen Points Fingerprint Standard in England and Wales" (1989) British Crown Copyright.
[15] "Editorial" (1990) 15 *Fingerprint Whorld* 72; Luff, K, "The 16-point Standard" (1990) 15 *Fingerprint Whorld* 73.

from the same or different sources. If a misidentification ever occurs there should
be a debriefing and the individual and the organisation should learn from the
mistakes. An expert should then say in court:

> I believe that these impressions come from the same finger. I can show you, if you wish,
> some of the most easily identifiable points of comparison but I rest my identification
> on my N years of experience, the agreement of my colleagues, and the fact that I have
> never, in blind-testing, misidentified a pair of impressions.

Even now we are assuming that for reasons of policy we will still not bring to court
relevant and admissible evidence in the form of impressions with similarities, but
about which an expert feels unable to say "these came from the same source".
There are, as discussed above, sound policy reasons for this. There is no reason of
principle, however, why evidence to the effect that "the similarities between these
impressions strongly supports the hypothesis of common origin" should not be
given and there may be good practical arguments for giving such evidence in the
most serious cases. The testing case will be when the defence wishes to produce
evidence of a partial print to show that someone other than the accused was
present.

The two vital questions raised by fingerprints are the same as those raised by all
other forms of scientific evidence. First, when are we justified in asserting that two
samples had a common origin without reference to other evidence? and, secondly, how can we quantify the value of the evidence when it only tends to support
a proposition of common origin? These are the questions to which thought needs
to be directed.

Conclusions

- Fingerprint identification is a matter of expert judgment, not counting of
  points.
- There is no reason in logic or law why a witness should not give evidence
  that a partial print "(strongly) supports the contention that the accused
  was present", but there are cost-benefit reasons for not doing so.
- The "standards" currently used in the United Kingdom and most other
  countries are conservative in the extreme and continue to deprive the
  courts of useful evidence.

8.2 Glass

Evidence about glass found on a suspect's clothing has been given in court for
several decades. Anyone near a breaking window, even the person who breaks it,
will collect glass fragments, many of microscopic size, on their clothing. Although
most of the glass will explode away from the breaker, many small fragments also
shower towards the source of the force.

The orthodox method of analysis

The traditional way in which glass evidence was given is described in chapter 6. First, a test would be carried out to find the refractive index of the glass from the broken window and from the suspect's clothing. The test often consists of placing the fragments in an oil which is warmed up. The refractive index of the oil at various temperatures is known. When the oil reaches the same refractive index as the glass, the glass seems to disappear.[16]

Usually, 10 fragments would be taken from the window to obtain an assessment of the variation in refractive index from one part of the window to another. A mean and a standard deviation for the refractive indices of the 10 fragments would be calculated. The fragments recovered from the suspect would also be tested, and if they fell within three standard deviations of the mean (as we would expect 99.9% of fragments from the same window to do) then the scientist would say that they could have come from the same source.

The next step was to consider the frequency of such a refractive index by referring to a database built up by the forensic science authorities from the cases which they dealt with, and from other glass samples which they were provided with. The database would be subdivided into curved and plane and coloured and colourless glass. The scientist would then report the fact that the glass could have come from the window in question, and give the frequency estimated from the database. From this information the court was supposed to infer something about the value of the glass as evidence.

It was this method of giving glass evidence that first caused disquiet with the traditional form of analysis of forensic scientific evidence. Forensic scientists had realised that the probability that glass would transfer to the perpetrator's clothing and remain there was a relevant factor, although the orthodox statistical analysis did not take this into account. Research into these problems had already taken place[17] when Lindley demonstrated the general problems with the significance test[18] and proposed the use of the Bayesian method as presented in this book.

It was realised that if one asked questions needed for Bayesian analysis, such as "What is the probability of the accused having this glass on him supposing he was near the breaking window?", one also needed to know how likely it was that the perpetrator would get glass on his clothing and retain it there until arrested. These probabilities came to be known as the probability of transfer and the probability of persistence. Once transfer and persistence are taken into account the value of the evidence tends to be reduced, especially if some time has elapsed between the event and finding the suspect.

Once one asked the question, "What is the probability that the accused would have this glass on him given that he was *not* near the breaking window?", one

---

[16] There are other tests such as elemental analysis (chemical composition), but these are expensive and complex and seldom resorted to.
[17] Pounds, CA and Smalldon, KW, "The Transfer of Fibres between Clothing Materials During Simulated Contacts and their Persistence During Wear" (1975) 15 JFSS 17 and 29.
[18] Lindley, D, "A problem in forensic science" (1977) 64 *Biometrika* 207–213.

needed to know not just the frequency of the detected refractive index but also how likely it was that the accused would have any glass on him at all. This might depend upon his job and recent activities, but if no defence explanation was offered the question would reduce to how likely it was that the ordinary person or "random man" would have glass on his clothing. This consideration would tend to increase the value of the evidence, since not everyone has glass on their clothing.[19]

One of the particular advantages of asking these questions was that it suggested lines of research needed to quantify the value of the evidence. This research was not in the technical area of measuring refractive indices or other indicators of the composition of glass or even in terms of increasing our knowledge of the frequencies of glass types, but in terms of gathering information needed to interpret the data obtained from tests.

Experiments were conducted to find some basis for quantifying the probabilities of transfer and persistence. The results showed that both depend upon the type of clothes worn, that the probability of transfer also depends upon the distance from the window and that of persistence upon the time which has elapsed since the event. As one might imagine, a cotton shirt acquires and retains fewer fragments than a woollen jersey.

Surveys were carried out to discover how many people ordinarily had glass on their clothing. These included examinations of clothing brought to dry cleaners, or clothing only of people suspected of involvement in offences involving glass, or outer clothing only, or examinations including shoes. Some results are given below but, in summary, it seems to be very rare indeed for people to have glass fragments on their clothing, so that the mere finding of glass is itself good evidence of involvement. In particular, it is extremely rare for people to have large amounts of glass on their clothing. More glass is to be found on shoes, but this is mostly bottle glass, not plane glass.

McQuillan and Edgar examined pairs of outer garments (*e.g.* jersey and trousers) worn by people in Belfast who had no known connection with crime.[20] According to the survey 23.8% of the sample had at least one fragment of glass on their clothing. Very few people had more than one fragment so that the scientists defined a "large group" as one containing three or more glass fragments. Only 2.9% of the sample had a large group of glass fragments.

These factors increase the value of this sort of evidence very substantially and certainly by far more than the numerator of the likelihood ratio is reduced by considering transfer and persistence.

One difficulty is the essentially judgmental nature of the assessments of probability of transfer and persistence. There may be no escaping this problem

---

[19] Evett, I, "A Bayesian Approach to the problem of interpreting glass evidence in forensic science casework" (1986) 26 JFSS 3. Evett, I and Buckleton, J, "The interpretation of glass evidence. A practical approach" (1990) 30 JFSS 215.
[20] McQuillan, J and Edgar, K, "A survey of the distribution of glass on clothing" (1992) 32 JFSS 333.

and the UK Forensic Science Service has developed an "expert system" to help scientists with their assessments. This system, called "CAGE",[21] asks the forensic scientist a number of questions to establish what is known of the incident in which the glass was broken, what kind of clothing is involved and the delay between the incident and the examination of the clothing. The system then searches the previous cases in its database and offers suggested figures for the various probabilities. Finally, the scientist is asked if he or she is willing for the current case and the scientist's own assessments to be added to the database.

Some scientists, accustomed to the claims of classical statistics to "objectivity" are unhappy with this aspect of CAGE. It is clear, however, that the classical statistical approach gave an incomplete assessment of the factors which go towards the probative value of glass evidence. Current research provides a much more comprehensive framework for considering the value of glass evidence.

8.3 Fibres

Often, an accused's clothing holds fibres that match those from the victim's garments, or fibres are found on the victim which match clothing owned by the accused. Fibres can be compared in a number of ways. They can be inspected with a comparison microscope or with an infra-red or visible light spectroscope. The dyes on the fibres can be identified using chromatography. Techniques are available for comparing the colour of even very small fragments of fibres. A database of colours of dyed fabrics has been collected. As each test is applied the tester will either be able or unable to distinguish between the scene sample and an item from the database.

The examination of fibres is, therefore, relatively straightforward. What is more difficult is to assess the evidential value of the fact that two indistinguishable fibres have been found. This has always been somewhat speculative, although it is felt that a two-way transfer (*i.e.*, when both victim-accused and accused-victim transfers are found) is very strong evidence. The defence has often argued that the garment in question is a common one, especially in the case of one-way transfers, and so the evidence is of little value.

The fundamental questions, such as the probabilities of transfer and persistence, are similar to those of glass evidence. It does not seem possible, however, to keep a database of clothing types in the same way that a database of glass types can be built up. Clothing is imported and manufactured by a far wider range of companies than those involved in the manufacture of glass. Compared to glass, styles in clothing change very quickly. Nonetheless, we know that some items of clothing such as blue jeans (throughout the world) and the Marks and Spencer

[21] Buckleton, J and Walsh, KA "Knowledge-based systems", pp 186–206, in Aitken, CGG and Stoney, DA *The Use Of Statistics In Forensic Science* (Ellis Horwood, Chichester, 1991).

blue sweater (in the United Kingdom) are produced in very large quantities. However, to say that finding fibres from these garments on someone's clothing is therefore useless as evidence would be to commit the defence attorney's fallacy (see chapter 6).

We do need some idea of what proportion of the population has fibres from a particular garment-type on their clothing. This data, incidentally, will automatically take into account not only the rarity of a garment but also its tendency to transfer fibres and for them to persist on the receiving clothing. This was explored in a "target fibre study" by Cook and Wilson in the United Kingdom.[22] They chose four common garments, including a Marks and Spencer blue V-neck sweater used by many schools as part of their uniform. They conducted two experiments. The first was to assess a transfer probability, and showed that when contact between two garments was simulated a large number of fibres were routinely transferred. The second examined tapings from 355 garments which had previously been examined in connection with crime. From all these garments only 12 fibres were recovered which matched those of the chosen "target" garments, of which nine were from the Marks and Spencer sweater. Only one taping had fibres from two of the targets on it.

These results suggest that is very unlikely that one will have a fibre, even from a very common garment, on one's clothing without recently having been in close contact with the garment in question. The total amount of clothing in circulation is enormous. Even the most common garments are only a small percentage of the total garment stock.

Other target fibre studies have been carried out.[23] These all indicate that finding a matching fibre strongly supports the hypothesis that the garments in question have recently been in contact. (That is, compared with an alternative hypothesis that there had been no contact.) If one wanted to become more specific it might be possible to conduct an individual target fibre study for particular garments involved in a crime. So, for example, if the victim of an offence was wearing a home-knitted red sweater and matching fibres were found on a suspect's clothing a survey could be carried out to discover how many people in the general population had such fibres on their clothing. Such a survey would be expensive to carry out for each case and the sample might have to be very large in order to find any matching fibres at all. For the present, then, we probably cannot do better than use the published target fibre studies to counter the suggestion that certain kinds of fibre might easily be found and to show that evidence of fibre transfer is strong evidence of contact.

---

[22] Cook, R and Wilson, C, "The Significance of Finding Extraneous fibres in Contact Cases" (1986) 32 For Sci Int, 267.

[23] For example, Grieve, MC, Dunlop, J and Haddock, PS, "An assessment of the value of blue, red and black cotton fibres as 'target fibres' in forensic science investigations" (1988) 33 JFS 1332 and see also Evett, I, Cage, PE and Aitken, CGG, "Evaluation of the likelihood ratio for fibre transfer evidence in criminal cases" (1987) 36 *Applied Statistics* 174.

8.4 Firearms examination[24]

Evidence from firearms examiners is often referred to as "ballistic evidence", although "ballistics" correctly refers to the study of the trajectory of bullets in flight and not to any other aspect of the operation of firearms.

Firearms examination may be needed for a number of purposes including:

- determining whether a particular bullet could have been fired from a particular weapon;
- determining whether a particular bullet could have come from a particular cartridge case;
- assessing the calibre and type of weapon used on a particular occasion;
- determining whether a particular cartridge case could have been fired in a particular weapon;
- assessing the distance from which a weapon was fired at a person or object;
- determining whether a weapon is safe or could have fired by accident.

We are concerned mainly with the first three purposes.

A firearms examiner may be able to describe the rifling of the barrel (the "class characteristics"). This will be of value to investigators, especially if the weapon is of a rare type, such as one that has a left-hand twist to its rifling or is a "microgroove" – one that has a large number of very small grooves, rather than the usual four or five large grooves.

When it is believed that a particular firearm may have fired a particular bullet, the firearm will be test-fired into a bed of some substance which will not distort the bullet. The test-fired bullet may then be compared with another bullet to see whether the two bullets have been fired from the same barrel. This is frequently carried out by mounting the two bullets on a comparison microscope and examining the microscopic marks on them.

When a rifled barrel is manufactured, the drills and cutters leave marks on the inside of the barrel. These, in turn, leave marks on any bullet fired down that barrel. Testing has shown that even bullets fired from barrels manufactured consecutively on the same machine can be clearly distinguished. The most revealing of these are the marks left on the lands (*i.e.* the ridges between the grooves). These marks are the reaming marks left by minute imperfections in the drilling and reaming tools (or fragments of metal picked up by them) when the bore of the rifle was drilled. The marks in the grooves, on the other hand, are left by a cutting tool and have been shown to be repeatable from one barrel to another.

---

[24] The factual information in this section is derived from Buckleton, JS and Walsh, KAJ "Firearms Evidence", in Freckelton and Selby, *Expert Evidence* (Law Book Co, 1992), section 86, where much more detail may be found.

From the moment it is manufactured each barrel leads a different life. The number of times it is fired, its exposure to the elements, how it is cleaned and any accidental damage will all affect the marks that the barrel leaves on bullets in a unique and unreproducible way.

As a result of all this it can safely be said that no two bullets fired from different barrels will appear the same. However, two factors mean that firearms identification is not easy. First, the barrel will change over time owing to the influences described above. If considerable time has elapsed between a crime and the test firing of a weapon there may be great differences between the test-fired bullet and the one from the crime, even though they were fired from the same barrel, especially if the barrel has been hidden underwater or buried in damp earth in the meantime.

Secondly, the bullet found at the scene of a crime will often only be a partial fragment. A bullet which strikes a hard object, such as a major bone, will be seriously deformed and some of it may be missing. This may mean that, rather than comparing two whole bullets, the examiner is comparing a partial fragment with a small part of a test-fired bullet.[25]

There are four main conclusions that firearms examiners commonly use:

- *The bullet was fired from the weapon* This conclusion is considered to be justified by a match on the class characteristics and close correspondence on the individual characteristics. There must be no unexplained differences.

- *The bullet could have been fired from the weapon* This requires that the class characteristics match and that there are no unexplained differences in marking.

- *The bullet could not have been fired from the weapon* where the class characteristics do not match or there are unexplained differences in individual characteristics.

- *Insufficient data* where a bullet from a crime scene is so badly damaged that no conclusions are possible.

Only if the conclusion is that the bullet "could have been fired from the weapon" will some consideration be given to how rare the weapon is amongst the suspect population. The evidential significance of a failure to exclude the weapon will be felt to be stronger where the suspect's weapon is of a rare type. This is as far as any attempt to quantify the value of the evidence has gone thus far.

Reflection reveals that these four conclusions are not watertight. In particular it should be possible to begin a rough quantification within the second type of conclusion. A scientist may believe, for example, that it is more probable that bullet X came from barrel X than that bullet Y came from barrel Y. In accordance with the general thrust of this book, we would, of course, prefer that the examiner said that the similarities tend to support the conclusion that the bullet was fired from that barrel and indicate how strong that support is.

[25] Booker, JL "Examination of the badly damaged bullet" (1980) 20 JFSS 153.

Furthermore the effect of the similarities needs to be combined with the relative rarity of the weapon. A firearm that is not tested until some time after the event will have altered its characteristics, and one may only be able to say that the weapon cannot be excluded. The power of this evidence is markedly increased if the firearm is rare. Suppose, in one case, that a murder is committed with a .22 micro-groove rifle, and a suspect arrested some time later on other grounds is found to possess such a rifle. Test-firing may reveal considerable differences in individual characteristics. In another case a murder may be committed with a five groove right-hand twist rifle, but when a suspect who turns out to own one is arrested fewer dissimilarities are found. The evidence may be stronger in the first case because of the relative rarity of such weapons.

Quantification has not proceeded far, however, because in some respects marks on bullets are similar to fingerprints. There is an infinite number of variations and no obvious way of constructing a probability model. Furthermore, since barrels wear with firing, two bullets from the same barrel are likely to be even more dissimilar than two fingerprint impressions. Several attempts to construct models have been severely criticised, usually on the ground that the model is highly specific to the circumstances of the study. Thus, Biasotti[26] compared a number of bullets fired from various weapons with each other and found that although a number of matching marks could be found, even on bullets fired from different weapons, a pattern of five neighbouring matching marks only occurred in bullets fired from the same weapon. A subsequent experimenter found that if there is a very large number of fine marks it is not unusual to find such patterns from different tools.

For a long time courts have been happy to rely upon the "experience" and "judgment" of firearms examiners. As with fingerprints, this is an essentially unscientific position. One response may be that proposed for fingerprints, namely blind-testing. This will work for cases where witnesses are prepared to "match" or "exclude" but it does not help in the "non-excluded" cases.

Logical analysis would suggest that a statement only that a bullet "could only have been fired" from a particular firearm is appropriate where there is a likelihood ratio of 1, that is to say the evidence is as likely if the bullets came from the same weapon as if they came from different weapons. However, this statement is being made in cases where there is a class match and the individual characteristics have considerable similarity. Evidence is thus being lost.[27] Experts should be willing to suggest that the similarities observed support, strongly support or very strongly support the hypothesis that the two bullets came from the same weapon. Research and thought should be directed to constructing an agreed framework for these conclusions.

[26] Biasotti, AA "A Statistical study of the individual characteristics of fired bullets" (1959) 4 JFS 34. Rowe, WF "Statistics in forensic ballistics", pp 168–177 in Aitken and Stoney (eds) *The Use Of Statistics In Forensic Science* (Ellis Horwood, Chichester, 1991).
[27] For this point we are indebted to Tim Gardner, LLB (Hons), student at Victoria University of Wellington.

8.5 Summary

- All that transfer evidence can help to prove is contact between the perpetrator and the victim or the scene.

- As with all evidence the value of transfer evidence depends crucially on the alternative hypothesis. If the defence admits such contact and explains it, then the value of this type of evidence may be greatly reduced or eliminated altogether. For example, fingerprints at the scene of a burglary can be explained by saying that one was a frequent visitor to the location. Transfer of fibres may be of little value in a rape case where the defence is consent or belief in consent. Glass may be of less value if the accused is a demolition worker.

- Although there are serious problems in assessing the value of some forms of transfer evidence, the adoption of the style of reasoning advocated here has clarified the issues and prompted lines of research which have greatly increased our understanding.

Chapter 9

BLOOD AND DNA EVIDENCE

Chapter 9

BLOOD AND DNA EVIDENCE

Samples of blood and other body tissues are examples of transfer evidence. A sample left at the scene may be used as evidence that the accused was there or a sample on the accused may be used as evidence of contact. Merely finding blood may be of evidential value. Blood at the scene may indicate that there has been a violent struggle rather than that someone has disappeared of their own will. Blood found on the clothing of an accused may, in itself, indicate that he has taken part in a violent crime. If, for example, the victim of a violent assault has run off before police arrive at the scene, then the mere presence of blood on the accused's clothing could be used as evidence hinting that he was involved in the assault. Where it is possible to analyse samples the evidential value of the mere presence of the tissue is often ignored. In fact, studies show that it is unusual for ordinary people to have any analysable quantity of blood on their clothing if they have not recently been involved in violent crime. In a pioneering study in 1978, Briggs found that only 3.2% of people had blood in analysable quantities of groups other than their own on their clothing.[1]

Controversy about blood and body tissue evidence tends to revolve around the analysis of the genetic characteristics. The evidence is potentially susceptible to much more refined analysis than glass or fibres because it is possible to build probability models which are reasonably representative of the genetic characteristic's distribution in the population. Nonetheless, DNA evidence, in particular, has been subjected to vigorous examination and questioning of its "reliability". It is important to discuss these types of evidence to show that the questions that are raised are not questions about DNA or blood-grouping but about *the process of inference.*

---

[1] Briggs, TJ, "The probative value of bloodstains on clothing" (1978) 18 Med Sci & L 79.

Thus, although we deal with some of the technical details in this chapter, it is not intended to turn lawyers into molecular biologists but merely to give a background to the techniques.

DNA (deoxyribonucleic acid), the "building block of life", is the material in which genetic information is stored and by which genetic characteristics are transmitted. It encodes the recipes needed to make the different proteins used in the body's cells. Each of us receives half of the DNA of each parent and it is the enormous number of possible combinations of characteristics which makes us each unique. Even so, practically all human DNA is identical in all human beings. This is not surprising considering that almost everyone is born with two legs, two arms, two eyes and so forth. The remaining genes differ from person to person, except in the case of identical twins.

Large parts of the DNA molecule have no known genetic or coding function. Perhaps, since these zones are not used for coding, they can vary a great deal from individual to individual without causing genetic disorders. Mutations or replication mistakes will cause no difficulties if they occur in such zones and so these areas of DNA have great variation in the population. The variations can be treated as independent of details obtained from eyewitnesses such as height, hair and eye colour.

Current "DNA tests" are tests for these non-coding parts of DNA – the parts of the DNA which do not appear to have any effect. Since the introduction of DNA testing some scientists have come to refer to traditional blood testing as "indirect DNA testing" since such testing identifies antigens[2], each of which is produced by a gene, and therefore is an indirect method of testing for the presence of particular DNA characteristics.

9.1 Blood groups

There are a number of antigens and groups of antigens associated with the blood which can be used for testing. The A, B, and O group is the most familiar and the earliest to be discovered. These define four main blood types, A, B, AB and O. Everyone belongs to one of these groups and most people know which blood group they have. The Rhesus factor, which appears in two forms labelled positive and negative, was identified a little later and is also well known. In combination, these give a total of eight readily identifiable blood types. Identification of these two systems together is sufficient to prevent serious reaction to a blood transfusion and so these factors are frequently given on identity cards or even on motorcyclists' helmets.

As the A, B, O and Rhesus antigens give us only eight blood types, they are shared by large proportions of the population and are by themselves of low discriminatory power. Kind[3] reports that for the general UK population the proportions of the different blood types are: A: 42%, B: 9%, AB: 3% O: 46%. The

---

[2] Proteins found in the blood that stimulate the production of antibodies.
[3] Kind, SS, *The Scientific Investigation of Crime* (Forensic Science Services Ltd, Harrogate, 1987).

proportions are different for different races. For example, Kind reports that 36% of the Asian part of the UK population are group B.[4]

There are a number of other systems of blood-grouping antigens, of which the most common are PGM, MNSs, Duffy, Kidd, Kell, Haptoglobins, Gcs and phosphoglucomutase. Sometimes an antigen is simply either present or absent. In other cases it can appear in a number of discrete forms known as "alleles". Thus, the PGM system can reveal any combination of two of the four alleles termed 1+, 1-, 2+ and 2-. The frequency of each such pair within any population can be estimated by sample surveys.

Each of these alleles (or forms) will be shared by quite large proportions of the population. Alleles which are independent of one another are deliberately chosen for forensic scientific work however, so that the proportions can be multiplied together. Hence, when a number of antigens can be tested, as with the whole fresh samples available in paternity cases, likelihood ratios of several hundred can easily be reached, although each antigen produces only a small number of alleles.

Example

The perpetrator's bloodstain at a scene is tested for PGM[5] with a result of 2+2+ and for Gc(IEF) with a result of 1F1S. This typing matches the accused's blood. What is the likelihood ratio for this evidence for the two hypotheses:

H_1 = the accused left the bloodstain;

H_2 = someone else left the bloodstain?

(We assume we know nothing further about the perpetrator except that he or she was a Caucasian.)

The frequency[6] of PGM 2+2+ in a typical Caucasian population is 0.026 (that is, 2.6% of the population has this blood group).

E_1 = the first test is PGM 2+2+ for both the stain and the accused.

This evidence by itself gives a likelihood ratio of:

$$\frac{P(E_1|H_1)}{P(E_1|H_2)} = \frac{1}{0.026},$$

since they would certainly match if the accused left the bloodstain (H_1). This likelihood ratio is 38.5.

We now add the second piece of evidence. The frequency of Gc 1F1S in a typical Caucasian population is 0.164.

---

[4] Thus, theoretically, a blood-group indication is weak evidence of race, although usually other, more powerful, evidence of race would be available in a case.

[5] (For specialists) specifically, IEF.

[6] Data is derived from tables in Mourant, AE, et al, *The distribution of the Human Blood Groups* (OUP, 1976); Gaensslen, RE, *Sourcebook in Forensic Serology, Immunology, and Biochemistry* (National Institute of Justice, US Dept of Justice, 1983); Woodfield, DG, et al, "Blood groups and other genetic markers in NZ European and Maoris", (1987) 14 Ann Hum Blg 29.

E_2 = the second test is Gc 1F1S for both the stain and the accused.

This evidence by itself gives a likelihood ratio of:

$$\frac{P(E_2|H_1)}{P(E_2|H_2)} = \frac{1}{0.164}.$$

This likelihood ratio is 6.1.

The combined effect of the evidence (we are informed that the two tests are independent) is given by the product of the likelihood ratios: $(38.5)(6.1)$ = 234.8.

''Indirect DNA testing' in the form of blood-grouping, therefore, still has a useful place in forensic work despite the much higher discriminatory power of direct DNA testing. Tests for these systems are relatively cheap and quick, certainly compared with earlier DNA methods, and provide a clear exclusion if the two samples are found to differ. Thus, when a large number of suspects are screened, conventional blood-typing can dramatically reduce the number of samples which have to undergo direct DNA testing. If presented in likelihood ratio terms, the results can also be combined with the results of DNA tests.

9.2 DNA evidence

DNA is of enormous potential value to forensic science for a number of reasons.[7] It satisfies the key requirements of being unique to the individual (except, probably, for identical twins) and unchanging during an individual's life. Provided one has good samples therefore, it would be possible to identify individuals, or determine parenthood to extremely high levels of probability. The determination of paternity is of obvious importance in affiliation cases and the determination of parenthood is important in immigration cases where a right to enter a country may depend upon a relationship with another person. The factor that makes DNA of enormous value in criminal detection is that almost all body cells contains one's complete DNA profile. Exceptions are sperm, eggs and hair shafts. An individual sperm or egg contains only one half of a person's DNA profile, but a large number of sperm or eggs will, in combination, contain the whole profile. While hair roots contain one's whole DNA, hair shafts contain only mitochondrial DNA which is inherited from one's mother.

It is important to realise that the one thing a forensic scientist does not do is peer down a microscope at a person's DNA. If one could do so one would see the famous *Double Helix* discovered by Watson and Crick.[8] This is made up of two intertwined strands of alternating phosphate and sugar units. The strands are linked by paired chemical complexes called *bases*, giving an overall effect rather

---

[7] Farley, MA and Harrington, JJ (ed), *Forensic DNA technology* (Lewis Publishers Inc, Chelsea, Michigan, 1991).

[8] Stentand, GA and Watson, JD (ed), *The double helix; a personal account of the discovery of the structure of DNA* (Weidenfeld & Nicolson, London, 1981).

like a twisted ladder. There are only four kinds of bases, A, T, C and G. These link up in *base-pairs*, which correspond to the steps of the ladder across the molecule. Each chromosome contains millions of base-pairs and it is the particular sequence of these that creates the individual's unique genetic code.

Nor do the testing processes used in forensic science yet give direct access to the sequence of base-pairs. Those in common use at present measure features such as the length of stretches of DNA between particular recognisable sequences of base-pairs. It is increasingly possible to determine the actual sequences of base-pairs and, in due course, it will be possible to identify sections of an individual's entire DNA profile, base-pair by base-pair. When, if ever, these techniques become cost-effective in forensic cases, extremely high likelihood ratios will be obtained.

The nine-step approach to examining DNA samples

Unfortunately, the process of examining DNA samples is currently time-consuming and demanding, taking times which can run into days and weeks. This means that it is expensive. This is one of the factors which dictates that currently it is only available as evidence in serious criminal cases. The steps in the process of examining a sample are outlined here.

Please note carefully that the technology changes extremely rapidly and that in any particular case methods may have been used which differ to some degree.

1   *Take sample*   The first step is to obtain a sample. In a paternity case this will be a large sample of clean, whole, fresh blood taken under controlled conditions. In a criminal case it will be whatever can be found at the scene of the crime in whatever quantity and condition it can be obtained. This is a key difference between criminal and paternity cases which should always be borne in mind. In several DNA cases defence lawyers have produced geneticist witnesses to say that the quality of the sample is so poor that they would not work with it. They have the luxury, which forensic scientists do not have, of being able to request repeat samples.

   The substances most commonly tested will be blood, semen including spermatozoa, skin, saliva or hair follicles. Very small quantities will be sufficient to produce some sort of result, although the greater the sample the clearer the results will generally be. Tests on very small samples may not be able to be replicated but results can be obtained from samples as small as 0.01 ml of blood.

2   *Extraction*   The sample is treated so as to separate the DNA molecules from the other material in the sample and to purify it.

3   *Restriction*   In the older systems the DNA was treated with a *restriction enzyme* or *restriction endonuclease*. This cut the DNA into fragments at points at which a particular sequence of bases is recognised. The huge number of combinations of these bases means that there is enormous variation in the lengths of the DNA fragments between specified sequences. The longer these fragments are, the heavier they will be.

4   *Amplification*   Selected parts of the DNA can be made to replicate themselves. When this is done restriction is not carried out as the amplification process selects the desired parts of the DNA and ignores the remainder. Amplification is carried out by a cycle of heating and cooling in a primer solution which causes a chain reaction. The cycle can be repeated 30 to 35 times to produce 10^6 - 10^7 copies of the target sequence. When this process was first introduced there were concerns about how faithfully replication occurred. This problem is, for practical purposes, solved by the introduction of short tandem repeat (STR)[9] technology. The amplification of very small samples requires even more careful attention to avoiding cross-contamination within laboratories.

5   *Electrophoresis*   The fragments are placed in a gel and an electric current is run through it. The negative electrode is placed at the end of the gel where the DNA has been placed and the positive electrode is placed at the opposite end. This causes the fragments to migrate up the gel towards the positive electrode. Naturally, the lighter fragments move faster and whenever the process is stopped the fragments will be sorted by length. Electrophoresis takes about two days.

    The DNA samples to be compared will be placed in different lanes on the same gel so as to ensure that they are tested under identical conditions. Included amongst the samples will be one from a familiar source such as a member of the laboratory staff, so that the functioning of the process can be checked. With STRs, small quantities of size-markers, that is molecules of accurately known weights, are included with the test samples so that the molecule weights can be compared accurately.

6   *Southern blotting*   The DNA is then transferred from the gel to a nylon membrane by a process known as *Southern blotting*. This is done because the membrane is much easier to work with than the original gel. The product is invisible at this stage.

7   *Application of a probe*   A chemical probe is then applied. This is a piece of DNA of specific make-up which will identify and bind to particular sequences of bases. These probes used to be made radioactive so that their positions could be traced on an autoradiograph. Today, a luminescent chemical is more commonly used.

8   *Autoradiography*   In the past, an autoradiograph (often referred to as an "autorad") was then developed by placing the membrane against an X-ray film and allowing a trace to develop. This took about five days. Today, luminescent chemicals allow the trace to be photographed immediately.

    The trace roughly resembles a supermarket bar code; the number of bands depend on the particular techniques used. The probe can be stripped from the DNA which can then be re-tested with a different probe.

9   *Measurement*   The trace is examined and the positions of the bands in the various lanes are measured accurately. Originally, measurement was done with a ruler but, increasingly, computer devices are available. One involves

[9] See page 165.

using a "mouse" consisting of a magnifying glass with a hair line. This is run over the autorad; whenever the hairline is precisely over a bar the scientist clicks the mouse and a line is recorded in the appropriate lane on the computer screen. The grid on the screen can then be used to compare the positions of bars.

At this point we have the measurements of the positions of the bands for each of the samples tested. The positions of the bands correspond to the molecular weight of the components of the DNA marked by the probes. Some of the bands – those corresponding to the size-markers if they were used – are of exactly known weight. The process is now a matter of comparison of the trace sample with the control sample, the bloodstain with the blood of the accused, for example.

In some cases, the bands will just not match and there is an exclusion. This is overwhelming evidence that the two samples are not of the same blood.

Where the bands seem to correspond in weight, more accurate measurements are needed and we measure the difference in position between corresponding bands. We might then get into the problem raised in chapter 7 of "What is a match?" – how far apart do the bands have to be for us to decide they are not of the same weight? Other complications occur when a band appearing in the control sample is missing, perhaps due to degradation, in the scene sample.

DNA technology

We now give a brief survey of some of the terms used in DNA analysis. Let us emphasise that this field changes very rapidly and techniques become obsolete faster than appeals move through the legal system. Some knowledge of past systems is useful. The list below is roughly in chronological order.

- *Multi-locus probes*   A multi-locus probe is a probe which binds to several different sequences of DNA. The overall result of using a multi-locus probe is rather like a supermarket bar code. There will be a number of bands and a dark blur at the end where the lightest bands congregate. Generally, only bands representing fragments of more than 4,000 bases are compared. Multi-locus probes give very high likelihood ratios but required a large amount of DNA to produce a result.

- *Single-locus probes*   As the name implies these are probes which identify a unique sequence of bases. The result of a single-locus probe will be a pair of bands unless the individual is a homozygote, *i.e.* someone who has inherited the same band from both parents, in which case only one band will be revealed. Single-locus probes are highly sensitive, requiring far smaller quantities of DNA to produce a result than a multi-locus probe. The technique of stripping enables several single-locus probes to be used one after the other. Sometimes, however, only one or two of the four or five probes used might produce results, in which case a relatively low likelihood ratio is yielded.

- *PCR or polymerase chain reaction* This is another term for amplification, explained above. The earliest PCR systems produced results on dot-blot tests, but single- and multi-locus probes could also be used on PCR product, in which case the systems was called AMP-FLP.

- *Dot-blot tests* These are test kits which produce a very rapid result. The test kit has a pattern of windows which either change colour or do not, indicating the presence or absence of certain alleles. The discriminating power of each of these tests is low, but several combined can produce high likelihood ratios.

- *(HLA) DQα* The genetic marker most commonly used in PCR/dot-blot processes examines a specific region of one chromosome containing the DNA for a protein called leucocyte antigen (HLA) DQα.[10] Scientists have identified six different forms of this protein. Every individual has two, determined by each of their pairs of chromosomes – a total of 21 possible pairs. Once this specific region is amplified it is used to seek out control DNA on strips and if the individual has this specific protein then it will be indicated by a blue dye. In the Caucasian population two individuals randomly chosen would have a 93% chance of being discriminated. This moderate power of discrimination means that it is useful for excluding suspects but not for definite inclusions. However, as more parts of the DNA sample are analysed the results can be combined to increase the discrimination. In the United Kingdom, at least, DQα has been overtaken by STRs (see below).

- *Mitochondrial DNA* In addition to DNA in the cell nuclei every mammalian cell has many mitochondria and each mitochondrion has its own copy of a different sort of DNA. This is much smaller than the DNA in the nucleus; it is in the form of a ring and is inherited only from the mother.[11] Potentially, this can be analysed even in minute degraded samples where the yield of DNA from the nucleus is too small for conventional typing.[12] In samples such as these mitichondria may still survive in typable quantities. Analysis of mitochondrial DNA has been successful on single shafts of hair and skeletons up to 3,000 years old. An example of its use was the recent identification of skeletal remains of the Russian Czar and his family.[13] Since mitochondrial DNA is inherited only from the mother it can give no information in paternity analysis.

---

[10] Already used in over 200 cases in the United States and adopted for operational use in limited situations by the Federal Bureau of Investigation in February 1992; (1991) 18 Crim Lab Dig 127. Also used by the Forensic Science Service in the United Kingdom.

[11] Sullivan, KM, *et al*, "The Use of Fluorescence Labelling Technology in the Forensic Analysis of PCR Products" (1991) 18 Crim Lab Dig 164.

[12] Jeffrey, AJ, *et al*, "Principles and Recent Advances in Human DNA Fingerprinting" in Burke, T, *et al*, *DNA Fingerprinting; Applications and Approaches* (Birkhauser Verlag, Basel, Switzerland, 1991), p 15.

[13] Gill, P, *et al*, "Identification of the remains of the Romanov family by DNA analysis" (1994) 6 *Nature Genetics* 130.

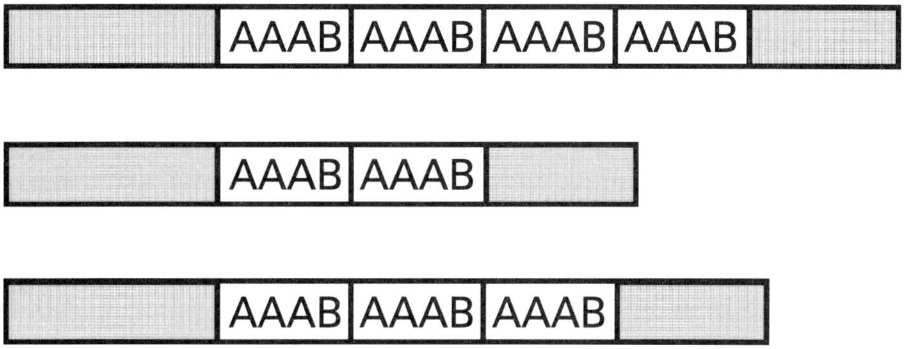

Figure 9.1 *Examples of an imaginary short tandem repeat (STR) section of the DNA molecules for three people. The shaded areas at the front and back are common to all sequences and enable the STR sections to be recognised and amplified using PCR. The central sections repeat the same short sequence of coding (here "AAAB") a few times. Each number of repeats is termed an allele. Since there are so few of these alleles, they can be distinguished easily but many people will share that number of repeats.*

- *STRs* Short tandem repeat (STR) loci are places where three to five base-pairs are repeated several times and the number of repeats may be different for different people. For example, one such locus (HUMCD4 – HUM standing for "human" DNA) has the base sequence [AAAAG] repeating from six to 14 times for different people. Although it does not effect its use as a forensic tool, it happens that this particular locus is part of a gene that codes for surface antigens.

These repeated sequences are accompanied by sequences at the start and end, which are the same in everyone. This enables the STR to be located and amplified. Each particular number of repeats is an allele. The frequencies of the different alleles varies with race. For example, about 28% of Caucasians but only 12% of Blacks have 12 repeats but 0% of Caucasians and 14% of Blacks have 10 repeats. Within the major racial groups, however, there seems to be little or no variation in frequency.

A multiplex system is used, meaning that DNA from several different STR loci (sections of DNA where STRs are found) can be amplified together in one process. In the United Kingdom forensic tests with four loci have been made.[14] These can give likelihood ratios of the order of 10,000. Tests using seven loci are now being introduced giving far higher

---

[14] Gill, P and Evett, I, "Population genetics of short tandem repeat (STR) Loci", *Genetica* (submitted 1994).

ratios. In academic work up to 13 loci have been tested, giving ratios of up to 100 billion.[15]

- *Future systems* In the future, sequencing of DNA may become feasible in forensic practice, at least in important cases. This will give immense likelihood ratios. It will even be possible to determine the ethnicity and visual appearance (hair colour, eye colour, and stature) of the individual responsible for a sample by examining the coding DNA. Testing for sex is already possible.

Interpreting DNA results

Once a result has been obtained it has to be interpreted. The first step is to consider whether any person tested can be *excluded* as the source of the sample. In a criminal case it is assumed that the sample taken from the suspect under controlled conditions will be better than the sample taken from the scene. If any bands are present in the sample from the scene which are not present in the sample from the suspect this will result in exclusion, unless it can be determined that the presence of the band is due to contamination. In a paternity case the DNA of mother, child and alleged father must be compared. Every band in the child's DNA must also appear in either the father or the mother. If a band appears in the child's DNA which appears in neither parent's then the alleged father can be excluded (assuming the mother really is the natural mother of the child).

If the suspect is not excluded the next step is to consider the value of the DNA evidence. This will depend upon the extent to which the DNA profile is capable of discriminating an individual from the general population. We must therefore consider the probability that we might have obtained the particular band weights from the suspect although he was not involved in the crime.

For each of the single-locus probes to be used the proportion of the different bands in the relevant populations must be determined before use as a forensic tool. Once this is done the probability of getting that band if the bloodstain came from a random member of that population can be used to determine a likelihood ratio. The population to be compared with is, as we said before, not necessarily that of the accused, although it may be. Since the probes used will be independent of each other (they may be associated with loci on different chromosomes) the likelihood ratios from different probes can be multiplied together.

STR results can be determined in the same way. For example, we find a bloodstain and test it using the STR method with 4 loci. Consider, first, only one of the loci. We find that the blood in the stain and blood from the accused, who is Caucasian, contains 12 repeats using HUMCD4 (which, as described above, has a frequency of 0.28 for this race). We have other evidence that the perpetrator is Caucasian. The likelihood ratio for this evidence comparing the two hypotheses that H_1, it is the accused's blood and H_2, it is from some other Caucasian, is

---

[15] Hammond, HA, *et al*, "Evaluation of 13 short tandem repeat loci for use in personal identification applications" (1994) 55 Am J Hum Gen 175.

(1)/(0.28) = 3.6. We now examine the other loci, which are known from testing to be independent, and find matches with corresponding likelihood ratios of, say, 6.1, 5.2, and 3.0. Since they are independent they can be multiplied, as explained in chapter 5. This gives an overall likelihood ratio of (3.6)(6.1)(5.2)(3.0) = 342.6, say about 342.

9.3 Was the mark from the perpetrator?

Up to now our presentation has implicitly assumed that a mark or a stain left at the scene of a crime (and not the victim's) actually came from the perpetrator. This, of course, will not always be true. Suppose a murder took place in a football team changing room and a number of bloodstains were found which did not belong to the victim. We might be uncertain whether the perpetrator had left any blood at all. Even in cases where only one stain is found at the scene of a murder there are at least theoretical alternatives, such as that the premises were entered for a second time during the night by another burglar who found the body, left in a hurry and cut himself on the way out.

In most cases the quantity and distribution of marks may make us reasonably confident that they were the perpetrator's, but the alternative hypothesis offered by the defence will also be important. At least theoretically, we must take into account the possibility that the mark was left by someone other than the perpetrator. This means that the likelihood ratio for transfer evidence, such as blood or glass or fibres, will be reduced if only by a small amount. This is because it is now not certain that the evidence would have been obtained if the accused was the perpetrator.

If r is the probability that the mark was left by the perpetrator, the probability that the mark was left by someone else is $(1-r)$. If the accused was the perpetrator and left the mark, the probability of the evidence would be 1. (This is what we have assumed all along.) If the accused was the perpetrator (H_1), but there is only probability r that the blood was left by him, then the probability of the evidence is $(1)(r) = r$ plus the probability of the evidence if someone else, not the perpetrator, left the mark. If there is no evidence as to who that person might be then he must be regarded as a "randomly selected member of the population", the probability of the analysis then being just the frequency of the characteristic, f_1. The numerator of the likelihood ratio, $P(E|H_1)$ is thus $r + f_1(1-r)$.

If someone else was the perpetrator (H_2) and we are regarding that person as a "randomly selected member of the population", then if the perpetrator left the mark the probability of the evidence would be f_1, and if it was not the perpetrator who left the mark the probability of the evidence would be also f_1. The denominator of the likelihood ratio, $P(E|H_2)$ is, therefore, $f_1 r + f_1(1-r) = f_1$.

The likelihood ratio is therefore $P(E|H_1)/P(E|H_2) = (r + f_1(1-r))/f_1$. In many cases r will be very close to 1 and in that case this likelihood ratio is approximately

$1/f_1$. This analysis can be extended to cases involving more than one mark at the scene.[16]

9.4 Case studies

We now look at the most famous DNA case, that of *Castro* which was the first and major test case in the use of this technique. We also examine two DNA cases, *Tran* and *Elliott*, which illustrate the difference in interpretation needed when a sample is found at the scene and one found on the accused.

The *Castro* case

Joseph Castro was accused of the murder of 20-year old Vilma Ponce and her small daughter in her apartment in New York.[17] A small, dried-up bloodstain was noticed on Castro's wristwatch at the time of his arrest which, he said, was his own. The prosecution carried out DNA sequencing of the 0.5 micrograms of DNA recovered from the degraded stain. The prosecution sought to present this evidence to prove that it was Vilma Ponce's blood and not Castro's. The testing was carried out by Lifecodes, a commercial DNA laboratory, which declared that there was a match with the victim's blood and that the frequency of the pattern found in the Hispanic population was about 1 per 100 million. This case aroused great controversy and debate in the scientific literature.

A *Frye* hearing[18] was held to decide whether the DNA evidence could be admitted. The court stated that its decision about admissibility depended upon three questions:

- Was there a theory for the DNA technique, generally accepted by the scientific community, that supported the reliability of its conclusions?

- Were the current techniques capable of reliable (and accepted) results?

- Did the testing laboratory in this particular case perform those accepted techniques in analysing the forensic evidence?

The court answered the first two questions in the affirmative but questioned the third. The judge was happy to accept DNA evidence in principle, but decided that in this particular case the accepted techniques had not been properly carried out by Lifecodes.

During the *Frye* hearing, Lander of MIT argued that the procedures for interpreting results were "so far below reasonable scientific practice in molecular biology as to be appalling".[19] Two experts who had testified for the prosecution later changed their position and declared that the results were "not scientifically reliable enough" to support the conclusion of a match with the victim's blood.

[16] Stoney, DA, "Relaxation of the assumption of relevance and an application to one-trace and two-trace problems" (1994) 34 JFSS 17.
[17] *People* v *Castro* (1989) 545 NY Supp 985 (SC, NY).
[18] See chapter 11. The *Frye* test has been superseded by *Daubert* v *Merrell Dow Pharmaceuticals* 113 S Ct 2786 (1993), also examined in chapter 11.
[19] Lander, E, "DNA fingerprinting on trial" (1989) 339 *Nature* 501.

This controversy has continued in the scientific literature[20] and Lander's position has been attacked by several commentators.[21]

The hypotheses and the evidence

We appear to have three hypotheses about the blood on Castro's watch:

H_1 = "the bloodstain was the victim's, Vilma Ponce" (prosecution hypothesis);
H_2 = "the bloodstain was Castro's" (first defence hypothesis);
H_3 = "the bloodstain was someone else's" (second defence hypothesis).

What is the evidence? E = "the DNA analyst declares a match between the stain on the watch and the victim's blood".

Consider first hypotheses H_1 and H_2. The three questions we must ask are:

● What is the probability of the evidence supposing H_1? $P(E|H_1)$. If the blood was Ponce's then we would hope that the samples would be very similar and $P(E|H_1)$ would approach 1.

● What is the alternative hypothesis, H_2? Castro initially claimed that the blood was his own and so this was the first alternative hypothesis to be considered.

● What is the probability of the evidence supposing H_2? Here, Castro's blood was available for test. The results showed (and there was no dissent to this conclusion) that $P(E|H_2) = 0$ because bands existed that Castro did not share. Thus, the defence's first hypothesis, that it was Castro's blood, was disproved. The likelihood ratio, $P(E|H_1)/P(E|H_2)$, was infinitely large.

We now have an equivalent set of three questions comparing H_1 with H_3.

● (As before) if the blood was the victim's, $P(E|H_1) = 1$.

● The alternative hypothesis, H_3, is that the bloodstain was someone else's (not Castro's and not the victim's). Since we have no other evidence about who this was we must assume it could have been anyone with whom Castro had associated recently.

● What is the probability of the evidence supposing H_3? Here the argument ensued.

Issues in the case

In the case itself three issues were raised.

1 *Quality Control* If the sample from the watch had been contaminated with blood from the victim then the probability of obtaining a match even though the sample on the watch came from someone else would be 1 and the evidence would be worthless. This is the most dangerous form of contamination. A risk of such contamination might be incorporated into the calculation

[20] An excellent technical review article is Roeder, K, "DNA Fingerprinting: A Review of the Controversy" (1994) 9 *Statistical Science* 222.
[21] Wood, GF, "Reasonable doubt (letter)" (1989) 341 *Nature* 100; Roberts, L, "Science in Court: A culture clash" (1992) 257 *Science* 732.

of the strength of the evidence by using an appropriate probability. If contamination was from any other source then it is highly unlikely that it would produce a "false match".

2 *Match criteria* The interpretation of the data was carried out using orthodox statistics which involved defining a criterion for a match.[22] There were two matters of argument: one was whether Lifecodes had adhered to its own matching rule when comparing the sample from the watch and from the deceased; the other was whether the match criteria used for comparing the two samples should have been the same as those used for calculating the probability of a match by chance.

Lifecodes had published a match criterion for comparing two samples. Such criteria are established by conducting many experiments in which several samples from the same person are compared. From the samples from each person a mean and a standard deviation could be calculated. The match criterion was that each band of the scene sample should be within plus or minus three standard deviations of the corresponding band in the suspect sample. This means that in 99.9% of comparisons of two samples from the same person, a match would be declared. However, it was argued by the defence that two of the probes actually differed by 3.06 and by 3.66 standard deviations. Lander comments, "Under the objective matching rule, the bands were non-matches".

When Lifecodes calculated the probability of a match by chance, however, they used a "bin" of plus or minus 2/3 of a standard deviation. From past data they estimate the frequency of bands occurring in each bin. The narrower the bin size, the smaller is the probability of two samples "matching" by chance. If the bin size used for calculating the probability of a match by chance is smaller than that used when comparing two samples, the likelihood ratio will be exaggerated. It is argued that it is wrong to use different bin sizes but this effect is apparent and can be easily corrected.

In chapter 7 we argued that matching ought not to be used. We should be concerned only with the probability of obtaining the actual profile found, supposing the alternative hypotheses. Using matching diverts argument to the issues of "appropriate" match criteria and (as in *Castro*) whether they have been adhered to. It is obvious that the wider the match criteria, the greater the probability of finding a match whether or not the samples come from the same person. The net effect will be that the strength of the evidence increases as the bin widths decrease, but so does the probability of a false exclusion.

3 *Population* To calculate the probability of a match by chance (using the language of the case itself) a database must be consulted. The database must be drawn from the "relevant" population. Since *Castro* concerned a mark found on the accused this population is the group of people with whom Castro had had recent contact since that is where he was most likely to have picked up a bloodstain. Much of the commentary assumes that the relevant

---

[22] Discussed more fully in chapter 6.

population was the Hispanic population. In the circumstances this may have been correct but the reasoning is never explained, with the result that many readers conclude that the relevant population must always be either the accused's or the victim's population.

A factor not mentioned in the discussion of *Castro* is that, assuming that few people have other's blood on their watches, the mere finding of blood on Castro's watch was evidence that should have been combined with the DNA analysis.

Castro was the first and most controversial DNA case. Since then the battle has continued in different courts, but DNA evidence is becoming accepted in the scientific arena as well as in most jurisdictions. The major arguments, as in the OJ Simpson case, are about the calculation of the probabilities of getting the evidence assuming the alternative hypotheses (or, in orthodox statistical terms, the probability of a match by coincidence). As we emphasised earlier, the problem is not the science but the interpretation of the results.

The cases of *Elliott* and *Tran*

Two Australian cases offer interesting examples of the reasoning in some DNA cases. *R* v *Tran*[23] involved analysis of a semen sample at the scene, while *R* v *Elliott*[24] involved analysis of a blood sample found on the accused and alleged to have come from the victim. These samples therefore need to be thought about in different ways, as argued by Buckleton, Evett and Walsh.[25]

Elliott was arrested as a suspect in a stabbing on the basis of other evidence and then found to have blood on his jeans. This blood was analysed and found to match the victim's so far as conventional grouping tests were concerned. One single-locus DNA probe produced a result which was said to give odds against a match by coincidence of 210 to 1.[26] This depended upon two assumptions, first that the population profile of Australian Caucasians is similar to that of North American Caucasians and, secondly, that Caucasians were the appropriate population.

Tran was accused of rape and murder. There was eyewitness evidence that the perpetrator was of Vietnamese appearance and Tran was picked out on an identity parade. A semen sample taken from the victim was analysed and a result obtained from one single-locus probe. There was some dispute between expert witnesses about whether this produced a sufficiently clear result. It was also disputed that comparison with the standard database from Caucasians, Afro-Caribbeans, and Asians was appropriate.

In both the *Elliot* and *Tran* cases the numerator of the likelihood ratio should be the probability of obtaining the test result given that the sample came from the accused or victim as the case may be. In each case it appears that some criterion was adopted for "declaring a match" and the numerator then assumed to be 1.

---

[23] *R* v *Tran* (1990) 50 A Crim R 233

[24] *R* v *Elliott*, unreported 70154/89, Supreme Court, NSW.

[25] Buckleton, JS, Walsh, KAJ and Evett, I, "Who is 'random man'?" (1991) 31 JFSS 463.

[26] The analysis was carried out using orthodox statistical methods and the scientist quoted a lower confidence bound for these odds, at 70%, to be 176.

An alternative procedure for assessing the numerator in the case of single-locus probes is offered by Evett, Scranage and Pinchin.[27]

In *Tran* the appropriate denominator is the probability that the test result would be obtained if it were not the accused who had raped the victim, bearing in mind other evidence tending to identify the perpetrator – *i.e.* the probability that the result would be obtained if it were another Vietnamese who was the perpetrator.

In *Elliott* the denominator is the probability that the accused would have blood producing this result on his clothing, although he had not stabbed the victim. As the judge pointed out, the odds against a match by coincidence were affected by the race of individuals with whom the accused might have been in contact. Using our terms, the appropriate alternative hypothesis was the probability of obtaining the result if the blood was from some other person with whom the accused had been in contact. This required investigation of the places the accused had been drinking in that day and whether or not they were frequented by Aboriginals.

If, as an example, 3% of people of Elliott's lifestyle have bloodstains on them and the probability of getting the DNA result from a random member of the contact population is 10%, then $P(E|H_2) = (0.03)(0.10) = 0.003$. Assuming the numerator, $P(E|H_1) = 1$, this would give a likelihood ratio of $1/(0.003) = 333$. If the alternative hypothesis had been that Elliott had merely rendered first aid, thus getting blood on him, the DNA evidence would have had a likelihood ratio of 1.

Further information is needed in order to assess the probability that Elliott would have blood on his clothing. Neither this probability nor the number of different bloodstains on his clothing is referred to in the judgment. The quoted odds against a match by coincidence would be increased by consideration of the probability that Elliott would have blood on his clothing and decreased if any other bloodstains were present. The greatest flaw in the argument is that there is no reference to a sample of Elliott's own blood being analysed.

9.5 Summary

- The mere presence of blood or body tissue can be of evidential value.
- Techniques for both conventional blood analysis and direct DNA analysis develop so rapidly that printed information on them is invariably out of date. In future, we expect techniques such as direct sequencing which will give extremely high likelihood ratios.

[27] Evett, I, Scranage, JK and Pinchin, R, "An Efficient Statistical procedure for Interpreting DNA Single-Locus Profiling Data in Crime Cases" (1992) 32 JFSS 307.

- Using such future methods it may even be possible to predict a perpetrator's physical description from the analysis of a sample left at the scene. It is already possible to determine sex in this way.

- The controversial issues raised in DNA cases such as *Castro* are not matters to do with DNA itself but with inference and reasoning.

Chapter 10

OTHER SCIENTIFIC EVIDENCE

Chapter 10

OTHER SCIENTIFIC EVIDENCE

Transfer evidence helps to prove that someone was in a particular place at a particular time. Other kinds of scientific evidence may be used to try to prove other issues, such as that someone wrote a cheque or made a copy. Psychiatric evidence may possibly offer explanations why someone did something when that is important for determining a case. In this chapter we consider a few examples of such evidence, not in order to discuss their techniques in detail, but in order to consider how they fit into the scheme of logical reasoning.

10.1 Behavioural and psychological evidence

Expert psychological evidence may be given in order to show that an accused is not fit to plead, or that an accused is insane and therefore entitled to be acquitted, or that an accused or a victim suffered from some syndrome. Where it is desired to show that the accused suffered from some syndrome this may be in order to advance a defence of duress, provocation or self-defence. A victim's syndrome may be evidence that the victim has suffered some particular form of abuse or assault.

Psychological and psychiatric evidence raise several problems relating to the ultimate issue rule, to hearsay and to the value of such evidence in proving a case.

Insanity and the ultimate issue rule

Insanity was defined at common law in *McNaughten*[1] and has since been defined by statute in a number of jurisdictions.[2] The common thread is a requirement that

[1] *McNaughten's Case* (1843) 10 Cl & F 200, 8 ER 718.
[2] For example, s 23 of the Crimes Act 1961 (New Zealand), s 16 of the Criminal Code (Canada).

the accused is suffering from "a disease of the mind". It is important to note that this is a disease of the *mind* and not of the *brain*.

At a philosophical level there is little agreement as to what constitutes the mind. Many psychologists and psychiatrists would not use the term, nor would they admit of a distinction between sanity and insanity. In fact these are all legal terms, not psychological. Furthermore, the inquiry at trial is not as to the accused's condition but as to whether, *at the time of the act alleged to constitute an offence*, he was labouring under insanity.

For these reasons witnesses should not be allowed to express an opinion about the sanity or otherwise of a defendant. Two classic contrasting English cases illustrate the problem.

In *Rv Charlson*[3], an otherwise loving father suddenly struck his son severely over the head with a hammer and threw him from a window. An expert testified that a brain tumour was a possible explanation for these actions and that, apart from the possible brain tumour, the accused was sane. Barry J directed the jury that, because of this, insanity was not an option and that if they believed that the accused had acted as he did because of the brain tumour they should acquit him. This direction has been severely criticised. The judge handed over responsibility for defining "sane" to the witness. Current caselaw on the application of the McNaughten Rules would clearly categorise the defendant's putative tumour as a "disease of the mind".

In *Rv Kemp*, on the other hand, Devlin J insisted that it was the task of the judge to decide what was a disease of the mind. "In my judgment the condition of the brain is irrelevant and so is the question of whether the condition of the mind is curable or incurable, transitory or permanent."[4] In that case doctors testified that the accused suffered from arterio-sclerosis and that this would have caused blockages of the arteries which, in turn, would have caused shortages of oxygen to the brain and blackouts. Devlin J decided that this was a "disease of the mind" since it affected the workings of the mind. This is regarded as the classical statement of the law.

This is not the place to discuss the very considerable conceptual problems that the law of insanity and automatism has got itself into. Such a discussion belongs in a work on the substantive criminal law. What is relevant to a book on scientific evidence is to set out the roles of the various players in the trial of an issue of insanity, both under the common law and under statutory provisions such as Federal Rule of Evidence 704(b).

The witness may have one or both of two roles:

(i)   to testify as to the observed signs and the reported symptoms and give a medical diagnosis;
(ii)   to explain the diagnosis and the physiological and psychiatric effects that the condition might have.

---

[3] [1955] 1 WLR 317, [1955] 1 All ER 859.
[4] [1957] 1 QB 399, [1956] 3 All ER 249.

The judge decides whether the condition referred to by the witness amounts to a "disease of the mind" and directs the jury accordingly. If the judge directs the jury that the condition does amount to a disease of the mind then:

The jury decides whether, at the time concerned, the accused was suffering from this disease of the mind and hence insane.

From this scheme it is easy to see that the expert who purports to give an opinion on an accused's sanity is not merely offending against the ultimate issue rule but also giving evidence on a matter on which he is not expert, namely whether a medical condition falls within the legal category of "disease of the mind".

The probative value of psychological evidence

Psychiatry and psychology have been vigorously attacked by lawyers, scientists and philosophers of science.[5] Whereas other forms of scientific evidence are based upon some consensual principles such as Newton's Laws of Motion or the rules of genetic inheritance, in psychology principles as fundamental as these are hotly disputed between various schools of thought.

Other problems are identified, such as the relative ease with which such witnesses can conceal beliefs about policy matters (*e.g.* whether persons not dangerous to others should be incarcerated) in their "expert testimony" and the potentially distorting effects of the patient–client relationship. Our concern is with our ability to infer what we want to infer from the evidence given by such witnesses.

In most forensic sciences it is possible to carry out controlled experiments. Thus, repeat samples from the same individual can be tested for DNA and experiments can be conducted to show that a person breaking a window is liable to collect glass fragments on his clothing. No such controlled experiments can be conducted in psychological matters. For obvious reasons we cannot abuse children and then examine their behaviour. We can never know for certain, therefore, that a child has been abused, and, just as importantly for evaluating evidence, we cannot know for certain that another child has not been abused.

Some controlled experiments have been conducted to assess the value of particular devices such as "anatomically correct dolls". In these experiments the way children alleging abuse react to the dolls is compared with the way a number of children believed not to have been abused react to them. There are still a number of difficulties in making use of the information from these experiments, however:

- There are still fundamental differences of opinion as to whether children should be simply observed playing with these dolls or whether they should only be used as an aid to precision of communication once a child has made allegations in an interview.

[5] *E.g.* Burger, WE, "Psychiatrists, Lawyers and the Courts" (1964) 28 Fed Prob 1; Ziskin, J, *Coping with Psychiatric and Psychological Testimony* (Law and Psychology Press, 1981); Ennis, BJ and Litwack, TR, "Psychiatry and the Presumption of Expertise" (1974) 62 Cal LR 693.

- These experiments are conducted under carefully controlled conditions by experienced and knowledgeable psychiatrists, but the interviews in a particular case may not be. It is relatively easy to replicate the conditions under which a DNA sample should be tested, in particular a change of tester should not affect the result. In psychological testing the same cannot be said; merely changing the interviewer can completely change the outcome of an interview.

- Interpretation of the tests is bedevilled by the use of significance testing and the search for tests which will act as "definitive markers of abuse". In this way useful information may be lost. In one test, for example, "44 per cent of the non-abused children and 30 per cent of the abused children spontaneously talked about and touched the dolls' genitals. Sixty-two per cent non-abused and 50 per cent abused children placed the dolls in clear sexual positions".[6] This test would appear to indicate that sexual play with the dolls produces a low likelihood ratio of about 1.4 in favour of the proposition that the child has not been abused (or, to put it another way, inhibition in playing with the dolls is evidence that the child has been abused). This is a low likelihood ratio and reveals that the test is of little use, but the authors of that test conclude that "there is no significant difference between abused and non-abused children", *i.e.* that the test is of no use at all.

- The alternative hypothesis apparently being tested is that the child is a non-abused child from the general population. However, many allegations of abuse arise from dysfunctional families involved in separation and custody disputes. The alternative hypothesis in such cases ought to be that the child is a non-abused child in such stressful circumstances.

Much psychological evidence is given in the form of "syndromes". These are collections of signs and symptoms which are frequently found together. The main purpose of the identification and publication of such syndromes is to assist in treating patients. A number of problems have arisen from the use of syndromes as evidence.

The first is that a syndrome is a statement that if someone is suffering from a particular condition or outside influence certain signs are highly likely to be found. For example, children who have been abused may be very likely to be evasive when questioned about their home life; this is to say that the probability of the sign is high supposing that the child has been abused. Unfortunately, certain formulations intended to be of help therapeutically were, at one stage, misused as diagnostic tools.[7] If the sign is to be used as evidence that abuse has occurred then

---

[6] Wakefield, H and Underwager, R, *Accusations of Child Sexual Abuse* (Charles C Thomas, 1988), pp 20–208.

[7] Levy, "Using 'Scientific' Testimony to Prove Child Sexual Abuse" (1989) XXIII FLQ 383; Hall, "The Role of Psychologists as Experts in Cases Involving Allegations of Child Sexual Abuse", *loc cit*, p 451.

we may be transposing the conditional unless, at the same time, we consider how likely the sign is under some alternative hypothesis. This form of transposition of the conditional seems to be common amongst less well-trained psychologists.

Secondly, the claim made for a particular sign which is part of a syndrome is that, for example, children *alleging* abuse are frequently evasive about their home life. Since we cannot conduct controlled experiments we cannot strictly say that abused children display this sign. Indeed, our judgment that a child has been abused depends often on a cluster of signs, each of which is the product of this kind of reasoning. The question is: can we infer that a child has been abused from the fact that he claims to have been abused and displays signs that other children who claim to have been abused display?

In the case of DNA or blood evidence there is a remote possibility that the DNA profiles of Paul McCartney or Prince Charles could be discovered and a search mounted for women with children whose DNA profiles were consistent with paternity by that man. There is a very much greater danger that a child might be coached to display the well-publicised signs associated with child abuse in a case, for example, of a mother fighting a custody battle. The probability of obtaining such evidence, given that the child has not been abused, must be increased by the widespread knowledge of such syndromes.

Thirdly, there is little data on the "base rates" for some of the observed phenomena. So far as child sexual abuse is concerned this is true even of physiological phenomena such as anal dilatation. This means that the denominator of the likelihood ratio cannot be calculated, even supposing that an appropriate alternative hypothesis can be agreed upon.

The assessment of the value of the expert's evidence is made more difficult by the fact that there is controversy as to whether there is a single "abused child syndrome", "rape trauma syndrome" or "battered women's syndrome", and as to whether these syndromes are sharply differentiated from other forms of post-traumatic stress disorder. Different people react differently to events and part of the expert's role is to help the court to interpret *this* person's behaviour.

Thus, we are trying to infer from present behaviour of the person to the proposition that he has, in the past, been subjected to abuse, or whatever. The background knowledge required to assess the likelihood ratio appears to be that *some* people behave in this way after being abused. The expert should then tell us the grounds on which he believes that *this* person is one of that class. This gives rise to two problems: first, only some people will react in this way to abuse; and, secondly, some other people may display this sign for some other reason. This brings up the question of the appropriate alternative hypothesis. Many psychologists, having been brought up on classical statistics, will discuss the probability of the signs occurring by chance, or in the general population. As mentioned above, this is not appropriate. Allegations of child abuse are likely to come from families which are dysfunctional; in fact, they frequently accompany family break-ups and custody disputes. The correct alternative hypothesis in such cases would be that the child was a non-abused child from a severely stressful family background. Research is required to assess such probabilities.

The second problem which has arisen from the use of syndromes as evidence is that the expert is observing and classifying the child now and the observations include the behaviour in question. These observations may be made against a background of belief already formed by the expert that the child has been abused. That this is a problem is shown by cases in which denials by children that they have been abused have been taken to mean that they have not yet come to terms with what has happened to them.[8] In other words, *any* form of behaviour is capable of being interpreted as a reaction to abuse. We must be careful, therefore, always to consider such evidence in likelihood ratio terms, which brings us back to the difficulty in determining the probabilities of the evidence under the hypotheses when we cannot conduct appropriately controlled experiments.

Psychological "syndromes" can be of greater value in court where diagnosis is not in issue. Thus a "battered women's syndrome" is increasingly recognised: apparently, it is characteristic of a woman terrorised by a man that she does not leave him. There are a variety of influences which explain this, of which the chief is probably economic. This question may arise when a woman is charged with assaulting or even killing a man. One item of evidence will be that the woman has lived with the man for a long period while apparently the victim of violence. One might have thought that the probability of this was low and that therefore the fact of the continued relationship was evidence against the proposition of violence. By testifying that such prolongation of the relationship is common amongst "battered women" a psychologist can make a jury realise that what it may have thought a valuable piece of evidence is actually almost meaningless.

In this case the jury is trying to assess a likelihood ratio for the evidence that the woman did not leave the man during a long period when he was supposed to be assaulting and terrorising her. They may believe that the probability of this is low. The psychologist is simply testifying that the probability of this is high. The witness is stating $P(E|H_2)$, where H_2 is the defence hypothesis that the woman was acting in self-defence or under provocation. This is a matter well within the witness's expertise and, in particular, does not purport to be a judgment that the woman was being terrorised. That question is for the jury to determine. This is a legitimate and proper use of "syndrome evidence". Use of syndrome evidence for diagnosis, however, raises the logical and inferential problems discussed above. It is increasingly evident that lawyers and judges are conscious of these problems but, not having been trained in the method advocated in this book, are unable to see the way forward. Further research is required to make such evidence useful, but neither the psychological professions (which tend to concentrate on classical statistical methods) nor the legal profession (which tends to think in terms of acceptance or rejection of the expert's opinion) seem to be moving in the right direction.

[8] See, *e.g. The Dominion Sunday Times* (Wellington, NZ) 26 March 1989, p 1.

10.2 Handwriting and document examination

Document examination attempts to provide answers to a number of questions such as:

- is the handwriting/signature on a document that of the purported author?;
- is the handwriting of an incriminatory document that of the accused?;
- on which typewriter, photocopier or printer was a document produced?;
- is the paper and ink type that which would be expected if the document is what it purports to be?

These questions fall conveniently into two groups: those concerned with handwriting and those concerned with the production of the document.

Handwriting

Nearly everyone is taught to write by a teacher or parent. In this way certain characteristics are transmitted through generations and become associated with particular cultures. It is well known, for example, that German handwriting is almost illegible to English-speaking people. In addition, each person starts to write in a slightly different way, owing to factors such as varying degrees of co-ordination, and subsequent changes in style may well occur. It is not unusual for teenagers to make deliberate alterations to their writing styles.

By adulthood most people have adopted a writing style which will remain more or less consistent for the remainder of their lives. Like other matters examined in forensic science this handwriting will exhibit class and individual characteristics. Given sufficiently extensive pieces of handwriting written "in the normal course of business" sufficient individuality may be displayed for an expert to form a judgment that two documents were written by the same person.

Handwriting analysis has so far defied detailed statistical examination.[9] Two main factors can be examined: pictorial impression and letter construction.

Pictorial impression includes matters such as slope, size, margins, spacing and position of writing in relation to lines. These factors are liable to considerable variation by the individual according to circumstances; indeed, if two signatures completely superimpose upon one another this would lead to suspicion that one was a tracing of the other. Pictorial impression is also easy to copy and easy to alter deliberately.

Letter construction includes the direction in which an "o" is formed and a "t" is crossed and the way in which letters which require more than one movement have

---

[9] Evett, I "Interpretation: a Personal Odyssey", pp 9–22, in Aitken, CGG and Stoney, DA (eds) *The Use of Statistics in Forensic Science* (Ellis Horwood, Chichester, 1991).

been written. Certain aspects of letter construction are believed to be consistent to the individual. For example, only about 10% of right handers and only about 30% of left handers will write an "o" clockwise, the majority of the population form an "o" anti-clockwise. Letter formation can be detected by microscopic examination of striations within the lines caused by flaws in the writing instrument and by the pressure variations in the lines. These factors cannot be detected in photocopies. This means that handwriting examiners are reluctant to consider photocopies of handwriting; it also means that a forger copying from a photocopy will be unable to reproduce the correct letter formation.

In fact, forgers almost invariably concentrate on the pictorial impression and omit to examine or copy details of letter construction. An apparently convincing document can therefore be revealed by examination of letter formation to be by someone other than the purported author. Likewise, people trying to disguise their handwriting will change the pictorial impression but, frequently, will not change the letter formation. Deliberate efforts to alter letter formation require great concentration and effort, and are difficult to sustain over more than a few lines.

In some jurisdictions handwriting examiners have adopted a policy of testifying only when they are prepared to say that two samples of handwriting are by the same author.[10] In other jurisdictions, experts will testify when they believe that it is "probable" that two samples of handwriting are by the same author. (Naturally, we would wish them to say that "the similarities in the two samples strongly support a contention of common origin".) What enables such assessments to be made?

There are certain characteristics which are obviously susceptible of statistical analysis. Examples have been given above of surveys of the formation of various letters, but even these surveys rely on a subjective division of letter formation categories and subjective judgments as to which category marginal cases belong. In general, however, handwriting examiners do not refer to such surveys when giving evidence and such characteristics are only part of what they rely upon in forming their views.

Handwriting examination provides another example of deference to the expert's "judgment" and "experience".[11] As in other areas this is essentially unscientific. Like fingerprints, however, handwriting is capable of infinite variation. Identified letter-types and styles depend upon the examiner's willingness and ability to distinguish, rather than upon anything intrinsic to the handwriting. Research should aim to provide some scientific basis for evaluations of identity but, in the meantime, blind-testing is probably the most fruitful way to satisfy ourselves of the standards of handwriting examiners.

Handwriting provides an interesting example of whether or not a study is a "science". There is empirical evidence to support the claims made by forensic

[10] *E.g.* New Zealand – personal communication, NZ Police Questioned Document Section.
[11] Phillips, JH and Bowen, JK, *Forensic science and the expert witness* (The Law Book Co Ltd, Victoria, 1989), pp 70–72.

handwriting examiners that handwriting exhibits characteristics which are individual and consistent. Handwriting is also used, however, to assess character. This
so-called "handwriting analysis" or "graphology" has no such scientific basis.
Different graphology texts will claim different meanings for the same characteristics and no satisfactory scientific testing has been carried out. In particular,
graphologists prefer to work from "free composition", and it is suspected that the
text influences their character assessments. Furthermore, graphology suffers
from all the problems inherent to any form of psychological assessment in that
the predictions it makes are not capable of scientific assessment and refutation.
So far as we know graphological evidence of character has never been accepted in
court.[12]

Document production

The second aspect of questioned document examination refers to everything
involved in the production of a document, from the composition of the paper
and ink to the marks left by any machine which has been used to add text or
illustration or to produce copies of the document. Again, the questions may be
whether a document is genuine or whether it has produced by a particular
machine. If, for example, a particular photocopier or laser printer can be
identified as that which produced a document it may help greatly in identifying
the person who copied the document.

In the past, typewriter identification was a well-known aspect of document
examination. No two typewriters would produce identical type, especially once
they had been in use for a period of time. Examination of characteristics such as
font design and size would reveal what kind of typewriter had been used, and
microscopic comparison of flaws in letters or the effects of use and cleaning could
enable the examiner to say, for example, that one typewriter had been used to
produce two documents.

Today, computer printers and photocopiers are more likely to be the source of
a document. These machines have detectable features which indicate the make
and type of machine, and also suffer from minute flaws which leave distinctive
marks on documents they produce. In the case of the photocopier these may be
caused by minute scratches on the glass plate or flecks of dirt. These will cause
marks, including marks of microscopic size, to appear on any piece of paper put
through the machine. Between the time a questioned document is supposed to
have been produced and a test document is put through the machine some of
these marks may have been removed if, for example, the glass plate has been
polished, and new ones may have been created. The examiner, therefore, has to
assess which of the marks on the paper are permanent marks from flaws in the
glass and which might have changed owing to maintenance and use of the
machine.

Yet again, the potential for variation is infinite and there is no easy answer to
the question of how many similarities, and how few dissimilarities, are enough for
a judgment that a particular document was produced on a particular machine.

Again, there is no reason in principle why witnesses should not give evidence when they are less than sure that two documents came from the same machine. That evidence should be in the form of a statement such as "the similarities strongly support the contention that this document came from this machine" rather than that the documents "probably came from the same machine".

10.3 Stylometry

Stylometry studies the style with which people use language.

In both classical and modern literature interpolations can cause considerable problems. There are well-known examples of large-scale suspected interpolations in the published versions of Shakespeare's plays. In the case of classical and biblical literature there is controversy as to whether certain "authors", such as Homer or Isaiah, were one person or several.

Those interested in these questions have always examined the style of writing, but in a subjective and judgmental style. Statisticians have been interested in the problem and the possibility of using objective measurements and statistics to tackle it.[12] More recently, some workers suggested using "cusum" or the "cumulative sum" technique.[13] This is a reasonably well-known statistical method for displaying small changes in level in sequences of data. Instead of graphing the actual measurements in sequence, the successive measurements are added together and this accumulated sum is graphed instead. This causes a change in level to become a change in slope which is usually much easier to see. For example, suppose a sequence of quality measurements is taken in a factory. These fluctuate unpredictably from day to day about an average level. One day a change occurs to the process which makes the quality level slightly worse. If the change is small it may take several days or weeks before it is noticeable on an ordinary graph. For example the (artificial) series of data in *Figure 10.1* has a change in level at the fifth point but this is nearly hidden by random fluctuations in the data values. A cusum chart of the same data indicates a slope change at that point, which would probably be noticed much earlier.

Taking merely the cumulative sum of the data would produce a graph which rose constantly with variations in the slope. The slope changes can be made more obvious by subtracting a constant value from each of the observations before calculating the cumulative sum. If this constant is chosen to be near the average value of the observations, the cusum graph will slope up and down as the level changes, making these changes even easier to see. In *Figure 10.1* the number 3 has been subtracted from each data value before graphing the cusum line.

---

[12] Yule, GU, "On sentence length as a statistical characteristic of style in prose" (1939) 30 *Biometrika* 363; Totty, RN, Hardcastle, RA and Pearson, J, "Forensic linguistics: the determination of authorship from habits of style" (1987) 27 JFSS 13.

[13] Morton, A, *Literary Detection: How to prove authorship and fraud in literature and documents* (Bowker, 1978); Morton, A and Farringdon, M, "Identifying Utterance" (1992) 1 Exp Ev 84– 91; Morton, A, *Proper Words in Proper Places* (Department of Computing Science, University of Glasgow).

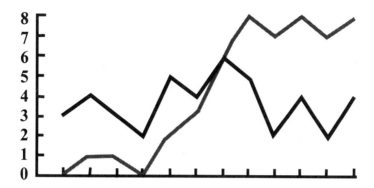

Figure 10.1 *A Cusum Graph. A set of data (the black line consisting of the values 3, 4, 3, 2, 5, 4, 6, 5, 2, 4, 2, 4) plotted in series. The corresponding cusum graph (grey line) is calculated by subtracting 3 from each value and then cumulatively adding the data. It shows the small change in average level of the data in the middle section as an obvious change in slope.*

In the context of stylometric analysis the sequential observations are the quantitative measures in each of the sentences. These measures could be of the number of words, or nouns or small words or particles, or indeed of any characteristic which appears to yield useful results, in a sentence. A cusum graph would show how the averages vary along the length of the document. If a block of sentences of very different writing characteristics is interpolated the corresponding section of the cusum chart will show a significantly different slope. When we revert to "genuine" text an ordinary graph will revert to a line in the same position that it would be if there were no interpolation. A cusum chart, on the other hand, will usually show that line continuing in a different position, higher or lower, making the differences even more obvious.

One should therefore distinguish between "stylometry", which is the measurement of style, and "cusum", which is a technique used, amongst other things, for stylometry. However, as it was stylometry which introduced cusum analysis to court, lawyers frequently refer to "cusum" analysis when they mean "stylometry". It would be unfortunate if doubts expressed about stylometric evidence were reflected onto the use of cusum analysis in other areas. Whether or not cusum is a valid and useful technique depends, as with all measuring devices, on what is being measured.

One of the leading exponents of stylometry is Morton. In *Literary Detection*[14], Morton suggests that the use of stylometry is not limited to classical and literary studies. He proposes that the technique should be used to authenticate utterances attributed to an accused. In particular, he discusses his study of confessions

[14] Morton, A, *Literary Detection: How to prove authorship and fraud in literature and documents* (Bowker, 1978).

in the defence of one Steve Raymond.[15] This case was a trial at first instance at the Central Criminal Court in England. Morton was called by the defence, without warning to the prosecution. Prosecuting counsel was given only 10 minutes in which to read Morton's opinion and consider the matter. Morton himself notes that "this would only be fair to a counsel who was highly numerate".[16] Even this comment misses the point. The most numerate counsel would not necessarily have any idea whether there was a scientific basis to what was being presented. This was an acute example of the difficulties caused by the fact that the defence did not have to give notice of expert evidence. This case should not be thought of as any sort of precedent, as validity and admissibility do not appear to have been argued at all. Not surprisingly, however, the fact that the evidence was admitted in this case has been used as an example of the use of stylometry being "accepted in court".[17]

Morton's evidence was again advanced at a very late stage in *R v St Germain*.[18] This case is not reported on this point, although it is well known in administrative law. The stylometric evidence was proffered in the Court of Appeal, where Scarman LJ referred to "the absence of a broad enough basis for this stylometric research" and said that Dr Morton "had been unable to advance his conclusions beyond that of hypothesis". The court would not allow the evidence to be adduced as fresh evidence and commented that even if it was heard it "would afford no ground for allowing the appeal or ordering a new trial".

In Australia Morton's evidence was also rejected in *R v Tilley*.[19] In that case Beach J, like the English Court of Appeal in *St Germain*, was prepared to regard stylometry in general as scientific, but he was not prepared to accept the contention that a person's oral utterances would be stylometrically consistent with his written work. Indeed, he regarded such an idea as "contrary to human experience"[20]and, therefore, requiring evidence, which was not forthcoming.

In that case Morton compared the recorded questions which the police officer had asked Tilley with Tilley's answers and with an essay written by Tilley at his request. He examined the incidence of four characteristics and found that the questions and answers were similar in these respects to each other and different from the essay, implying that the police officer had been the author of the answers as well as the questions. In the course of questioning this evidence, the prosecution referred to letters apparently written by the accused and which shared the characteristics of the answers. Beach J noted that a number of conclusions could be drawn from this, but regarded it as a matter going to the weight of the evidence rather than to admissibility. A question that does not seem

[15] See *Literary Detection, loc cit*, p 204 *et seq*. No ruling relating to the admissibility of the stylometric evidence appears to have been recorded .

[16] *Ibid*, p 204.

[17] For example in *St Germain*, although, there, the limitations expressed in Niblett, B and Boreham, J, "Cluster analysis in court" [1976] Crim LR 175 were noted. In *Raymond* statements made to police, some acknowledged as authentic and others questioned, were being examined.

[18] Unreported, 9 May 1977, Court of Appeal, Roskill, Scarman and Croom-Johnson JJ, 5150/B/75.

[19] [1985] VR 505.

[20] *Ibid*, 509.

to have been considered was why those four characteristics had been chosen and whether any others had been examined and, if so, with what results.

Such evidence was also rejected in the US *cause célèbre*, the case of *Patty Hearst*.[21] Hearst, the daughter of a newspaper magnate, was kidnapped and was accused subsequently of becoming converted to her kidnappers' "cause" and working with them. She alleged that she had been forced to make various statements which she had not composed personally. This evidence was rejected on the ground that "psycholinguistics" failed the *Frye* test of acceptance in the relevant scientific community.

Despite these rejections, stylometric evidence was admitted in the two recent English cases *McCrossen*[22] and *Mitchell*.[23] In *McCrossen* there are two curiosities about the judgment which may reflect the course of argument. Taylor LJ (as he then was) referred to the "acceptance" of stylometry in Australia. His Lordship did not cite cases. If this reference included *Tilley* it is unfortunate that the court does not seem to have been informed that the evidence in *Tilley* was actually rejected because it attempted to compare written and oral utterances – as did the evidence in *McCrossen*. The second curiosity was the absence of any reference to *St Germain*. Taylor LJ refers to three trials at first instance at which Morton had been accepted as an expert witness, but does not appear to have been informed about the Court of Appeal case in which his evidence had been rejected.

In *McCrossen* there was no substantial challenge to the stylometric evidence and it was admitted, despite the concerns which the court expressed as to its truly scientific nature. In *Mitchell* the Crown produced evidence from Professor D Canter. Professor Canter had been unable to obtain original data from either Morton or Dr Farringdon (who gave evidence in *Mitchell*). He therefore had to conduct his own tests which he analysed using classical statistical techniques. These indicated that the tester had been no more successful in identifying single and multiple authored texts than might have been expected by chance.[24] Professor Canter's published data was re-analysed by the present authors using Bayesian techniques. This analysis confirmed that the tests were, indeed, valueless as evidence of either single or multiple authorship; in fact, some of the evidence pointed the wrong way.[25]

The Court of Appeal appeared inclined to admit the evidence in *McCrossen* and *Mitchell* because the jury might think it capable of raising a reasonable doubt. It is submitted that this is not a coherent or proper position. First, it leaves to the jury, or the judge at first instance, the task of deciding whether the evidence ought to be given any credence at all. In other words, the court ducked the issue of judicial regulation of admissibility. The question whether the evidence should be regarded as having any relevance or probative value at all is one for the judges and for

---

[21] *US* v *Hearst* 412 F Sup 893 (1976).

[22] *The Queen* v *McCrossen*, unreported, 10 July 1991, CA (Crim Div) 90/1256/Y2.

[23] *R* v *Mitchell*, unreported, 26 March 1993, CA (Crim Div) 82/2419/E2.

[24] Canter, D, "An Evaluation of the 'Cusum' Stylistic Analysis of Confessions" (1992) 1 Exp Ev 93–99.

[25] Robertson, BWN and Vignaux, GA, "Correspondence: 'Forensic Stylometry' " (1993) 2 Exp Ev 47.

the Court of Appeal, not for the jury. Secondly, it is incoherent to suggest that the evidence might be admissible because it is being adduced by the defence to raise a reasonable doubt. If evidence is rationally capable of affecting the decision it must be relevant and admissible unless excluded by some rule of evidence. If the evidence is not relevant it cannot be rationally capable of affecting the decision, which means that it cannot raise a reasonable doubt.

In *Mitchell* the court adjourned the hearing so that the experts could meet to resolve their differences. Unfortunately, no such resolution took place. The Court of Appeal was disinclined to investigate the reasons for this and simply passed the job of determining the scientific validity of the technique to the trial judge. This, again, seems to avoid responsibility. One of the major problems in assessing the value of stylometric evidence is the failure of its proponents to provide data to support their assertions in a form in which it can be analysed by others. If it was the case that the experts could not resolve their differences because the witness was unwilling to provide such data to the prosecution then this would be a ground for doubting the technique.

There can be no doubt that if stylometric analysis was proved to have any scientific basis it would be a valuable forensic weapon. A number of uses can be imagined, including in the prosecution of terrorist and organised crime. It is not clear, however, that stylometry is at present capable of yielding useful evidence. Stylometric evidence appears only to have succeeded in obtaining acquittals in trials at first instance where the prosecution was unprepared to deal with the evidence; no one else appears able to reproduce the results which the proponents claim, and they have consistently failed to publish their data or to make it available to the prosecution in a way that enables their claims to be analysed.

We must emphasise that this dispute is not comparable to disputes that have arisen over DNA evidence. In DNA cases the argument has been that the evidence may be prejudicial because of over-stated statistics. In stylometry cases the issue is whether the evidence has any value at all. Both the English Court of Appeal and Beach J in Australia were presented with evidence which indicated that stylometry was valueless in determining questions of authorship. In each case, however, the court evaded the responsibility of making a decision on this issue. Beach J rejected the evidence for reasons peculiar to the case, and the English Court of Appeal handed the task of deciding whether the evidence had any value to the jury. The challenge mounted by the prosecution was that stylometric evidence was of no value and irrelevant to the determination of the case. This is a matter for judges not juries.

10.4 Summary

- Types of scientific evidence related to human behaviour are much harder to evaluate since many of the principles cannot be verified in the same way as they can in the physical sciences. In some cases analysis may reveal that the evidence is of no use.

- Nonetheless, analysis of such evidence in logical terms clarifies the issues, prompts relevant questions and indicates where further research is required.
- Like all evidence these types of evidence should be combined with other evidence. They should not be considered in isolation and either "accepted" or "rejected".

Chapter 11

IMPLICATIONS FOR THE LEGAL SYSTEM

Chapter 11

IMPLICATIONS FOR THE LEGAL SYSTEM

So far we have discussed the logical structure for the interpretation of scientific evidence and investigated particular types of scientific evidence and particular problem cases. We now turn to the law and the court system to see whether they get the best results from expert witnesses or, if not, what changes might be needed.

Discussion of expert evidence in legal texts is often conducted under headings such as "The Qualifications Rule", "The Area of Expertise Rule", "The Common Knowledge Rule", "The Basis Rule" and "The Ultimate Issue Rule". The matters discussed under these headings often seem closely related. Many cases could be analysed as having been decided under two or more of these rules and, in some cases, where the judges have been clear which of these rules they were referring to, the case would have been better decided under another. The regulation of expert evidence seems to be very confusing. In this chapter we look at these questions in the light of the logical analysis used in earlier chapters. We hope that the result will be a clearer identification of the central issues.

11.1 What is expert evidence?

Expert evidence is customarily regarded as an exception to the opinion rule. This basic rule of evidence is that witnesses may only testify as to what they have perceived with one of the five senses. Inference from those perceptions is the job of the court. The opinion rule assumes that there is a clear distinction between fact and opinion but, as Thayer said, "In a sense all testimony as to matters of fact is opinion evidence: *i.e.* it is a conclusion from phenomena and mental impressions".[1] In particular, it is accepted that a person may express an opinion on a matter so evanescent or so complex that the facts on which the opinion is

---

[1] Thayer, JB, A preliminary treatise on the law of evidence (Little, Brown & Co, Boston, 1898).

founded cannot be unravelled.[2] Thus, Wigmore defines the "modern opinion rule" as:

> "... wherever inferences and conclusions can be drawn by the jury as well as by the witness, the witness is superfluous; and that thus an expert's opinion is received because and whenever his skill is greater than the jury's, while a lay opinion is received because and whenever his facts cannot be so told as to make the jury as able as he to draw the inference."[3]

The underlying idea is that the witness should provide evidence as near as possible to "raw data". It is then possible for the fact-finder to construct a likelihood ratio by considering how probable those facts are under the competing hypotheses. If the witness goes further than the raw data then he is providing evidence which is either superfluous, because the jury could have worked it out, or misleading, because it contains some inarticulate assumption.

When opinion evidence is allowed

There will be occasions, however, when the jury cannot assess the evidence for itself. If this is because of the complexity and evanescence of the factors then even a lay witness may be allowed to state his opinion. There will also be statements which would be meaningless to an average juror such as "the bandweights in these two DNA samples differed by 2 standard deviations". Lacking any background knowledge one could only assess a likelihood ratio of 1 to such a statement as, in one's state of ignorance, it seems as likely if the suspect is the perpetrator as if he is not. An expert is therefore permitted to testify as to the likelihood ratio and its components.

There are not two clear categories of evidence: those where jurors can assess the values as well as anyone else and those where experts are better than jurors. This being the case, any division of subjects into those which are suitable for expert testimony and those which are not is arbitrary and will depend, at least in part, on suppositions about costs and benefits. The marginal case at present appears to be the value of eyewitness testimony, with jurisdictions having different rules about the admissibility of expert evidence on this subject.

Is expert evidence, evidence of opinion?

In assessing these probabilities an expert will often be relying purely upon observations, either from first hand or from the literature, and might not be expressing an opinion at all. This will be the case especially with the kind of scientific evidence which we are concerned with. Such evidence is clearly "expert evidence", since the witness goes at least one step further than a lay witness. The lay witness merely expresses "E". The expert witness is allowed to express $P(E|H_1)$

[2] Tapper, CF, *Cross on Evidence*, 7th ed (Butterworths, London, 1990) 489.
[3] Wigmore, JH, *Wigmore on evidence*, Volume VII, chapter 67, section 1917: Opinion Rule – History (Little, Brown & Co, Boston, 1983).

and $P(E|H_2)$, $P(E|H_3)$ etc. Thus, the probabilities of obtaining a DNA profile if the samples had common or different origins will each be derived from a study of test results. Neither is an opinion. If the witness goes on to state the likelihood ratio or, as we suggest, actually guides the court in combining it with the prior, this is just arithmetical calculation, which is not "opinion" and, therefore, according to the traditional view, not expert evidence at all.[4]

The idea that mathematical calculations are not expert evidence is an example of the illogical consequences of the restricted notion of expert evidence as an exception to the opinion rule. Given sufficient time and care, anyone could carry out calculations that were limited to addition, subtraction, multiplication and division if they knew what to do and in what order. Nonetheless, knowing what is the right calculation is clearly not a matter within common knowledge. The calculations relating to DNA are matters of expert evidence; indeed, as we shall see in the next section, it is sometimes argued that even forensic scientists do not have the required expertise to testify to such matters.

Even the expertise required to know what tests are worth carrying out and to ensure that they are correctly carried out is usually a matter of training rather than opinion. Further, this latter expertise makes the forensic scientist an expert investigator, not an expert witness. When he testifies about observations in court the scientist is giving direct evidence of perceptions. Imagine a case in which a scientist conducts a test in the presence of a student. A sample is held in a flame and the flame turns blue. The scientist draws the attention of the student to the colour and then falls dead. The sample is completely consumed by the test. The student would surely be permitted to testify that when the sample removed from a marked bag was burned the flame turned blue, but a qualified scientist would have to testify as to the significance of the colour change, that is to assess the probability of it occurring under various hypotheses as to the composition of the sample.

Avoiding the need for opinions

Clearly, then, much of "expert evidence" does not involve "opinion" at all. Furthermore, we have argued that many of the conclusions a witness might express can be broken down into evidence that can be expressed in logical terms. Thus, a scientist might say that because a substance produced a blue flame it contained copper. This clearly breaks down into the propositions that: a blue flame is highly likely if it was copper; highly unlikely if it were anything else except barium; copper is common and barium is rare. The scientist might assume that the prior probability for barium was low and hence conclude that the substance was copper. This conclusion is inappropriate. Some factor in this particular case might make barium a real possibility, for example that the substance was found in the radiography department of a hospital. In other words, evidence external to the test (prior evidence) could affect the conclusion.

[4] *Reckitt & Colman Products Ltd* v *Borden Inc (No 2)* [1987] FSR 407.

It would be better to have analysed the evidence in likelihood ratio terms rather than to have given a conclusion which embodies assumptions that may not be appropriate to the particular case. In this way the "raw data" is made available to the jury, which can use it to draw inferences relating to the hypotheses being considered in the instant case, and expression of "opinion" is avoided. The "Birmingham Six" case is an example of an occasion where a scientist stated a conclusion without considering an alternative hypothesis which was actually crucial to the value of the evidence.[5]

Is "expert opinion" different from "lay opinion"?

On the other hand some witnesses, such as handwriting and fingerprint experts, are working in fields which have so far defied attempts at comprehensive analysis.[6] These experts are allowed to give an opinion that the two samples come from the same source not *although*, but *because* they are unable to analyse that judgment in logical terms. There are other occasions when the factors on which the opinion is based are so complex that we cannot disentangle them, and defer, instead, to the expert's "experience" or "judgment" and in these cases the witness will also be allowed to express an opinion.

Opinion evidence, therefore, falls into one of three categories:

- *superfluous*, because the facts on which it is based have been set out and the jury can draw their own inferences from them. Not all superfluous evidence is wasted effort, however. It may be much quicker for the witness to provide the answer to a mathematical calculation than to leave the jury to work it out with pencil and paper;
- *misleading*, because some assumption as to the prior probability or the appropriate alternative hypothesis has been concealed in the conclusion;
- *vital*, because the factors on which it is based are so complex or evanescent that they cannot be analysed by the witness.

Thus, expert witnesses are not exempt from the opinion evidence rule. An "opinion" is required only when the factors on which it is based are too complex or too evanescent to be analysed. It makes no difference whether the opinion is "expert" or not.

We can now amend Wigmore's statement of the modern opinion rule as follows:

"Whenever probabilities for the evidence under the competing hypotheses can be assessed by the jury as well as by the witness, the witness's assessment is superfluous, and thus an expert's assessment is received because and whenever his skill is greater than the jury's, while an opinion (lay or expert) is received because and whenever the facts cannot be so told as to make the jury as able as the witness to assess the probabilities or the likelihood ratio."

---

[5] Mills, H, "The Birmingham Six judgment – Court Restricts Blame to Science and the Police", *The Independent*, 28 March 1991.

[6] Evett, I "Interpretation: a Personal Odyssey", pp 9–22, in Aitken, CGG and Stoney, DA (eds) *The Use of Statistics in Forensic Science* (Ellis Horwood, Chichester, 1991).

Nor are expert witnesses traditionally regarded as exempt only from the opinion evidence rule. Experts may refer to their colleagues' work and to the literature in forming their views. The information on which they base their probability assessments may therefore be hearsay.[7] In jurisdictions in which witnesses are not usually allowed to sit in court prior to giving evidence, expert witnesses may do so and may answer hypothetical questions which may be based upon other witnesses' evidence.

Expert evidence a subject in itself

Special provision is increasingly being made for expert evidence in rules of procedure. In England, for example, there is a comprehensive code of procedure regulating expert evidence in civil cases[8] and in criminal cases the defence is required to give notice of expert evidence.[9] To operate these provisions a definition of expert evidence is required and, as we have seen, it is inadequate for that simply to be in terms of an exception to the opinion rule. Expert evidence is better regarded as a subject in its own right. This means that a definition of expert evidence must be attempted.

Expert evidence, therefore, is evidence the relevance and probative value of which depends upon the witness having some special knowledge or skill, other than having directly perceived a fact.

11.2 Who is an expert?

The traditional common law approach is that no special qualifications are required of an expert witness. In *Folkes* v *Chadd*[10], Lord Mansfield said, "Mr Smeaton understands the construction of harbours, the causes of their destruction and how remedied. In matters of science no other witnesses can be called". It was sufficient for Lord Mansfield that Smeaton understood these matters. It was not required that he attained that understanding in any particular way, such as formal education or the practice of a profession. In fact in *R* v *Silverlock*[11], a century later, a solicitor who had studied handwriting as a hobby was permitted to give evidence of handwriting comparison. The court said:

> "... the witness who is called upon to give evidence founded on a comparison of handwritings must be *peritus*; he must be skilled in doing so; but we cannot say that he must have become *peritus* in the way of his business or in any definite way. The question is, is he *peritus*?"

The adjective *peritus* seems arcane but it is useful because any English word such as "skilled", "experienced" or "knowledgeable" begs questions which will be

---

[7] *R* v *Abadom* [1983] 1 WLR 126.
[8] *Rules of the Supreme Court* ("*The Supreme Court Practice*") (Sweet & Maxwell, London, 1994), Order 38.
[9] Police and Criminal Evidence Act 1984, s 81.
[10] *Folkes* v *Chadd* (1782) 3 Doug KB 157, 99 ER 598.
[11] *R* v *Silverlock* [1894] 2 QB 766.

considered below. For the English courts, then, the question is not what has the witness *done* in the past but is the witness *now* able to give useful evidence. Expert witnesses should always begin a formal statement by qualifying themselves, giving full details of their education, training, publications and experience, including experience as an expert witness. The court may use any or all of these factors in deciding whether the person is an expert.

We can examine this in likelihood ratio terms by regarding the fact that the witness has made the statement as the item of evidence. For example, the witness says that "X is the case" and we could ask ourselves the probability that the witness would say this supposing that it were true and supposing that it were not true. In the extreme case where one knows nothing whatever about a subject any such utterance is just as likely whether or not it is true. Thus, if we were to ask a geography teacher the capital of Mongolia and be told Ulan Batar we would regard this as strong evidence that Ulan Batar is indeed the capital. On the other hand if a young child were to say this and we knew nothing about it we might conclude it was just as likely that the child had made it up (an experience one of the authors remembers from his childhood).

An organised body of knowledge?

There have been suggestions that an expert must be *peritus* in some recognised branch of study or organised body of knowledge. This may be implicit in "general acceptance" tests but is occasionally mentioned as a specific requirement. For example, in the Australian case, *Bugg* v *Day*, Dixon J criticised the evidence of a motor repairer as to the speed at which an accident had occurred on the grounds that it was not based on "a branch of knowledge or an art in which the witness was skilled".[12] More recently, in New Zealand, in *R* v *B*, McMullin J referred to as a "precondition of admissibility" that "the subject-matter to which the expert opinion relates must be a sufficiently recognised branch of science at the time the evidence is given".[13] This requirement, for which no authority was cited, imposes an additional requirement to that of relevance, and risks diverting argument into whether something is an organised body of knowledge. It would even rule out some expert evidence which is routinely accepted. For example, evidence of local Maori custom may be given by elders whose only qualifications are that they are members of the relevant tribe and have lived in the area for some time.

Outside the United States, authority for the requirement of an organised body of knowledge is weak. Apart from a comment by Vaughan Williams J in the course of argument in *R* v *Silverlock* these *dicta* are almost all confined to Australian cases. However, the High Court of Australia and even individual judges have ruled inconsistently on the issue.[14]

---

[12] (1949) 79 CLR 442, 462 (HCA).
[13] *R* v *B (an accused)* [1987] 1 NZLR 362, 367 (CA) per McMullin J.
[14] The record of the High Court of Australia on this issue is fully analysed in Freckelton, I, *The Trial of the Expert* (OUP Melbourne, 1987), pp 21–24.

Forensic scientists as expert witnesses

Forensic scientists usually qualify themselves in terms of their education and training. Their initial qualifications may be as chemists, physicists, biochemists, etc. This seems to deny that forensic science is a discipline or an organised body of knowledge in its own right. It is then argued by some that evidence such as DNA evidence should be given by as many as three witnesses, a microbiologist, a geneticist, and a statistician.[15] None of these disciplines, however, ordinarily involves the kind of problems faced by forensic scientists.

Forensic scientists may be involved in a number of tasks. They may have to:

- gather samples from a crime scene;
- test the samples;
- analyse the results;
- make those results into evidence relevant to the particular case.

Problems can arise at any of these stages (in *Tran* there was argument whether certain DNA bands dimly visible on the autorad should be used as evidence).[16] The first three stages are essentially technical – the most challenging part is the last stage. It is this last stage which makes forensic science distinct. This makes it all the more troubling that in *Lucas* the judge should have held that the forensic scientists were experts in testing DNA but not in statistics.[17] The real problem in that case was that the evidence given by the forensic scientist included a "probability of paternity", but the evidence given by the expert statistician was also unhelpful in a number of ways.

Is forensic science different from other sciences?

Scientists in other disciplines are concerned with what predictions can be made on the basis of a series of replicable experiments often analysed by traditional statistical techniques. Even statisticians, who regard themselves as expert in interpreting data, classically only claim to predict the frequency of events in the long run. Forensic scientists, on the other hand, must try to assess the value as evidence of single, possibly non-replicable items of information about specific hypotheses referring to an individual event.

Scientists who do not have to consider such questions are arguably not *peritus* for forensic scientific purposes, however eminent they may be in their own field. Conversely, forensic scientists who think of themselves primarily as experts in blood or glass or whatever, must make themselves conversant with the interpretational techniques required. If forensic scientists were to describe themselves as such, their competence as specialists in forensic scientific issues would be recognised and this would reduce the impact of the highly formally qualified

[15] For example, by Martin Sides QC when presenting his paper, "Admissibility of Expert Opinion Evidence" at the Australian Institute of Criminology Conference on Law, Medicine and Criminal Justice, Queensland, 6–8 July 1993.
[16] *R* v *Van Hung Tran* (1990) 50 A Crim R 233.
[17] *R* v *Lucas* [1992] 2 VR 109.

scientists called against them. It would also avoid allegations that they are testifying as to matters outside their own field as, for example, when a forensic scientist qualified as a biochemist answers what appear to be statistical questions about the evidence.[18]

The axioms of probability and the likelihood ratio should not be seen as "statistical techniques"[19] but as the interpretational armoury of forensic science.

11.3 What is a science? The *Frye* test

Questions will still arise when forensic scientists wish to take advantage of new technical developments. Forensic scientists will generally only use methods whose underlying theories are published and fully accepted in the relevant field; but occasionally practitioners in other fields such as dentistry[20] or literary style attempt to apply their own knowledge to forensic scientific problems. Courts will always be faced with questions about the validity of new forms of scientific evidence and the usefulness of the techniques used to extract such evidence.

The fundamental principle of the law of evidence is that evidence which is relevant is admissible unless it is excluded by some other rule or its probative value is outweighed by its prejudicial effect. The first question to be asked of any scientific evidence therefore is whether it is relevant. We have argued in this book that it is relevant if it helps to distinguish between appropriate hypotheses; in other words, it produces a likelihood ratio other than 1.

Additional requirements for forensic scientific evidence?

A question which is then asked is whether there is any other hurdle which scientific evidence or, more particularly, new forms of scientific evidence, must clear before being admissible. If yes, we must identify the rule of exclusion; if no, we must explain how a court can decide whether a new form of evidence is relevant.

In England, attempts to impose such additional requirements have been resisted and the question whether new forms of scientific evidence should be admitted, "is, at root, one of probative value".[21] Indeed, in two recent cases the English Court of Appeal refused to reject purportedly scientific evidence, saying that the jury might have found it to be of probative value, although the court itself had failed to come to any assessment of its own.[22] In both cases it was the defence which sought the admission of the evidence, and in both cases the court was satisfied that the totality of the evidence was overwhelmingly in favour of the accused's guilt. They are, therefore, weak authority for the application of a lower

[18] *R* v *Raheke* (1993), unreported, 2 July 1993. (High Court Napier).
[19] As in *R* v *Hammond*, unreported, 7 December 1992, CCC920108.
[20] *R* v *Carroll* (1985) 19 A Crim R 410 (bite-mark offered as evidence of identity).
[21] Hodgkinson, T, *Expert Evidence* (Sweet and Maxwell, London, 1990), p 133.
[22] *R* v *McCrossen*, unreported, 10 July 1991; *R* v *Mitchell* 82/2419/E2, CA, June 1993.

standard for the admission of scientific evidence than for evidence generally, but certainly indicate that the English Court of Appeal is not looking to impose additional requirements on scientific evidence.

In other jurisdictions tests have been imposed which are interpretable as requirements additional to the basic requirement of relevance. The most well-known of these is the US *Frye* test. This test has been referred to throughout the common law world, despite the long-standing debate, now resolved in *Daubert*[23], as to whether it was superseded by the Federal Rules of Evidence. The *Frye* test required that "the things from which the deduction is made must be sufficiently established to have gained general acceptance in the particular field in which it belongs".[24] This led to vigorous argument in US courts about whether a technique had achieved "general acceptance" as an issue quite separate from its probative value.

In New Zealand, at least one case (involving psychological evidence in an accusation of child abuse) appeared to indicate that scientific evidence should be conclusive rather than merely relevant.

> "As child psychology grows as a science it may be possible for experts in that field to demonstrate as matters of expert observation that persons subjected to sexual abuse demonstrate certain characteristics or act in peculiar ways which are so clear and unmistakable that they can be said to be the concomitants of sexual abuse. When that is so the courts may admit such evidence as evidence of direct observation."[25]

The natural reading of this passage is that the evidence will only be admissible if it is conclusive of abuse. However, a number of points can be made. First, the judge was dealing with a statement that the witness believed that the child had been abused. It would have been preferable if the witness had been able to state, as we recommend, by how much her observations increased the assessment of probability of abuse. This, and other problems with the case, were discussed in chapter 2.

Secondly, the word "concomitant" may mean simply "associated with" rather than "useful for distinguishing". If observed behaviour is a "concomitant" of a number of conditions then, although its probability given any one of those conditions may be high, it would be no use for distinguishing between them. If the word "concomitant" in the passage is being used in this sense then the passage is an example of the prosecutor's fallacy at work.

Thirdly, if, on the other hand, "concomitant" is used to mean "conclusive" then the passage imposes a requirement impossible to achieve. There is probably no form of human behaviour which always occurs as a consequence of any particular event and which never occurs otherwise.

---

[23] *Daubert* v *Merrell Dow Pharmaceuticals Inc* (1993) 113 S Ct 2786.
[24] *Frye* v *United States* (1923) 293 Federal Reports (1st series) 1013, 1014 (CA).
[25] *R* v *B (an accused)* [1987] 1 NZLR 362, 368 (CA), per McMullin J.

Finally, this requirement, so far as psychological evidence in child sex-abuse cases in concerned, was overturned by legislation which itself, arguably, over-reacted by mandating the admission of evidence of no probative value.[26]

Attempts to impose requirements for admissibility additional to relevance are fraught with difficulty. Such requirements are typically either enhanced probative value or some set of criteria purporting to define science. In the first case the obvious question is, "How highly probative must evidence be to be admissible?". To this there is no analytically determinable correct answer. References can be found in the literature to a requirement to prove points "beyond reasonable doubt".[27] There is no judicial authority for such a requirement, nor is there any reason why scientific evidence should have to be, as a matter of rule, of greater probative value than other evidence in order to be admitted.

The application of rules defining "science" simply diverts argument into the mechanical application of the chosen criteria, without consideration of the probative value of the evidence. When the cases are examined it seems that whatever verbal incantations are used by the court, decisions are, in practice, made on an assessment of probative value.[28] The most useful way to proceed, therefore, seems to be to consider how we can assess the probative value of new or contested forms of scientific evidence.

11.4 The end of the *Frye* test – *Daubert* v *Merrell Dow*

In *Daubert* v *Merrell Dow Pharmaceuticals Inc*[29] the US Supreme Court decided that *Frye* had, indeed, been superseded by the US Federal Rules of evidence. As a matter of law that decision only applies inside the US Federal system; in fact, the argument might be made elsewhere that it depends upon a statutory amendment to the common law and that the *Frye* test (if it was ever accepted) still stands in other jurisdictions. However, the rule of evidence that the court was applying was that scientific, technical or other specialised evidence may be given if it will "assist the trier of fact to understand the evidence or to determine a fact in issue".[30] The court considered how a judge can determine whether evidence will "assist the trier of fact" and it seems likely that its criteria will be useful in other jurisdictions when courts are trying to assess the probative value of the evidence.

---

[26] Evidence Act 1908, s 23G(2)(c) (NZ). Discussed in Vignaux, GA and Robertson, BWN, "Authorising irrelevance? Evidence Act 1908, section 23G(2)(c)" (1990) 2 FLB 67–68, publisher's corrigendum, p 74.

[27] *E.g.* Magnusson, E and Selinger, B, "Jury Comprehension of Complex Scientific Evidence: The Inference Chart Concept" (1990) 14 Crim LJ 389.

[28] Freckelton, *The Trial of the Expert* (OUP Melbourne, 1987), p 64. See the discussion of *Gumbley* v *Carrington* in chapter 5 in which in one case the strength of the case as a whole was clearly high and in the other weak.

[29] (1993) 113 S Ct 2786.

[30] US Federal Rules of Evidence, Rule 702.

The Supreme Court listed some key factors which did not purport to be a definitive checklist or test. None of the factors is intended to be determinative of admissibility. The court emphasised that the inquiry was a flexible one, the object was to determine "the scientific validity – and thus the evidentiary relevance and reliability – of the principles that underlie a proposed submission". These factors were:

(i) Whether the theory or technique can be, and has been, tested.
(ii) Whether the technique has been published or subjected to peer review.
(iii) Whether actual or potential error rates have been considered.
(iv) Whether the technique is widely accepted within the relevant scientific community.

We discuss these points in turn.

Whether the theory or technique can be, and has been, tested

This seems to combine two entirely different questions. Whether the theory or technique has been tested is closely related to publication and peer review and we consider it below. Whether it is capable of being tested is a separate question. The court quoted statements to the effect that the "criterion of the scientific status of a theory is its falsifiability or refutability or testability".[31] To be testable a theory must enable one to make predictions that are capable of being either true or false.

A forensic scientist has to be able to assess the probability of the observations supposing certain conditions. A vital part of these conditions will be the underlying scientific theories involved. For example, when we discuss the probability that a particular DNA profile would be found "supposing that the accused left the mark", we really mean "supposing that the accused left the mark *and* that DNA is unique (except for identical twins) *and* that it is unchanging *and* that the DNA in a person's blood is the same as in their skin, etc". The probability for observations can only be assessed supposing clearly defined conditions. We cannot, for example, assess the probability that the daytime population of "downtown Chicago" is over one million since each of us might have different ideas about the boundaries of "downtown Chicago". It is therefore important that all conditions, including the theories in the light of which evidence is considered, are phrased in terms that are capable of being true or false, and this is what is meant by "testability".

The prediction that no two people (other than identical twins) have the same DNA is potentially testable in that it is theoretically possible to examine the DNA of every human being and to determine that the proposition is or is not true. Conversely, the proposition that no two objects are identical is not falsifiable since whenever we fail to detect a difference between two objects it may be because the

---

[31] Popper, K, *Conjectures and Refutations: the Growth of Scientific Knowledge* (Routledge and Kegan Paul, London, 1989), p 37.

theory is wrong or we may merely lack the technology or the understanding to detect the differences.

Psychological and psychiatric theories often fail this test. For example, there is a theory that some personality problems in adults are due to childhood abuse, the memory of which has been suppressed. This theory is clearly unverifiable. Even if a subject fails to remember abuse under hypnosis, this could, according to the theory, indicate either that the person is not a suitable hypnotic subject or that the suppression is even deeper.

We should note here that scientists and lay people may mean different things by the word "theory". To a scientist a "theory" may include something for which the evidence is overwhelming, such as the theory of gravitation; but the word "theorem" in science is reserved for rules that follow necessarily from axioms.

Whether the technique has been published or subjected to peer review

One result, obtained by one person on one occasion, might be explained in all sorts of ways. Thus, a tradition has built up in science that a theory should be tested by independent replication of the experiments. These experiments will attempt to reproduce the effect of the original, but are bound to be subject to differences in conditions – if only that they are carried out by different experimenters. If the same results are consistently obtained this will eliminate possible alternative explanations, for example that the original result was caused by particular humidity and barometric conditions. Replication also guards against the possibility that the original experimenter is either dishonest or deluded.

We have already stated that the scientific theory justifying the evidence is one of the conditions under which the probability of the evidence is calculated. This means that the theory must also be part of the conditions under which the prior probabilities are assessed. If we force the reasoning process back far enough we must at some point be concerned with the probability that the theory is true given the accumulation of data about it and our background knowledge. This will have to be compared with the probability that some other hypothesis is true given the same information. A single set of observations obtained by a single experimenter cannot distinguish between hypotheses such as: "the theory is correct", "the experimenter twisted the data to fit the theory", "the experiment was affected by some external influence". Prior information about the experimenter may help us to distinguish between these hypotheses and there is no doubt that people do take this into account. The best approach, however, is an attempt to replicate the results. If the same results are obtained by different experimenters under apparently the same conditions this will eliminate some alternative hypotheses, and if the same results are obtained under conditions known to be different this will eliminate the hypotheses that those conditions affected the outcome.

A prelude to replication is usually publication in a scientific journal, where the details of the experiments and results are described. Reputable journals subject papers to peer review so that even before the paper is published other scientists in the field have checked the material for obvious flaws. Publication also increases the chances that if there are any flaws in the theory or procedure someone will find them.

The requirement for publication, or even of wide peer review, cannot apply to the tests conducted by a forensic scientist in an individual case. It is the techniques and theories used that should have been verified beforehand.[32] Where possible, material can be handed to the defence for independent testing although, as we have said before, it is usually the interpretation rather than the measurements themselves that are important to the defence.

Forensic scientific techniques develop very rapidly and an obvious problem arises when a new technique which has yet to be subjected to wide peer review becomes available. If more established tests produce useful results then the new test will often be conducted in parallel but not used as evidence. A dilemma arises (as it does in medicine) if the new test is the only one that produces useable results, perhaps because it is more sensitive. Should the forensic scientist take evidence to court which is not based on a peer-reviewed technique or should the evidence be concealed?

The court in *Daubert* emphasised that publication was only one element of peer review and was not an absolute requirement for admissibility. This is just as well, since delays between submission of papers to scientific journals and their publication can be more than one year. In the meantime the results may have been widely disseminated by discussion at conferences or via the new electronic "invisible colleges".

Whether actual or potential error rates have been considered

The court seems to have had in mind techniques which lead to a witness saying, for example, "these two speech recordings are of the same person". It would certainly be possible to test experts and to measure how often they made misidentifications in these circumstances. We might then calculate a likelihood ratio which expresses the evidential value of the expert's utterance.

We have argued that experts should not give such evidence except in instances where it is impossible to measure the strength of the evidence in the usual way. In all other cases, the fact that a piece of evidence increases the probability of a hypothesis which actually turns out not to be true is not an "error". For example, comparison of two DNA samples may, in a minute number of cases, give a small likelihood ratio in favour of the proposition of common origin when, in fact, the samples are from two different people.[33] More obviously, the fact that two blood samples match on ABO analysis, although they come from different individuals, is not an "error". Thus, if a likelihood ratio approach is adopted we are usually concerned, not with a technique's "error rate", but with its discriminatory power.

---

[32] See the discussion of *HM Advocate* v *Preece* in chapter 6.
[33] Evett, IW, Scranage, J and Pinchin, R, "An Illustration of the advantages of efficient statistical methods for RFLP analysis in forensic science" (1993) 52 Am J Hum Gen 498.

An error does occur when a test produces a result which it ought not to produce, owing to some contamination of the sample, a mistake in technique, or an undetected variation in testing conditions. This is a matter of quality control and the emphasis should not be on measuring an error rate but on identifying and rectifying the flaw in the process which resulted in the particular error.

At any time there will be an irreducible "error rate" owing to, for example, the precision with which we can control the strength of the electric field along a DNA gel. This may be subject to fluctuations which we cannot detect, let alone control. If the approach advocated in this book is rigorously adopted the effect of these fluctuations is taken into account automatically. Let us see how this is so.

When we compare a DNA sample from the scene of a crime with that from a suspect there may be differences in band position even though the two samples actually come from the same person. The probability of such a displacement occurring, supposing that they do come from the same person, will be determined from a large number of experiments in which similar pairs have been compared. One of the possible reasons for displacement is minute differences in the density of the gel from lane to lane. If this occurs it will also have occurred during the previous experiments and one of the reasons why the numerator of the likelihood ratio may only be, say, 0.9, instead of 1.0, is that these tiny differences do occur. This possible source of "error" is taken into account automatically by a reduction in the numerator of the likelihood ratio. The appropriate question is thus not, "What is the error rate?", but simply, "What is the likelihood ratio?".

If the reader is not convinced, imagine a test which is so difficult to conduct consistently that any result might be obtained from any sample. In this case the probability of getting any particular result would be the same whether or not the sample originated from the suspect. The likelihood ratio would be 1.0 and the test would be useless as evidence.

Whether the technique is widely accepted within the relevant scientific community

Acceptance within the relevant scientific community will usually follow from the testing and replication of such experiments. When there is no such acceptance the court's decision about relevance is much harder and may even be impossible. However, the US Supreme Court in *Daubert* stated that evidence should not be rejected, as some courts have done, merely because a dispute exists within the relevant scientific community.[34]

---

[34] As the California Appeal Court did in *People* v *Wallace*, unreported, 25 March 1993, No A051967, (CA). See also *Commissioner for Government Transport* v *Adamcik* (1961) 106 CLR 292 in which the High Court of Australia held that a doctor who had made a study of the psychosomatic causes of disease could not be prevented from testifying that leukaemia might be triggered by the trauma of a road accident merely because it was not an opinion widely shared in the medical community.

Stylometric evidence provides an example of lack of acceptance of the conditions on which the assessments are based, and this was more fully discussed in chapter 10.

Most problematic issues will arise in the inference process rather than in the testing procedures. Where DNA evidence has been rejected, especially in the United States, it is usually because of dispute as to "the appropriate method of calculating probabilities". Inference from evidence should be governed by general principles of logic and not by techniques peculiar to the testing of a particular type of evidence. It may be that one day judges will be sufficiently well-versed in logical inference to be able to evaluate scientific evidence for themselves. In the meantime, however, it appears that scientific witnesses will be relied upon for this and so it is vital to determine what is the "relevant scientific community" within which the methods of inference must be widely accepted. As discussed above, most geneticists, biologists and statisticians do not use the inferential techniques advocated in this book because they are not required to answer the sort of questions with which forensic scientists are confronted. Courts should not, therefore, be discomforted by evidence that there is dispute within genetics or biology about the use of Bayesian probability theory.

One way of reducing dispute would be to restrict witnesses to expressing the strength of the item of evidence rather than drawing a conclusion from it. It is notable that many cases where courts are concerned about whether a technique is "scientific" are cases in which the witness has stated a conclusion. Such cases include *McKay*[35] (whether a person subjected to a truth drug was telling the truth), *Gumbley* v *Cunningham*[36](whether a driver's blood alcohol level had been over the limit four hours prior to the test) and the stylometric cases (see chapter 10). In all these cases the witnesses went much further than simply stating the evidentiary value and, in at least some, attention to the principles of inference explained in this book might have dispelled the concerns.

Conclusions on *Daubert*

Some of the criteria in *Daubert* overlap heavily[37] and also display the kind of thinking about scientific evidence from which this book is trying to escape. In general, however, the effect of the case is to abolish any special requirements relating to scientific evidence and to return to basic principles of relevance and probative value. The court then goes on to offer some guidance as to how to think about the probative value of scientific evidence and the criticism above relates only to the details of that guidance, rather than to the basic principle.

---

[35] [1967] NZLR 139.
[36] [1988] 2 QB 171, DC.
[37] As argued in Allen, RJ, "Expertise and the *Daubert* Decision" (1994) 84 J Crim L & C 1157.

11.5 Preparing evidence: the effect of defence alternative explanations on the expert

Forensic scientists have traditionally been expected to work somewhat isolated from the remainder of the investigation. The picture the non-scientist investigator has is of a detached professional who considers the scientific evidence unsullied by any potentially biasing knowledge of the case as a whole. Scientists are frequently provided with little information about the case by police who, along with counsel when the case comes to court, expect the scientific evidence given to have its own intrinsic value unaffected by the issues counsel has decided to dispute. This has either led to or been caused by the classical statistical technique of only considering as an alternative hypothesis that the evidence arose "by chance".

It will be evident that scientific witnesses cannot work at their best in this way. They must certainly guard against bias. They must not form a view as to who the perpetrator was and pursue evidence to prove that theory to the exclusion of all else – however, nor should a good police investigator.

In order to interpret the evidence both to police and courts, scientists need understand the whole of the case and the issues raised. The evidence can only be interpreted in the light of the rest of the case, as we have seen. If the background is changed, the value of the evidence could change radically. In particular scientists need to know of any circumstances or evidence that tends to identify the perpetrator's ethnicity. The scientist needs to be able to consider, and may be able to advise police and counsel on what alternative hypotheses to evaluate the evidence against. Failure to do so can lead to great waste of time and money. One of the authors investigated the death of a pedestrian in a road traffic accident. The laboratory report baldly stated a (not very high) blood/alcohol content. Considerable effort was spent trying to discover where the deceased had been drinking. The defence called the analyst and it was only in the court corridor that he explained that the small quantity of alcohol could be explained by the cleaning and treatment which the deceased had received at hospital!

These considerations, however, lead to a clash with the traditional requirements of the common law system. Theoretically, a plea of not guilty in a criminal case puts everything in issue. In practice the defence will usually choose to run on one or two possible alternatives to the prosecution story, but it is traditionally under no obligation to tell the prosecution in advance what those lines will be. The stock-in-trade of the prosecutor is predicting what the line of defence will be and being prepared to deal with it. In 99% of cases this is not particularly troublesome, but in certain notorious cases, such as *Arthur* and *Raymond*,[38] this system led to the court not receiving the evidence it required.

---

[38] *R* v *Arthur* (1981) discussed at [1985] Crim LR 706. For *Raymond* see 10.3.

The best known of these is probably *Arthur*, in which a doctor was charged with attempting to murder a Down's syndrome baby. An eminent pathologist appearing for the prosecution, Professor Usher, was confronted in cross-examination with the results of tests he had not known about. This caused him to weaken his own evidence in the witness box, but, subsequently, he publicly stated that if he had had the opportunity for proper consideration he would not have retracted any of his own evidence.

Defence disclosure

In reaction to such cases, England and a number of other jurisdictions enacted that the defence in criminal cases had to give notice of expert evidence. The content of the defence expert reports will help the prosecution to predict the likely line of defence, but it must still be prepared to meet alternative possible defences. Indeed, the scientific evidence itself may suggest alternative hypotheses, such as that the perpetrator was the accused's sibling.

The notification of expert evidence will avoid the debacles that occurred in *Raymond* and *Arthur* but the clear implication of this book is that this provision does not go far enough. This arrangement does not reveal possible lines of cross-examination and so the scientific witness still has to be prepared to deal with a number of alternative hypotheses. This requires extensive (and expensive) preparation since it would not be possible to do the computations required to re-evaluate DNA evidence, for example, in the witness box. This, in turn, may require a change in attitude by the scientific witnesses who are used to coming to court armed only with the one set of figures.

The next move is to require the defence to reveal in advance its planned line of defence. Such proposals invariably arouse great opposition from defence lawyers, but they need not involve any great issues of principle. The defence should always be free, of course, to take up any new line of defence suggested by surprising evidence from a prosecution witness.

In some jurisdictions steps in this direction have been taken. Pre-trial conferences in criminal cases have become a regular feature in New Zealand, but these lack any statutory support and some defence counsel do not co-operate with attempts to "cut down the issues". In England the Royal Commission on Criminal Justice – the "Runciman Commission" – proposed in 1994 that defence in trials on indictment must give notice of the line of defence, and this proposal has caused the expected heated arguments.[39]

---

[39] See the index to *New Law Journal*, 1993/4 for numerous short articles and letters.

11.6 Court-appointed experts

Discussion of expert evidence frequently leads to the suggestion that expert witnesses should be appointed by the court rather than by the parties. This is put forward to solve the perceived problem that:

> "... it is often quite surprising to see with what facility and to what extent, [skilled witness's] views can be made to correspond with the wishes or interests of the parties who call them."[40]

It is also believed that appointing "neutral" experts would solve the problem of conflicting expert evidence. This cause has been espoused by figures as distinguished and as separated in time as Wigmore[41] and Lord Woolf. There are a number of reasons why this suggestion may be neither necessary nor sufficient to deal with the problems identified.

First, we have argued in this book that apparent conflicts of expert evidence can often be resolved when the logical approach is followed. Once scientists are explicit about their alternative hypotheses and about the information on which their assessments are conditioned the reasons for any conflicts should become clear. On the other hand, if "court-appointed experts" fail to give their evidence in the form advocated in this book then the courts will be faced with just as great difficulties as before.

Secondly, we have also argued that the process of inference required in legal cases should be the particular domain of forensic scientists. We have seen cases in which confusion has been caused by the evidence of highly qualified statisticians and geneticists. The impression still lingers amongst lawyers and scientists that forensic science is simply an application of other scientific techniques. It would be unfortunate if those responsible for appointing the panel from whom the court would choose experts failed to realise the special nature of the inferential problems which confront the forensic scientist. On this argument those appointed would have to be forensic scientists, but nearly all of them work for the official forensic science services. Even after being appointed to a panel they will need to keep abreast of developments in their field, and facilities to do this are likely only to be available in the official services. There is, therefore, probably little to be gained in perceived impartiality.

Thirdly, the defence, especially in criminal cases, is bound to retain the right to consult experts of its own and even to produce them as witnesses. The potential for conflict of expert evidence will always remain.

In short, the way forward is to educate all scientists, whoever might employ them and, for that matter, all lawyers, in the principles of logical inference. If this

---

[40] Taylor, J, *Taylor On Evidence* (Maxwell and Son, 1885). In fact, Taylor said that expert witnesses gave "Perhaps the testimony which deserves least credit with a jury" but then he also had an index entry "Irish Witnesses – credibility of".

[41] Wigmore, JH, "To abolish the partisanship of expert witnesses as illustrated in the *Loeb-Leopold* case" (1934) 15 J Crim Law & C 314.

is not done then changing the way witnesses are selected will not help and, if it is done, such a change will not be necessary.

11.7 Summary

- The value of an item of evidence is determined by its likelihood ratio. The qualifications rule, the area of expertise rule and the basis rule all indicate factors which should be taken into account in assessing the likelihood ratio.

- The axioms of probability and the likelihood ratio should not be seen as "statistical techniques" but as the interpretational armoury of forensic science.

- In order to assess the value of the evidence the forensic scientist needs to know what the alternative possible explanations for the evidence are. This requires familiarity with the case and disclosure by the defence.

- Forensic science is a discipline in its own right concerned with assessing the value as evidence for competing hypotheses of single items of evidence. Non-forensic scientists are not necessarily expert in such matters.

- Expert evidence is not an exception to the opinion rule. Experts may only express an opinion under the same circumstances as non-experts.

- Court-appointed experts will not solve the problems that have been identified with forensic scientific evidence. Education in the principles of logical inference will.

Chapter 12

CONCLUSION

Chapter 12

CONCLUSION

12.1 General

The general view is that there is a failure of communication between scientific witnesses and lawyers. Lawyers contend that scientists do not understand the legal process, while scientists claim that they are prevented from giving the evidence that ought to be given.

Most seem to assume that the solution is that lawyers should understand more about science and scientists should understand more about the law. It is our contention, on the other hand, that logic, probability and inference provide the language in which the two groups should communicate with each other. Not only that but, as we have tried to explain in this book, each group also needs to understand the principles of inference in order to think about its own work carefully.

This approach will solve many of the problems perceived to dog scientific evidence. Conflicts of scientific witnesses will mostly evaporate and with them the appearance of partisanship; consideration of new forms of scientific evidence will be given some rational basis; difficult decisions of the past can be re-analysed in understandable terms. All the "rules" said to govern expert evidence, such as the field of expertise rule, the basis rule and the ultimate issue rule, will be translated into a demand that courts accurately assess the probative value of the evidence as measured by the likelihood ratio.

We cannot pretend that within the covers of this book we have provided an answer to every possible question. There may well be ways in which the presentation of this argument can be improved and there are doubtless questions which we have not begun to answer. Indeed, increasing our understanding of scientific evidence through logical analysis may well confront us with complexities of which, hitherto, we have been blissfully ignorant. There is a world of difference between simply reporting the frequency of a particular kind of glass and considering how probable it is that someone would have this glass on them if they were not the perpetrator of the offence.

What we hope to have done is to light the path by which rational discussion of the subject can proceed. For far too long progress in understanding scientific evidence has been bogged down. Scientists have used statistical techniques which make it impossible to combine their evidence with the other evidence in the case and lawyers have approached the subject by offering slogans of elusive meaning such as that "the evidence must be regarded with caution". A logical analysis offers the tools required for rigorous examination of the subject and for increasing the value of scientific evidence to the legal system. In fact, the logical approach adopted in this book takes us further than that. It helps to answer the question, "Is forensic science a science?".

Forensic science as a science

The view is widely held that there is no unity to forensic science. Eminent forensic scientists have themselves complained that forensic science is seen merely as an application of the knowledge generated by other sciences, lacking any underlying theory or principles.[1] This is illustrated by the fact that many working forensic scientists regard themselves as chemists or biochemists. Apart from anything else this creates the difficulty that when the prosecution call a forensic scientist the defence will frequently be able to retain a more highly qualified chemist, biochemist or geneticist.

We argue that forensic science does indeed have a unity. This is because it is concerned with drawing inferences relating to an event that is the concern of a court from individual items of non-replicable data. Scientists and statisticians working in other fields use techniques that do not provide and, in many cases, deny the possibility of, answers to such questions. Forensic scientists therefore should think in such terms, should qualify themselves in court as forensic scientists and should more actively question the qualifications of other scientists to give evidence.

This implies that the research which is urgently required is not research into newer and better hardware (although that is always useful) but fundamental research which supports the interpretation of the evidence available. The Target Fibre Study is one example of the sort of research which is valuable. Research is also required into the way in which experts such as fingerprint technicians make their decisions. This will not only improve our understanding of the value of the evidence but also enable the practitioners to develop their professional expertise in a scientific manner.[2]

Many professional expert witnesses have failed to develop in this way since they have either been, like fingerprint technicians, trained to think about absolute identification or, in the case of forensic scientists, trained in orthodox statistical

[1] Kirk, PL, "The ontogeny of criminalistics" (1963) 54 Criminology & Political Science 235; Osterburg, JW, "What problems must criminalistics solve" (1963) 59 J Crim Law & C 427.
[2] Evett, IW, "Criminalistics – The Future of Expertise" (1993) 33 JFSS 173.

techniques which have left them content, for example, to study the frequency of the refractive index of glass without considering the other factors that affect its value as evidence. Once the approach advocated here is adopted, practitioners are forced to ask these questions and are challenged constantly to consider how they form their judgments and how they can be of more help to the court.

It is important to note that the approach we advocate does not diminish the role of the jury in any way. In the end it is still for the jury in a criminal case to assess the prior probabilities for the various hypotheses on the basis of the other evidence and, therefore, even to decide what hypotheses are worth considering. In fact, as our discussion of the ultimate issue rule shows, the logical approach enables the witness to give the maximum assistance to the court whilst preserving the traditional relationship between expert and juror.

12.2 Conclusions

- The important point about expert evidence is its correct interpretation by the court. This is best achieved by the expert using the likelihood ratio to describe the strength of the evidence and by the lawyers understanding what it means. Understanding the logic of inference is more important to lawyers than technical knowledge about scientific processes.

- What inferences can be drawn from a particular kind of physical scientific evidence are not the preserve of that kind of scientist. Inference is a matter of logic and can and should be understood by everybody involved with the legal process.

- Problems in cases involving scientific evidence usually arise from problems of interpretation rather than from experimental errors. Where scientific evidence is misleading this is more likely to be because of a misapplication of the principles of inference than because of a technical failure in laboratory processes.

- Witnesses cannot state a conclusion about an issue, for example whether a stain was left by a particular person or whether a child has been abused, on the basis of one item of scientific evidence. Scientific evidence relating to an issue should be combined with other evidence relating to the same issue. The best way of doing this is to receive the evidence in likelihood ratio form. It can then be combined with the other evidence by simple multiplication.

- Items of scientific evidence do not have an intrinsic value which can be divined by a scientist examining some material in isolation from the rest of the case. Evidence has a value only in context. Its value depends on its ability to distinguish between specific hypotheses.

- Since the probative value of the evidence is a measure of its ability to distinguish between hypotheses, it is important for forensic scientists and legal practitioners to consider appropriate alternative hypotheses. In a criminal trial, one hypothesis will be the prosecution case; the alternative will usually be the defence case.

● Forensic scientists should give evidence in a way which clearly expresses its value and enables the court to combine it with the other evidence in the case. Evidence should not therefore be given in the form of probabilities for assertions or the results of significance tests, because these cannot be combined with other evidence. The best way to express the weight of an item of evidence is in the form of a numerical value, the likelihood ratio.

An understanding of these principles will enable lawyers and courts to interpret all forms of scientific evidence that are currently quantifiable, without necessarily having to acquire detailed knowledge of the intricacies of particular scientific techniques. For them to do this it is necessary that forensic scientists understand these principles and express their evidence in the appropriate way. Understanding these principles will also enable those working in areas that are not readily quantifiable, such as fingerprints and handwriting analysis, to identify lines of research required to increase our understanding of those forms of evidence.

There are implications for the reform of legal procedure which follow from these principles. Lawyers have commonly talked of accepting or rejecting evidence rather than of combining it; and court procedure underestimates the extent to which the opposing case must be known in order for evidence to be evaluated rationally. The likelihood ratio also offers a resolution of the legal system's longstanding ambivalence about scientific evidence. It illustrates that scientists cannot give us certainty, and it makes clear the respective roles of witness and juror.

12.3 The magic questions

We leave the reader with the five questions that should be asked of all scientific evidence. If these five questions are asked and correctly answered the fundamental difficulties that practitioners and commentators have with scientific evidence should evaporate.

● What is the probability of this evidence if our story is true?
● What are the appropriate alternative hypotheses?
● Why are they the appropriate alternative hypotheses?
● What is the probability of the evidence given the alternative hypotheses?
● What is the value of the evidence?

Appendix

PROBABILITY, ODDS AND BAYES' RULE

Probability and odds

Probability is treated in this book as a measure of the degree of belief in a proposition based on rational analysis of information. Propositions about the world may be either true or false, but because we have limited information we will seldom know which. We express our uncertainty in the form of probabilities for propositions. Thus "the light was red" or "it will rain today" or "the suspect was present at the scene" are all assertions about the world which will be true or false. We can talk about the probability that "the light was red". We talk about the probability of propositions, assertions or hypotheses.

An assessment of probability is usually expressed as a value between 0 and 1 but can equally be represented as a corresponding percentage between 0 and 100%. We switch between these forms at will.

A probability of 0 indicates complete disbelief in an assertion or hypothesis given the information one has. Thus, my probability for the assertion "I will live for ever", given what I know about the world, is 0.

A probability of 1 (or 100%) indicates absolute belief. My probability for the proposition that "the sun will rise tomorrow", given my experience and what I know about the working of the solar system, is 1.

A probability between 0 and 1 indicates less than certainty. An assessment of probability of 0.5 or 50% means that we consider the event to be as likely as not to happen. An assessment of more than 0.5 means that we consider the event more likely to happen than not. Thus, my probability that there will be rain today may be about 0.25 (25%) given the weather forecast I heard this morning and looking out of the window at the clouds. In ordinary language "I think there is quite a possibility of it raining but it 'probably won't' ".

One must bear in mind always that the probability one has for an assertion depends on the information one has. My probability that it will rain may be different if I have heard a weather forecast that says it will be dry than if I have not. The information is called the condition.

An assertion will have a negation. Thus, the assertion "it will rain today" has a corresponding negative assertion "it will not rain today". In this instance one can calculate the probability of the negative form of the assertion since it will either rain or not. It is done quite simply. The probability that there will *not* be rain (given the information we have) is 0.75, which is 1 minus the probability that there will be.

Odds

Odds are another way of describing probability. Odds tell us how much more likely it is that one assertion is true than its negation. In other words, odds are the ratio between the probability that an assertion is true and the probability that it is false. In the example above the probability that it will rain is assessed as 0.25 and the probability that it will not rain as 0.75. The ratio 0.25/0.75 is a ratio of 1 to 3, in other words we believe it is three times more likely to be dry than to rain. We can then say that the odds are 1 to 3 that it will rain (or that the odds are 3 to 1 *against* rain).

Most people usually talk about the odds *against* a proposition, such as that Phar Lap will win the Derby. Scientists, however, usually talk about the odds *of* a proposition. If we believe that the odds against two blood samples "matching" are a million to one, the scientist will usually talk about odds of 1 to a million.

To convert odds of *a* to *b* to a probability we use the formula:

$$P = \frac{a}{a+b}$$

where *a* is the figure "in favour" and *b* is the figure "against". Thus, in the rain example above, the odds of rain were 1 to 3. In that case $a = 1$ and $b = 3$. So the probability of rain = $1/(1+3) = 1/4 = 0.25$.

Generally in this book we use odds. They have two key advantages.

- The odds form makes it easier to see the importance of the alternative hypothesis and to use the likelihood ratio for the evidence based on two specific hypotheses.

- Odds are more comprehensible when we are dealing with extremely high or low probabilities. There does not appear to be much difference between probabilities of 0.999 and 0.9999, but we can immediately see that there is a great difference between the corresponding odds of roughly 1 to 1,000 and 1 to 10,000.

Odds do have some mathematical disadvantages which we shall indicate further on in this Appendix.

Sometimes, odds are written as a fraction (such as 2/3) and, particularly when the odds are some whole number to 1 (such as "3 to 1"), the odds are stated just as a number, such as 3. In this book we try to remember to state odds for or against a proposition in the form "3 to 1".

The symbols

It is often convenient, particularly when developing general methods of argument, to represent different assertions or hypotheses by different letters. Thus we would state:

$$A = \text{"it will rain today"}$$

and then refer to A in our discussions. The symbol not A (often conventionally written, ~A or $\bar{A}$) is the negation of this, meaning that it is not true that "it will rain today" or, more directly, "it will not rain today".

In symbolic form, a probability value and its conditions are written as P(A|B). This reads "the probability of assertion A assuming that assertion B is true".

- "P" stands for "probability";

- A and B are assertions or hypotheses; A is an assertion for which we are assessing a probability;

- B is the *condition*;

- "|" means "assuming that" or "given".

Thus, the construction "|B" means "assuming B is true". It is important to note that *all* probabilities are conditional upon the information used to assess them. Thus, we might say that:

A = "it will rain today";
B = "the weather forecast said 'fine weather' ";
P(A|B) = 0.25 means that (my assessment of) the probability that "it will rain today" supposing that "the weather forecast said 'fine weather' " is 0.25 or 25%.

Our probability for rain might have been different if the weather forecast had been different and different again if we had failed to hear the weather forecast. The probability one assesses always depends on (is conditional on) the knowledge available.

We have already noticed above that if P(A|B) = 0.25 then P(not A|B) = 0.75. This is the axiom of complementarity. Since it is certain that an event either occurred or did not, the probability assessments for all the possible ways it might have occurred plus the proposition that it did not occur must add up to 1. If we stipulate that an event occurred and consider our probabilities conditional upon that (*e.g.* we might regard it as practically certain that a person was murdered and condition all the possible methods on that) then the probabilities for all the possible methods must add up to 1.

It is important to be clear what probabilities must be complementary. In chapter 2 we discussed the example of a breath-testing device. Let:

B = "a red light shows"; and

A = "the person is over the limit"; and
not A = "the person is *not* over the limit".

Then the probabilities that the person is over the limit and the person is *not* over the limit (given that the red light shows) must sum to 1.

$$P(A|B) + P(\text{not } A|B) = 1$$

However, probabilities which have different conditions do not have to add up to 1. Thus, the probability that we got a red light if the subject was over the limit was 0.95 but the probability of getting a non-red (*i.e.* a green) light if the subject was *not* over the limit was 0.995 and these do not sum to 1. The difference can be seen clearly if we use symbols:

$$P(B|A) = 0.95$$
$$P(\text{not } B|\text{not } A) = 0.995$$

So, if we change the conditions the probabilities do not have to add up to 1, but if we are discussing the probabilities of different hypotheses, one of which must be true, under the *same* condition then all the probability assessments must add to 1.

The laws of probability

We have already discussed the axiom of complementarity above. There are two other axioms, or laws, of probability. These explain how to assess the probability that both of the two assertions are true, or that at least one of two assertions is true.

The statement that A and B are both true is written (A and B) or (AB). If we want to assess how probable it is that A and B are both true given that C is true, then the multiplication rule, or product rule tells us that we first assess how probable A is (assuming C is true) and then assess how probable B is given not only that C, but also that A is true. In symbols:

$$P(A \text{ and } B|C) = P(AB|C) = P(A|C) \, P(B|AC)$$

Thus, A might be "it will rain today" and B might be "Phar Lap will win the Derby tomorrow". C will be all my other information on both the weather and horse.

I have already assessed the probability of rain today (given all the information in C) as 0.25. I know the horse runs well when the going is soft, so, assuming it will rain, I assess the odds that it will win if it rains as 4 to 1 (on), a probability of $4/(4+1) = 0.8$.

If I want to assess the probability that it will rain today *and* that Phar Lap will win tomorrow:

$P(AB|C) = P(A|C)P(B|AC) = (0.25)(0.8) = 0.2$ (or odds of 1 to 4 or 4 to 1 against).

Sometimes the product rule is written as:

"$P(AB|C) = P(A|C) P(B|C)$ provided that A and B are independent".

This leads to confusion in DNA cases where it is said that the product rule does not apply if A and B are not independent. The answer is to use the more general form of the rule, which applies in all situations.

At this point one of the disadvantages of the odds form of representing probabilities is displayed. Odds *cannot* be multiplied in the same way as we have just multiplied the probabilities.

The statement that A or B (or both) is true is written (A or B) or (A+B). If we want to know how probable such a combination is given some condition, C, then we use the addition rule or sum rule. First, we consider how probable it is that A and B are each true. We might then consider just adding those two probabilities together but inside our assessment of $P(A|C)$ is the probability that A is true when B is also true and vice versa. We would therefore double count the probability that both would be true. To deal with this we subtract the probability that both are true. In symbols:

$$P(A \text{ or } B|C) = P(A+B|C) = P(A|C) + P(B|C) - P(AB|C)$$

So, taking our horseracing example, assuming all the knowledge we have, C, we assess the odds that the horse will win $P(B|C)$ as 1 to 1 (a probability of 0.5). The probability that it will either rain or the horse will win *or both* is $P(A+B|C) = 0.25 + 0.5 - 0.2 = 0.55$.

If A and B cannot both be true together then the term to be subtracted, $P(AB|C)$, is 0 and the formula simplifies to $P(A \text{ or } B|C) = P(A+B|C) = P(A|C) + P(B|C)$. This would be the case if A and B are *exclusive* assertions.

The form we have given above is the general form.

Once again, the odds form of displaying probabilities cannot be combined in this simple way.

The likelihood ratio

The likelihood ratio is a number which is the ratio of two probabilities for the *same* assertion assuming *different* conditions. It is a number that can take any value above zero. It measures the weight of the assertion as evidence in distinguishing the conditions. To use the example given above for the breath-tester, let:

B = "a red light shows"; and
A = "the sample is over the limit"; and
not A = "the sample is *not* over the limit":

$$\frac{P(B|A)}{P(B|\text{not}A)} = \frac{0.95}{0.005} = 190$$

Contrast this with odds which is a ratio for *alternative* assertions under the *same* conditions.

If the likelihood ratio is greater than 1 it indicates that the "red light" makes the proposition that the sample is over the limit *more* probable than it was before. If it is less than 1 it makes the proposition *less* probable.

Bayes' Rule

Bayes' Rule is a mathematical theorem that enables one to assess new probabilities for assertions in the light of new evidence. It can be expressed in either a probability form or an odds form.

Probability form

Bayes' Rule in this form gives the probability of A given evidence B and reads:

$$P(A|B) = P(A)\frac{P(B|A)}{P(B)}$$

This gives the value of $P(A|B)$ in terms of $P(B|A)$ and two other probabilities. It can also be viewed as calculating the probability of A given evidence B from three components:

- the prior probability of A, $P(A)$;
- the probability of the *evidence* assuming the truth of A, $P(B|A)$; and
- the probability of getting the *evidence* in any possible way, $P(B)$.

Odds form

Bayes' Rule gives the odds of A given evidence, B:

$$\frac{P(A|B)}{P(notA|B)} = \frac{P(A)}{P(notA)}\ \frac{P(B|A)}{P(B|notA)}$$

Here, the first ratio on the right-hand side is the odds for A before we have the evidence B (the *prior* odds) and the second ratio is the likelihood ratio for evidence B given the two alternative assertions A and not A. The left-hand side is the *posterior* odds.

Thus, if the likelihood ratio is greater than 1 the posterior odds are increased compared with the prior odds; if it is less than 1 the posterior odds are decreased.

Extending the conversation

One useful technique for assessing probabilities is to use information we have about conditional probabilities to calculate combinations. To take the horse-racing example again, if we know the probability that it will rain (and therefore the probability that it will not) and the probability of the horse winning if it rains and if it does not, we can extend the conversation to the different cases of rain. Let:

C = "our background knowledge";

A = "it will rain today" and P(A|C) = 0.25, hence P(not A|C) = 0.75;

B = "Phar Lap will win today".

P(B|AC) = 0.8 was given in the example before. Thus, the probability that it rains today and the horse wins is P(AB|C) = P(A|C)P(B|AC) = (0.25)(0.8) = 0.2.

Similarly, P(B|not A C) = 0.4 is the probability that the horse will win if it does not rain today. (This is a new piece of information we have added for the example.) From this, the probability that it does not rain today and the horse wins is P(not A B|C) = P(not A|C)P(B|not A C) = (0.75)(0.4) = 0.3.

We seek to determine P(B|C) and we do this by *extending the conversation* to the cases of rain and not-rain. B is true if (it rains and the horse wins) or (it does not rain and the horse wins). B = (A + not A)B = (AB)+(not A B). We have just calculated all the probabilities we need.

Then, P(B|C) = P(AB|C) + P(not A B|C) = 0.2 + 0.3 = 0.5.

So, the probability that the horse wins is 0.5: odds of 1 to 1.

Combining evidence

Bayes' Rule tells us how to update our odds when we have a piece of evidence B. How do we incorporate a second piece of evidence, E, for example? If we write out Bayes' Rule for updating the odds when we have both pieces of evidence B *and* E, or (BE):

$$\frac{P(A|BE)}{P(notA|BE)} = \frac{P(A)}{P(notA)} \frac{P(BE|A)}{P(BE|notA)}$$

The second term on the right-hand side is the likelihood ratio for the combined evidence (BE). We might give this likelihood ratio in court but we might also wish to express this in terms of the likelihood ratios of the two pieces of evidence separately. This is straightforward when the two pieces of evidence are independent (such as blood type and DNA profile) for then the likelihood ratio for (BE) is the product to the likelihood ratios for B and E separately. It is more complicated when they are dependent (such as DNA profile and race). We can use the product rule: P(BE|A) = P(B|A)P(E|BA), so the likelihood ratio becomes:

$$\frac{P(BE|A)}{P(BE|notA)} = \frac{P(B|A)}{P(B|notA)} \frac{P(E|BA)}{P(E|BnotA)}$$

This is a product of two likelihood ratios, the second, for E, having B as an additional condition. However, if B and E are independent then P(E|BA) =

P(E|A) and the expression can be written as a simple product of two likelihood ratios as we discuss in chapter 5:

$$\frac{P(BE|A)}{P(BE|notA)} = \frac{P(B|A)}{P(B|notA)} \quad \frac{P(E|A)}{P(E|notA)}$$

We must always remember that this is a special form; the correct form is the one given before.

Derivation of the probability laws

The laws of probability (also known as the axioms) are often simply assumed and examples of their operation are given using manipulations of bags full of coloured balls or of packs of cards. This leads to the belief that probability only works for choosing lotto numbers or for long-runs of "random events" and is not useful for considering single events or decisions.

On the contrary, the laws of probability are *generalisations of basic principles of logic* and can be derived without reference to coloured balls, packs of cards, etc. There are certain requirements with which any system for rationally expressing strength of belief must comply. These desiderata include:

- if a conclusion can be reasoned out in more than one way every possible way should lead to the same results;
- equivalent levels of belief should be represented by equivalent plausibility statements;
- closely approximate levels of belief should have closely approximate expressions; divergent levels should have divergent expressions;
- if I believe A more strongly than B and B more strongly than C then I must believe A more strongly than C.

A system of belief representation which obeys these requirements will express levels of belief with real numbers. Only in this way can some uniformity of meaning and some method of comparison be ensured. Furthermore, it can be shown that the only set of quantitative rules which satisfy these requirements consistently is the set of axioms of probability.[1]

Nothing restricts the operation of these laws to long runs of "random events". They are the rules for handling information efficiently and should be used even when we are thinking about single assertions.

---

[1] We explain the derivation more fully and give further references in Robertson, BWN and Vignaux, GA, "Probability – the Logic of the Law" (1993) 13 *Oxford Journal of Legal Studies*, 457–478.

SELECT BIBLIOGRAPHY

Aitken, CGG and Stoney, DA, *The Use of Statistics in Forensic Science* (Ellis Horwood, Chichester, 1991).

Balding, DJ and Donnelly, P, "Inference in Forensic Identification" (1994) 158 JRSS(A) 158.

Bates, F, "Describing the Indescribable – Evaluating the Standard of Proof in Criminal Cases" (1989) Crim LJ 331.

Buckleton, J and Walsh, KA "Knowledge-based systems" pp 186–206, in Aitken, CGG and Stoney, DA (eds) *The Use of Statistics In Forensic Science* (Ellis Horwood, Chichester, 1991).

Chakraborty, R and Kidd, KK, "The Utility of DNA typing in Forensic work" (1991) 254 *Science* 1735.

Diaconis, P and Freedman, D, "The persistence of cognitive illusions" (1981) 4 *The Behavioural and Brain Sciences* 333.

Essen-Möller, E, "Die Biesweiskraft der Ähnlichkeit im Vater Schaftsnachweis; Theoretische Grundlagen" (1938) 68 *Mitt Anthorop, Ges (Wein)* 598.

Evett, IW and Buckleton, J, "The interpretation of glass evidence. A practical approach" (1990) 30 JFSS, 215–223.

Evett, I, "Interpretation: a Personal Odyssey", pp 9–22 in Aitken, CGG and Stoney, DA (eds) *The Use of Statistics in Forensic Science* (Ellis Horwood, Chichester, 1991).

Evett, I, "A Bayesian approach to the problem of interpreting glass evidence in forensic science casework" (1986) 26 JFSS 3–18.

Evett, I, "Bayesian inference and forensic science: problems and perspectives" (1987) 36 *The Statistician* 99–105.

Evett, I, "Evaluating DNA Profiles in a Case Where the Defence is 'It was my Brother'" (1992) 32 JFSS 5.

Evett, I, Buffery, C, Willott, G, and Stoney, D, "A guide to interpreting single-locus profiles of DNA mixtures in forensic cases" (1991) 31 JFSS 41.

Evett, IW and Williams, RL, *A Review of the Sixteen Points Fingerprint Standard in England and Wales* (British Crown Copyright, 1989).

Evett, IW, "Criminalistics – The Future of Expertise" (1993) 33 JFSS 173.

Evett, IW, Scranage, J and Pinchin, R, "An illustration of the advantages of efficient statistical methods for RFLP analysis in forensic science" (1993) 52 Am J Hum Gen 498.

Freckelton and Selby, *Expert Evidence* (Law Book Co, 1992).

Freckelton, I, *The Trial of the Expert* (Oxford University Press, Melbourne, 1987).

Galton, F, *Finger Prints* (MacMillan and Company Ltd, London, New York, 1892).

Gigerenzer, G, Swijtink, Z, Porter, T, Daston, L, Beatty, J and Kruger, L, *The Empire of Chance* (Cambridge University Press, 1989).

Grieve, DL, "Reflections on Quality Standards – an American Standpoint" (1990) 15 *Fingerprint Whorld* 108.

Hamilton, FJ, Cordiner, SJ and Chambers, GK (1990), "A survey of Band-sharing in the New Zealand Population with multi-locus probe" 33-15, DSIR Report No CD.

Hammond, HA, Jin, L, Caskey, CT and Chakraborty, R, "Evaluation of 13 short-tandem repeat loci for use in personal identification applications" (1994) 55 Am J Hum Gen 175–189.

Harrison PH, Lambert, JA and Zoro, JA, "A survey of glass fragments recovered from clothing of persons suspected of involvement in crime' (1985) 27 *Forensic Science International*, 171–187.

Hodgkinson, T, *Expert Evidence: Law and Practice* (Sweet & Maxwell, London, 1990).

Good, IJ, *Probability and the Weighing of Evidence* (Charles Griffin & Co, London, 1950).

Jaffee, L R, "Of Probability and Probativity" (1985) 46 U Pittsburg Law Rev, 925–1082.

Kirk, PL, "The ontogeny of criminalistics" (1963) 54 Crimlgy & Pol Sci 235.

Kleinmuntz, B and Szucko, JJ, "A field study of the fallibility of polygraphic lie detection" (1984) *Nature*, 308, 449–450.

Levy, RJ, "Using 'scientific' testimony to prove child sexual abuse" (1989) 23 FLQ 383.

Lewontin, RC and Hartl, DL, "Population Genetics in Forensic DNA Typing" (1991) 254 *Science* 1745.

Ligertwood, ALC, *Australian Evidence* (Butterworths, Sydney, 1989).

Lindley, D, "A problem in forensic science" (1977) 64 *Biometrika* 207.

Lindley, DV, "Subjective Probability, decision analysis and their legal consequences" (1991) 154 JRSS(A), 83–92.

Magnusson, E and Selinger, B, "Jury Comprehension of Complex Scientific Evidence: The Inference Chart Concept" (1990) 14 Crim LJ, 389–400.

McLeod, N, "English DNA Evidence held inadmissible" [1991] Crim LR 583–590.

McQuillan, J and Edgar, K, "A survey of the distribution of glass on clothing" (1992) 32 JFSS 333.

Montrose, J, "Basic Concepts in the Law of Evidence" (1954) 79 LQR 527.

National Research Council of the National Academy of Sciences Committee on DNA, *DNA Technology in Forensic Science* (1992).

Osterburg, JW, "What problems must criminalistics solve" (1963) 59 J Crim L & C 427.

Pearson, EF, May, RW and Dabbs, MGD, "Glass and paint fragments found in men's outer clothing – a report of a survey" (1971) 13 JFS 283.

Popper, KR, *Conjectures and Refutations: the Growth of Scientific Knowledge* (Routledge and Kegan Paul, London, 1989).

Robertson, BWN and Vignaux, GA, "Probability – the Logic of the Law" (1993) 13 OJLS 457.

Roeder, K, "DNA Fingerprinting: A Review of the Controversy" (1994) 9 *Statistical Science* 222.

Rosenkranz (ed), *ET Jaynes: Papers on Probability, Statistics and Statistical Physics* (Dordrecht:Reidel, 1983).

Stockdale, R, "Running with the hounds" (1991) 141 NLJ 772.

Stoney, DA and Thornton, JI, "A Critical Analysis Of Quantitative Fingerprint Individuality Models" (1986) 31 JFS 1187.

Thayer, JP, *A preliminary treatise on the law of evidence* (Little, Brown & Co, Boston, 1898).

Thompson, WC and Schumann, EL, "Interpretation of Statistical Evidence in Criminal Trials" (1987) 11 *Law and Human Behaviour* 167.

Thorwald, J, *The Marks of Cain* (Pan Books Ltd, London, 1965).

Walsh, KAJ and Buckleton, JS, "On the Problem of Assessing the Evidential Value of Glass Fragments Embedded in Footwear" (1986) 26 JFSS 55–60.

INDEX